Shakespeare and Italy

Copyright 2001 by Jack D'Amico. This work is licensed under a modified Creative Commons Attribution-Noncommercial-No Derivative Works 3.0 Unported License. To view a copy of this license, visit http://creativecommons.org/licenses/by-nc-nd/3.0/. You are free to electronically copy, distribute, and transmit this work if you attribute authorship. However, all printing rights are reserved by the University Press of Florida (http://www.upf.com). Please contact UPF for information about how to obtain copies of the work for print distribution. You must attribute the work in the manner specified by the author or licensor (but not in any way that suggests that they endorse you or your use of the work). For any reuse or distribution, you must make clear to others the license terms of this work. Any of the above conditions can be waived if you get permission from the University Press of Florida. Nothing in this license impairs or restricts the author's moral rights.

Florida A&M University, Tallahassee
Florida Atlantic University, Boca Raton
Florida Gulf Coast University, Ft. Myers
Florida International University, Miami
Florida State University, Tallahassee
University of Central Florida, Orlando
University of Florida, Gainesville
University of North Florida, Jacksonville
University of South Florida, Tampa
University of West Florida, Pensacola

View of an Ideal City, Anonymous, Italian, late fifteenth century.
Reproduced with the permission of the Walters Art Gallery, Baltimore.

University Press of Florida
GAINESVILLE · TALLAHASSEE · TAMPA · BOCA RATON
PENSACOLA · ORLANDO · MIAMI · JACKSONVILLE · FT. MYERS

Shakespeare and Italy

The City and the Stage

Jack D'Amico

Copyright 2001 by Jack D'Amico

All rights reserved

06 05 04 03 02 01   6 5 4 3 2 1

Library of Congress Cataloging-in-Publication Data
D'Amico, Jack.
Shakespeare and Italy: the city and the stage / Jack D'Amico.
p. cm.
Includes bibliographical references and index.
ISBN 0-8130-1878-1 (alk. paper); ISBN 978-1-61610-112-1(pbk.)
1. Shakespeare, William, 1564-1616—Knowledge—Italy.
2. Theaters—Stage-setting and scenery—England—History—16th century. 3. Theaters—Stage-setting and scenery—England—History—17th century. 4. Shakespeare, William, 1564-1616—Stage history—To 1625. 5. Italy—Foreign public opinion, British. 6. English drama—Italian influences. 7. Italy—In literature. I. Title.
PR3069.I8 D36 2001
822.3'3—DC21   00-048825

The University Press of Florida is the scholarly publishing agency for the State University System of Florida, comprising Florida A&M University, Florida Atlantic University, Florida Gulf Coast University, Florida International University, Florida State University, University of Central Florida, University of Florida, University of North Florida, University of South Florida, and University of West Florida.

University Press of Florida
15 Northwest 15th Street
Gainesville, FL 32611-2079
http://www.upf.com

To the memory of my father

Contents

List of Illustrations ix

Preface xi

1. Some Versions of Italy 1

2. The Piazza 21

3. City Streets 57

4. Interior Spaces 73

5. The Court 95

6. The Garden 119

7. The Temple 138

8. City Walls 152

9. The Journey to Italy 161

Bibliography 177

Index 193

Illustrations

Frontispiece: *View of an Ideal City*

Map: *Theatre Map of London, 1520–1642* 2

1. *Hampton Court Palace, a View from the North (Centre)* 96

2. *The Gardener's Labyrinth* 120

3. *Florence* 140

4. *A View from St. Mary's, Southwark, Looking Towards Westminster* 162

Preface

The idea of writing a book on Shakespeare's conception of Italian life developed out of my work on English and Italian theater of the Renaissance. The essays I wrote comparing dramatic structure and theatrical setting suggested to me that Shakespeare not only set a certain number of his plays in Italy, perhaps following his sources, but had a coherent understanding of Italian life that could be articulated, in its general outlines, through a close study of the plays. What I take to be Shakespeare's Italy was a society uniquely open to exchange and transformation, a distant place that was, at the same time, a variation on the urban world of London, a world that could be recreated through the poetic language and dramatic structure of the plays and presented to an audience through the theatrical medium of the stage.

In this book I explore the urban geography of the imagined Italian city-state, the piazza, the city streets, the interior spaces, the garden, the temple, and the city walls, as represented in the plays that are set in Italy. I trace the ways in which Shakespeare's vision of a society more open to exchange is merged with the world of his audience in these variations on a prototypical city-state, which become the focus of individual chapters.

The book was written with the informed, imaginative reader and spectator in mind, the scholar, the student, the theater- or moviegoer, and the general reader who is entertained and enlightened by Shakespeare's plays. All references are to *The Riverside Shakespeare*.

Acknowledgments

A major portion of this book was completed with the generous assistance of a sabbatical leave and a Summer Faculty Research Grant from Canisius College. I am most grateful for the support I received from my colleagues among the faculty and the administration of the college.

To my brother go thanks for the use of his apartment during my sabbatical and for the direction and encouragement that only a younger brother can give to an extravagant and wheeling sibling.

In the preparation of the manuscript I relied on the talents and graces of Elizabeth Mangus, Marisa Loffredo, and Veronica Serwacki. I was equally fortunate to be assisted by Amy Gorelick of the University Press of Florida.

Anthony Caputi read the manuscript at various stages in its development and offered his ever cogent insight into what a book of this kind ought to be. Dain Trafton applied his learning and bracing critical acumen to matters of style and content, and Alan Hager was generous with suggestions for enlarging the scope of the argument. I am grateful to all three, good friends and more.

Finally, the last stages of work on the manuscript were completed at the American University of Beirut, where my wife Susan and I enjoyed the hospitality of Lebanon.

1
Some Versions of Italy

THIS BOOK EXPLORES what Shakespeare imagined about Italian life in cities such as "fair Verona," where he set the scene in *Romeo and Juliet* (prologue 2). Through Italy, I argue, Shakespeare could imaginatively project the promise and the danger of a more open society. In the sources he used, or his more general knowledge of Italian life, he perceived certain dominant characteristics of family, government, and society. The analogous structures of everyday life in and around London played an important role in his conception and its representation on the stage, for his Italy was not a place to which one escaped from the everyday, but rather a place where familiar structures were subtly reconfigured. In this process the analogy between the Italian city as theater and the stage itself took on a special significance. His Italian cities recast the familiar much as his theater did, for openness and freedom of movement, distinctive features of his stage, characterize life in his Italian city-states.

In his plays, Shakespeare uses many devices to merge his Italy with London and its surrounding landscape. He moves between the distant setting and the local scene to refresh the imagination, reminding the audience of how strange the features of their city appear when seen from a new point of view and of how familiar the urban landscape of a foreign city becomes when represented on London's stage. He may have conceived of Italian life as particularly theatrical because of what he knew of the customs and temperament of its people, but I think his conception

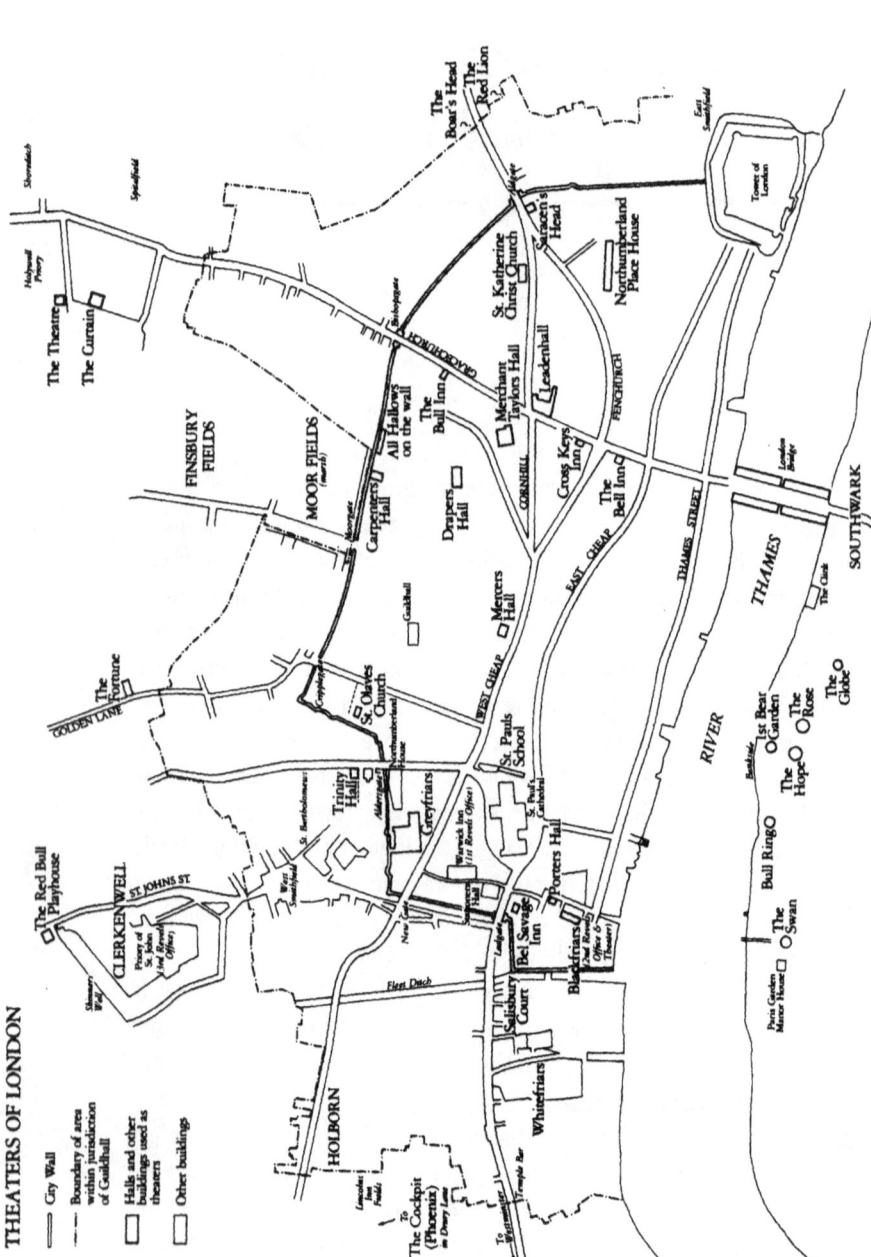

Map: *Theatre Map of London, 1520–1642* from *The Living Monument* by Muriel C. Bradbrook. Reproduced with the permission of Cambridge University Press.

owed as much to his sense of the inherent theatricality of urban life. The Italian city-state is London reduced to typical theatrical spaces, such as the piazza, the street, and the garden. The fact that Shakespeare's conception of the Italian city-state draws on salient features of London also acts as a brake on stereotypes. The city-states Shakespeare recreates on his stage are as much Italy Anglicized as the *Inglese Italianato*.

There have been a number of excellent studies of what Shakespeare may have known about and where he may have gained his knowledge of Italy. To explore how he uses the basic elements of his stage to create the Italian city-states of his comedies and tragedies, I structure the argument around key centers of life within the city. This approach breaks up the treatment of individual plays but creates, I think, a fresh perspective on the way Shakespeare treats these Italian settings and the unique social and political forms he imagines within them. It also allows us to consider how the basic elements of his urban perspective change in different kinds of plays and at different points in his career.

Shakespeare's stage does not present the audience with a theatrical set that fixes the image of place; it is open to the shifting perspectives that can be generated by language, props, structures placed on the stage (Hotson 131), costume, music, and the ingenious use of the facade, the pillars, the heavens, and the trap. The reconstructed Globe theater in London promises to enrich our sense of the theatrical dynamics of Shakespeare's stage. While attending performances of *Henry V* and of *The Winter's Tale* at the reconstructed Globe, I was struck by the fact that the frequent and subtle shifts in wind, sunlight, clouds, and temperature, combined with the movements of the audience, remind one, as much as the chorus does, of the theatrical enterprise of creating an imagined world on a stage in a particular part of the city of London. Audience and performers gathered within the walls of the gallery share a locus that has the potential to become any imaginable setting. But at the same time the theaterplace, like a marketplace, is never canceled, even as the exchange of places takes shape in the imagination. This double consciousness of the imagined and the present repeatedly removes and returns the sense of place, transports while reminding the spectators of where they are. The shared enterprise of theater works despite and because of distractions— airplanes now and street vendors then.

One is also struck by the imposing effect of the stage facade, the gallery, pillars, and heavens all painted to create an architectural structure rich in classical allusions, with its splendid capitols, arches, and astrological figures viewed from the wooden benches that never let you forget where and who you are. This architectural frame, when combined with costume and language, can certainly be used to evoke settings that are geographically and culturally distant from the audience, whether that other place is imagined to be Bohemia, France, the English court, or Italy.

The Choruses of *Henry V* and *The Winter's Tale* articulate a relationship between the audience and the play that remains constant at some level throughout the performance. The sense of presence creates an equally important and strong sense of participation. Certain lines naturally lend themselves to the kind of stage business that creates a sense of inclusion. The audience does not merely observe the distant goings-on but participates in the trial of Hermione, or the exposure of the English traitors Cambridge, Scroop, and Northumberland. With time, directors will, I think, learn that staged attempts to prompt audience involvement create a false note. The stage itself does the job and should be allowed to draw in an audience, or to create those distractions that the play and the improvisational skills of the actors must digest. The unique combination of a gallery that encloses while leaving the audience exposed to the open air is repeated in the great thrust stage, which centers the action amidst the spectators and is at the same time enclosed by its splendidly painted pillars and heavens. The structure sets up a very basic dynamic of inclusion and exclusion, confinement and exile that extends from the action of the play to the relationship between the play and the audience. Just as Hermione, at one moment the pregnant center of Sicilia, can suddenly be exiled from the court and imprisoned, the audience can just as suddenly be drawn into the action that unfolds in this seemingly distant court, made to participate in the trial of Hermione and to feel implicated in her suffering.

∽

Shakespeare does not write city comedy or citizen comedy, terms that have been used to describe plays about citizens, portrayed sympathetically or satirically, plays which share London settings, themes, and character types, and which may have been written with particular theaters and playgoers in mind (Gurr, *Playgoing* 165; Leggatt 4; Gibbons 24). Shakespeare works within an imagined urban space that contains a full range of character types, whose interests are not focused on the dominant preoccupations of city comedy, marriage and money. The Italian city-state as he conceives of it includes variations on the court as well as the marketplace. The cities are not merely, nominally Italian, for through them Shakespeare dramatizes a distinctively open way of life that remains constant in comedy and tragedy, in the street or within the household.

In his essay "Shakespeare and Italy, or, the law of diminishing returns," Manfred Pfister discusses the limitations of many studies of Shakespeare's Italy and makes the following suggestion: "Starting perhaps from Robert Weimann's analysis of the spatial dialectics of *locus* and *platea* in Shakespeare and the popular theatre of his time, one would have to study how the construction of the fictional other, the other place, is fore-grounded in the theatrical representation itself and what purposes this serves" (300). This approach would trace the relationship between *platea*, the nonrepresentational and nonlocalized setting identified with the open space of the thrust stage, and locus, cities such as Messina, Venice, or Padua. Weimann identifies the *platea* with a popular tradition of theater that typically undercuts the illusion of place through direct address, wordplay, and parody. In this scheme, the English clowns dominate the *platea*, while the Italian locus remains somewhat distanced from the audience. Leo Salingar contrasts the realistic dialogue of Italian comedy with Shakespeare's use of verse to create a richer, more learned language, which distances his characters, who are "presented to their first spectators as foreigners from distant, semi-fictitious countries" (*Traditions* 220).

But there is also interplay, as Giorgio Melchiori suggests when he says that "the very *lazzi* ultimately derived from the *commedia dell'arte* are metamorphosed, are translated into the language of the society in which Shakespeare and his audience moved" (105). In the prologue to *Romeo and Juliet*, Shakespeare's Chorus draws the audience into the "two hours' traffic" between the Italian story and the world of the audience: "The which if you with patient ears attend, / What here shall miss, our toil shall strive to mend." The Chorus appeals to that imaginative venture of theater which requires the patient auditors to participate in a joint enterprise that will mend any particular misses. In this venture neither the stage, nor the scene that is Verona, can be easily segmented into the familiar and the alienated. Whatever he knew, or may have believed about Italy, that country became for him the paradigm of a certain kind of society, an urban world teasingly familiar and yet different in the degree of its openness to exchange and transformation. What he imagined of that world and could bring his audience to imagine through the instrument of his theater were cities whose quick pace tests but never quite loses touch with familiar hierarchies.

Shakespeare has a conception of Italy that cannot be reduced to the "other," if by that we mean a version of the most common prejudices and stereotypes of his age. And it is his stage that provides the basic theatrical vocabulary for his representation of urban life in the Italian city-states of Verona, Venice, Messina, and Padua. As recreated on his stage, the piazza, the street before a house, the garden, and the courtly or domestic interiors articulate his understanding of the unique character of Italian society. To reverse the perspective somewhat, I want to look at how the stage bridges the worlds of England and Italy by means of what we might call spatial analogies. The cities he represents in his plays mean something to the English audience because they are made up of recognizable features of English urban life, things like walls, houses, gates, and gardens. The life lived within these imagined cities has a distinctive character with which the audience can, for the two hours or more of the play, imaginatively traffic (Bruster 35).

In her discussion of the relationship between London and Italy, Angela Locatelli maintains that "every setting, no matter how distant and exotic, is meant as analogous (whether a similarity or opposition is created) to London, and its strangeness is given as the equivalent of London's booming diversity, a diversity which was absolutely necessary to its acquisition of the status of 'capital' or primarily significant 'locus' in the state" (71). In a similar vein, Murray J. Levith observes that "Italy serves in part as metaphor for Shakespeare's England—the metropolitan virtues and vices of Italian places are those of the Queen's and King's cities" (11), and

G. K. Hunter asserts that "the foreigner could only 'mean' something important, and so be effective as a literary figure, when the qualities observed in him were seen to involve a simple and significant relationship to real life at home" (*Identities* 13). Cities grew as centers for the exchange of everything from goods and services to information, status, and identity (Mumford 255). This characteristic of the city becomes enhanced in Shakespeare's Italian settings and is closely identified with the urban geography of open spaces and intersections, the central square, the market, the crossroads, the port, and the city street.

The analogy between market and theater has been explored in a suggestive way by Jean-Christophe Agnew, who argues that "we need to know how the market was made meaningful at the very moment that meaning was becoming marketable" (12). The movement from "the personal and ceremonial apparatus of the marketplace" to the "relatively impersonal framework of a money and credit market" was mirrored in a theatrical world whose protean character blurred the distinctions of rank, gender, and nation that were, for many, the basis of social order (49). Lombard Street is a place-name that reminds us of the Italian merchants who took over financial operations after the Jews were expelled from London in 1290 (50). But the shift from a marketplace that contained trade to an expanding marketplace required the English to follow the aliens: "All along the sixteenth-century 'commercial axis' that linked the Antwerp and London exchanges, new forms of liquidity were developing that overflowed, where they did not burst, the mold of medieval commerce" (49). And theater created a parallel axis of imaginative travel. Lena Orlin sees the early modern market as "implicated in the move away from a culture of relatively high self-sufficiency and self-containment to one of getting, trading—and travelling—to achieve the new standard of living" ("The Performance" 186). While this new standard might have been identified as the destabilizing other, the Italian city of Shakespeare's plays has its laws and its hierarchies, its walls and gates that can channel or thwart the dynamic energies of the urban world.

The city enclosed within its walls is an important characteristic of Shakespeare's urban geography (Braudel 492–95), but in many ways his conception of Italian cities and their relationship with the outside world comes closer to the vision of Giovanni Botero, who sees trade as the very essence of the city and a part of God's divine plan: "It seems in very truth that God created the water, not only for a necessary element to the perfection of nature, but more than so, for a most ready means to conduct and bring goods from one country to another. For His Divine Majesty, willing that men should mutually embrace each other as members of one body, divided in such sort His blessings as to no nation did he give all things, to the end that others having need of us, and contrariwise we having need of others, there might grow a community, and from a community love and from love an unity between us" (Botero 6, trans. Peterson 237). This point of view is shared by Herman Kirchner in his "Oration on Travel" from *Coryat's Crudities*. Journeys, he argues, are necessary because heavenly providence has dispersed the gifts and delights of the world so that "we must needs undertake journeyes and voyages to those renowned places, wherin this fragrancy and most heavenly plenty doth harbor" (Coryat 1:125).

The city is the goal of the traveler because the city is by its nature a place of accessible variety and exchange. The London Shakespeare knew was a city of great commercial and industrial activity which provided access to the court, the Inns of Court, and to various forms of entertainment—the drinking, whoring, and theatergoing that were not limited to the urban world but which flourished there. And his immediate world, the world of commercial and artistic venture, began to attract a variety of ambitious, talented men to London in the 1570s.

Steven Mullaney and John Gillies examined the place of the stage within the "marginalized" space of London and mapped the dangerous, transgressive elements of the theatrical other. The plays reflect some of the anxieties aroused by much that was considered dangerously fluid in the rapidly changing economic, political, and social life of London. For many, theater itself might have been as foreign as the Italy represented on the stage. Traditional values—patriarchal, aristocratic, agrarian—mixed with a variety of new currents—Protestant, mercantile, and urban. Responses to these crosscurrents were as varied as the historical and critical scholarship that has studied them. As I see it, Shakespeare does not equate the potential for exchange in his Italy with a form of transgressive otherness that had to be circumscribed to maintain traditional values in the emerging nation-state. This general view of the transgressive, with many learned and subtle variations, has been explored by Philip Armstrong, Stephen Greenblatt, Richard Helgerson, A. J. Hoenselaars, and Alvin Kernan, among others. Italy brought with it the promise of the new humanism and the dangers of the old Catholicism, the intrigues of the court and the glories of art.

Shakespeare projects an imagined spirit of openness into the Italian settings and creates urban centers in which the privileges of rank and the rigidity of the social system are softened, if not entirely forgotten. The reality of status, as pervasive within the Italian city-states as within England, undergoes a theatrical sea change, which enhances the potential for a reshaping, if not a transformation, of society. Scholars may differ regarding the social composition of the audiences that patronized the public theaters and the patrons who attended the private, but the players found a way to address those whose interests were vested in power and wealth, as well as those who would have identified London, the theater, and Shakespeare's Italian cities as analogous centers of exchange.

Whatever dangers might have appeared in this shifting landscape—threats to the old hierarchy, to patterns of identity, and to ethical codes of conduct—Shakespeare's theater provided an example of how transformation could work toward something of great constancy. The plays held together as works of art, and the theatrical enterprise prospered. Italy is theater played out in piazzas, houses, gardens, and streets. We know that Shakespeare often omits reference to what might have been well-known places, such as Piazza San Marco, or the Roman theater in Verona, while he shapes geography to conform to the place of performance in London, a place near a river or a port and not far from a market. I will elucidate how he does this in the chapters that follow. Like every foreign setting we are asked to imagine in Shakespeare's theater, his "fair Verona" is both a distant place and a familiar place, an Italian city to be sure, but a city introduced to the audience in the English vernacular of the play's opening lines.

∼

To create the urban settings of Venice, Verona, or Padua, Shakespeare drew on characteristics of the parishes and wards of London shared by the Italian communes: "Propertied urban inhabitants were attached tenaciously not merely to a city but to a street, a parish, an ambience—to a radius of perhaps 150 meters" (Martines 37). But there is an important difference. Shakespeare's Italy is not an emerging nation-state dominated by a central court; his Italian city-states are not satellites revolving around Rome. Some, perhaps most notably Venice, are very distinctive urban centers, and they are all, in a sense, variations on what Lewis Mumford calls "the walled container" (321), enclosed within walls that create an identity, defining a space within which one can be protected, or from which one can be banished. The Italian city-states of Shakespeare's theatrical world retain their separate identities, but they also exist in a greater social and political landscape that encourages social, commercial, and political transactions between these urban centers. William Thomas in *The History of Italy* gives a favorable account of the temperate climate, the "havens open to trade of all nations" (8), and the cosmopolitan character of the cities and of the ideal Italian gentleman: "to his superior obedient, to his equal humble, and to his inferior gentle and courteous; amiable to a stranger and desirous to win his love" (12). Reading Thomas Coryat, who provides an instructive analogue, one has the impression that the traveler moves within an archipelago of cities and towns that dot Lombardy, each offering a unique combination of walls, towers, palaces, churches, and gardens, each with its own customs, antiquities, and works of art and of manufacture. Harry Levin remarks that "Shakespeare delighted in the diversity of the Italian city-states, the movement and interaction from one community to another, often subject to the quasi-epical intervention of their civic dynasties" (22).

Peter Burke calculates that by 1300, twenty-three cities in north and central Italy had a population of 20,000 apiece and that by 1550 there were forty towns with over 10,000 and twenty with over 25,000 inhabitants. Within the towns were to be found gentlemen, merchants, moneylenders, guildsmen, artisans, tradesmen, shopkeepers, and laborers. A striking number of these towns, many of which became city-states, were also centers of study—with thirteen universities among them (*Italian Renaissance* 53). Cities located on or near the seaside, on great rivers, or along the Roman Via Emilia became natural centers of commerce, as well as of banking (223). According to the *Cambridge Economic History of*

Italy, "The two areas which in 1500 represented the richest and most advanced concentrations of trade, industry and wealth were the quadrilateral formed by the Italian cities Milan, Venice, Florence and Genoa; and the strip of the Netherlands that ran from Ypres . . . to Antwerp. It was not merely coincidence that these were the areas where the tradesmen of the cities had been most successful in emancipating themselves from feudal interference and in keeping at bay the newer threat of more centralized political control offered by the new monarchies" (Rich 492).

I see these cities as analogous in many ways to the theaters that existed in and around London, enclosed within walls and yet set in the open air, gathering places for nobles, merchants, and craftsmen, centers at the margins of the more conservative traditions that prospered because they found a way to draw on various traditions, from the academic world of the universities to the oral and folk traditions of street theater.

How does Shakespeare exploit the place of his stage, its location outside and yet close to the city, and the space of the stage, its internal dimensions, to create a theatrical impression of Verona or Venice or Padua? The geography of the stage maps the foreign setting, giving it a shape that corresponds in general terms to the dimensions of the public amphitheater. The open stage becomes a street or square; the facade and the galleries, with perhaps a house constructed on stage, combine to create a sense of the walls that enclose a city or a household. It is a basic characteristic of Shakespeare's approach to theatrical space that the audience never mistakes the stage for a set. John Russell Brown says of Shakespeare's stage-picture: "Sometimes it is a self-contained whole, bounded by apparent limits; at other times it is limitless and flowing, suggesting continuations beyond the bounds of the stage" (133).

The Italian city takes shape around a square, a space that gathers to it the students, merchants, and lovers who move with considerable freedom within the urban landscape. These distant and yet familiar urban spaces mirror the freedom and mobility that drew young men to London. The Italian setting allows Shakespeare to pick up various threads and weave them together in an imagined place open to the exchange of letters, bills of credit, and even of identities.

As we, the contemporary English-speaking students of Shakespeare's plays, move into this urban landscape, we need to examine the assumptions that we bring to the imaginative experience of Italy, assumptions that derive from a literary and cultural tradition that took shape between Lord Byron and E. M. Forster. Some of these assumptions about the attractions and the dangers of travel to Italy existed in Shakespeare's day, and they have been canvassed thoroughly. Italy could be seen as both the center of humanist learning and the dangerous seat of Catholicism, the country of Castiglione's graceful courtier and of the evil "Machiavel" (Raab 56).

Some of these stereotypes Shakespeare works into the plays. But it is the interconnected nature of Italian urban centers rather than their dangers that is central to Shakespeare's theatrical conception. We know that commerce and banking created important links that extended between the Italian cities and beyond them to northern nation-states and to eastern trade routes. In a related way the growth of humanism in Italy connected the courts, the academies, and, eventually, the universities that flourished in various urban centers, particularly in the region of Lombardy. John Stephens maintains that the "learned academicians and aristocratic circles . . . . conceived of themselves inhabiting a 'republic of letters' in which reason united scholars in a commonwealth, as it had before them for Erasmus, Petrarch and Valla" (149). This intellectual commonwealth reached beyond the medieval class of "clerical intellectuals" to include a diverse class of public servants and princes, men such as Niccolò Niccoli, Federigo da Montefeltro, and Lorenzo de' Medici (149).

The ladies and gentlemen who participate in the dialogue recreated by Baldassare Castiglione in *The Book of the Courtier* inhabit this republic of humane letters. They have gathered in Urbino from other important city-states such as Verona, Genoa, and Florence. As Sir Thomas Hoby says in his prefatory "epistle" to Lord Hastings, his translation brings the courtier who in other languages "hath a long time haunted all the Courtes of Christendom" to the court of England, where Lord Hastings is to serve as his patron (Castiglione 2). The courtier, through this book, enters into a dialogue on courtly fashions, as well as on the moral and political issues of governing the self and the state. This commonwealth of humane letters connects Italian city-states, European courts, and the world of the ancients, as Hoby makes clear in his discussion of how "Castilio hath folowed Cicero" (3).

Roger Ascham, who believes that Castiglione's book "advisedly read and diligently followed but one year at home in England, would do a young gentleman more good, iwis, than three years' travel abroad spent in Italy" (Ryan 55), enters into this dialogue in a significant way. He begins his *Schoolmaster* with "A Preface to the Reader" that transfers the dialogue setting to London, where, during the plague of 1563, a group of friends gather in Sir William Cecil's chamber; "[for] the most part [they] were of Her Majesty's most honorable Privy Council and the rest serving her in very good place" (Ryan 5). Lucky to find himself that day "in the company of so many wise and good men," Ascham briefly recounts a discussion between Sir William Cecil, Sir Richard Sackville, and Sir Walter Mildmay (founder of Emmanuel College) of the "'strange news ... that divers scholars of Eton be run away from the school for fear of beating'" (6). A second conversation between Ascham and Sir Richard Sackville takes place at a window in the queen's privy chamber, where Ascham and the queen had been reading "that noble oration of Demosthenes against Aeschines for his false dealing in his embassage to King Philip of Macedonia." The details are important because they show that Ascham appreciates how dramatic setting contributes to the rich texture of the dialogue form. His conversation with Sackville ranges over many subjects related to the "bringing-up of children" and leads to the request that Ascham "'put in some order of writing the chief points of this our talk'" (8). Though the book that follows (posthumously published in 1568) does not continue the dialogue form, Ascham does not hesitate to move beyond narrow questions of pedagogy to address those who consider themselves members of the court of humane letters: "Point forth six of the best-given gentlemen of this court, and all they together show not so much good will, spend not so much time, bestow not so many hours, daily, orderly, and constantly, for the increase of learning and knowledge as doth the Queen's Majesty herself" (56).

Given the important differences between the archipelago of Italian city-states, whether princely courts or republics, and the emerging nation-states of England, France, and Spain, the Italian model of commerce in goods and money, as well as of intercourse in arts and humane letters, influenced English life and was certainly available to Shakespeare. One of the two works of Machiavelli's translated and printed during Shakespeare's lifetime, *The Art of Warre . . . Set Forthe in Englishe by Peter Whitehorne* (1560), takes the form of a dialogue between Cosimo Rucellai and Fabrizio Colonna set in the "Orti Oricellari," the walled gardens of the Rucellai family (Raab 52). The friends who met there from 1517 to 1520 included Cosimo and Zanobi Buondelmonti, the men addressed in the proem to Machiavelli's *Discourses* (de Grazia, *Machiavelli in Hell* 113), as well as Luigi Alamanni, Batista della Palla, and Lorenzo di Filippo Strozzi, to whom *The Art of War* is dedicated. Machiavelli's evocation of a conversation that develops from its dramatic setting under the shade trees in the garden exemplifies the commonwealth of humane letters that Stephens describes.

Despite the very real restriction on speech created by princely tyrants and by the requirement that courtiers themselves be prudent, these works can be seen as contributing to the ideal image of a spirited exchange of ideas within the Italian cities. Shakespeare draws on these admittedly complex impressions of the Italian courts and cities to create a sense of fluidity within the urban settings of his plays. At the same time, the plays do not neglect the many barriers that crossed the urban world. Though symbolically flanked by the open port and the potentially open marketplace, and alive with the exchange of goods and ideas, the cities also have the capacity, like the stage, to wall in open spaces, to close gates, doors, and windows.

∾

Whether performed at court or in the public theater, the plays were set on a stage that allowed for quick transitions from interior to exterior settings, from a garden to a bedroom, from the outward thrust of adventure to the felt pressure of the established structures that control the household and the city. Despite the absence of scenes painted in perspective, there are times when we will be reminded of the *città ideale,* or ideal city of Italian Renaissance painting, for the walled cities we imaginatively enter contain temples, palaces, gates, monuments, and tombs. But the fixed, monumental character of the city as seen in the idealized space of Renaissance painting is not the dominant characteristic of Shakespeare's

Italian city-states. The sense of place is more dynamic, capable of being imaginatively and theatrically reshaped in each scene. The open character of the society that Shakespeare creates in the Italian plays is not, as cultural assumptions then and now might suggest, simply the result of a loosening of restraints, moral and societal, in that other, Mediterranean climate that makes life, for those who view it from the outside, somehow more primitive, closer to nature and to the instincts. Shakespeare infuses his Italian city-state with a sophistication and a sense of freedom that expands experience without undermining existing social structures.

Kenneth R. Bartlett provides a concise survey of English travelers to Italy, from the Tudors who considered Italy as "the graduate school of humanism and the *vita civile*," to the gentlemen who looked for "the patina of culture, manners and social finesse which had made the image of the *cortegiano* a model of aristocratic behavior throughout Europe, but especially in England" (49). The generally positive image of Italy presented in William Thomas's *History of Italy* (1549) and his *Italian Grammar* (1550) finds its opposite in the critical passages from Ascham's *Schoolmaster* (1570). The great cities of Italy, such as Rome, once "the best breeders and bringers-up of the worthiest men, not only for wise speaking but also for well-doing, in all civil affairs, that ever was in the world" (Ryan 60) are now, according to Ascham, enslaved to vice so that those English who travel there exemplify the Italian proverb *"Inglese italianato è un diavolo incarnato;* that is to say, 'You remain men in shape and fashion but become devils in life and condition'" (66). And the freedom of Italian cities takes on a decidedly sinister cast from Ascham's perspective: "And being brought up in Italy, in some free city, as all cities be there, where a man may freely discourse against what he will, against whom he lust—against any prince, against any government, yea, against God himself and his whole religion—where he must be either Guelf or Ghibelline, either French or Spanish, and, always compelled to be of some party, of some faction, he shall never be compelled to be of any religion, and if he meddle not overmuch with Christ's true religion, he shall have free liberty to embrace all religions and become, if he lust, at once, without any let or punishment, Jewish, Turkish, papish, and devilish" (74). Ascham sees freedom degenerating into political factionalism and religious apostasy.

Kenneth Bartlett makes the point that although later visitors "might not have shared [William] Thomas' laudatory vision of the peninsula, they could not escape the contours which his great book gave to their intellectual maps" (56). As David Frantz points out, the positive and the negative images of Italy owed much to the written word: "On the one hand the English admired and imitated much in the way of Italian learning, general culture, and especially literature. On the other hand, they abhorred and feared Italy as a land of Catholicism, lewd living, and lewd writing" (*"Festum"* 141). Both the idealization and the vilification of Italy are fictions drawn from literature or the equally imaginative accounts of travelers. George B. Parks, in his excellent survey of this ambivalence, makes the point that Ascham "decried the wickedness glorified in Italian fiction then becoming popular in English translation." He observes that the enthusiasm for things Italian first expressed by William Thomas "is best attested by the numerous editions in England of Castiglione's *Courtier*, in the English of Thomas Hoby (1561) and the Latin of Bartholomew Clerke (1571)" ("Decline and Fall" 342). The more colorfully negative representations of Italy, frequently quoted out of context, attack the dangers of travel itself, as we see in the banished English earl from Thomas Nashe's *The Unfortunate Traveller* (1594) who includes Italy in the forbidden ports of call: "Italy, the Paradice of the earth and the Epicures heaven, how doth it forme our young masters? ... From thence he brings the art of atheisme, the art of epicurising, the art of whoring, the art of poysoning, the art of Sodomitrie"(McKerrow 2:301). David Frantz argues that just as Nashe "ridicules literary forms and conventions that present a positive view of things Italian, so too will he ridicule 'tragicall tales' and 'eligiacall histories' that portray a negative view of Italy" (*"Festum"* 155–56). What Nashe expects of his readers, that they understand the character of the speaker as part of the characterization of a place, would certainly apply to spectators responding to the dramatic perspectives represented within a play. In his *Pierce Penilesse* (1592), Nashe attacks the seemingly infinite forms of devilish pride and hypocrisy to be found at home and abroad, including Italy, "the Academie of manslaughter, the sporting place of murther, the Apothecary-shop of poyson for all Nations" (McKerrow 1:186). On the other hand, Frances Yates tells us that "Italians forced to live in England for business or other reasons had long regarded their sojourn here as a banishment in a barbarous island" (*Florio* 31).

And one must add that Shakespeare's knowledge of the Italian language may have been sufficient to provide him direct access to works in Italian available in London, such as Ser Giovanni Fiorentino's *Il Pecorone*, an important source for *The Merchant of Venice*, of which no English translation has been found (Shaheen 161–69). George Pettie's translation, *The Civile Conversation of M. Steeven Guazzo* (1581), introduced standards of fashionable conduct from Italy, and John Florio, Italian tutor to the earl of Southampton, was actively promoting Italian literature and culture in England with his language manuals, *Firste Fruites* (1578) and *Second Frutes* (1591), and his Italian-English dictionary, *A Worlde of Wordes* (1598) (Yates, *Florio* 36; Frantz, "Florio's Use" 48). Between 1584 and 1589 the printer John Wolfe was publishing editions of Pietro Aretino and Machiavelli, using false Italian imprints (Sellars 110; Hoppe 244). In 1584, as part of what G. K. Hunter calls a commercial venture designed "to exploit English fascination with Italian wickedness and the desire to read, even if in a half-understood language, works never likely to be available in English" ("Italian Tragicomedy" 127), Wolfe brought out Machiavelli's *Il prencipe: con alcune altre operette* and *I discorsi di N. Machiavelli sopra la prima deca di T. Livio*, and in 1587 *Historie fiorentine*, *Libro dell'arte della guerra*, and *Lasino doro* (with separate title pages for the plays *Mandragola* and *Clitia*). With Giacopo Castelvetro, Italian exile, teacher, and nephew of the critic Lodovico Castelvetro, Wolfe responded to the interests of a courtly, literary circle in London, printing Aretino's *Quattro comedie* and sexy *Ragionamenti* in 1588 and 1589, followed by Giovanni Battista Guarini's *Pastor fido* and Torquato Tasso's *Aminta* in 1591 (Clubb 50; Henke, *Pastoral* 47). Sheila E. Dimsey asserts that the printing of *Il Pastor fido* one year after the first edition of Guarini's pastoral appeared in Venice (1590) illustrates "the keenness with which literary London of Elizabeth's time followed any new development in Italian letters" (424).

In addition to the printed translations of Machiavelli—Peter Whitehorne's *Arte of Warre* (1563, 1573, 1588) and Thomas Bedingfield's *Florentine Historie* (1595)—seven manuscripts of *The Prince* have survived, comprising three separate translations, and three of *The Dis-

courses, two incomplete (Orsini 5–33). And to this list of Italian works available in England one must add Giordano Bruno's five Italian dialogues printed in 1584–85 by John Charlewood, with false imprints (Yates, *Giordano Bruno* 259). As Felix Raab asserts, "Everything indicates that, at least from the middle 'eighties onwards, Machiavelli was being quite widely read in England and was no longer the sole preserve of 'Italianate' Englishmen and their personal contacts, as had been the case earlier" (52–53). Reflecting on Shakespeare's knowledge of Livy via Machiavelli, Anne Barton notes that "it would be more surprising if it could be proved that Shakespeare had managed to avoid reading Machiavelli than if concrete evidence were to turn up that he had" (122). Shakespeare's use of the *novelle* of Giraldi Cinthio, Matteo Bandello, Ser Giovanni Fiorentino, and Boccaccio, translated or in the original Italian, has been sifted by Geoffrey Bullough, Kenneth Muir, Howard C. Cole, and Charlotte Pressler. Leo Salingar remarks that "the greatest creative writer whose influence can be felt widely diffused through Shakespeare's plays, however indirectly, is Boccaccio" (*Traditions* 323), and Mario Praz asks rhetorically whether Shakespeare avoids the more stereotypical horrors and thrills of the Senecan-Italian dramatic tradition "because the acquaintance he had with Italian things enabled him to take a more sober view of Italian society than the current one circulated by religious and conservative fanatics and cherished by the thriller-seeking crowd" (148). It is likely that Shakespeare was familiar with the reputation, the dramatic techniques, and the stock figures of the *commedia dell'arte* (Campbell 32) and quite possible that he or a fellow actor, such as the peripatetic Will Kemp, might have had direct contact with Italian actors (Henke, *Pastoral* 56–57; Louis B. Wright 518).

The final question is what all of this may have to do with our understanding of the plays. What "Italian things" among the sources and possible barometers of opinion do we use, for example, to frame the opening of *The Taming of the Shrew*? Following Ascham, we might be prepared to imagine the audience suspicious of an Italian educational program, especially when Tranio steers his master from "Aristotle's checks" to a curriculum that satisfies an important breadth requirement still in effect among students—"No profit grows where is no pleasure ta'en" (1.1.39). But from William Thomas in 1549 to Thomas Coryat in 1611, the positive reputation of the universities of Italy, and especially of Padua for civil law, remained constant: "more students of forraine and remote nations doe live in Padua, then in any one University of Christendome. For hither come in, many from France, high Germany, the Netherlands, England, etc. who with great desire flocke together to Padua for good letters sake, as to a fertile nursery, and sweete emporium and mart town of learning"(Coryat 2:297–98). For Shakespeare's dramatic purposes, the idea of the confluence of students from various cities as to a market town of learning and experience seems more important than the particular kind of doctrine that might have been picked up there.

The value of a humanist education could not, on the other hand, be separated from some general notions of the dangers of travel to Italy. In his edition of Ascham, John E. B. Mayor quotes a letter from the Privy Council (December 16, 1580): "The Queen's Majesty found the daily inconvenience growing to the realm by the education of young gentlemen, and others her subjects, in the parts beyond the seas: where for the most part they are nourselled and nourished in Papistry" (222). The bawdy Italian *novelle* might have aroused apprehension as well as thrills. And the Italy of Machiavellian policy, or courtly manners, might have appeared dangerously subversive, whether seen as a passing fad or as a genuinely attractive departure from the cultural and ethical norm in England. As Lawrence Ryan points out, "This notion of Italy as a place of Circean enchantment was hardly new with Ascham, but his is the most vigorous and memorable expression of a prejudice that was shared by many Elizabethans and is by no means dead among English-speaking peoples even today" (Ascham, Ryan xxx).

The dangers and enchantments of Italy cannot be easily separated from complex attitudes toward travel and theater. The Italy of Shakespeare's plays is represented as a collection of urban spaces that enhance a potential for metamorphosis that could easily be identified with the experience of travel to London or from within London to the theater itself. Jonas Barish maintains that the antitheatrical prejudice belongs to "a conservative ethical emphasis in which the key terms are those of order, stability, constancy, and integrity, as against a more existentialist emphasis that prizes growth, process, exploration, flexibility, variety and versatility of response. In one case we seem to have an ideal of stasis, in the other an ideal of movement, in one case an ideal of rectitude, in the other an ideal of plenitude"(117). To the extent that Shakespeare's Italy is identified with theater itself, it would seem to stand in opposition to the conservative ethical values Barish defines. But as he also shows, for certain of Shakespeare's characters—Falstaff, Hamlet, Edgar, and Cleopatra—"multiplicity seems an enlarging and liberating principle, conferring something like heroic stature" (127).

We must be careful not to let our interest in the attitudes that comprise a textured background obscure our reading of the plays (Jones 252). Within Shakespeare's Italian city-states change often constitutes the means by which voyagers help others achieve stability: "But Nature to her bias drew in that" (*Twelfth Night* 5.1.260). London was the great meeting place of change and stability, the city itself an urban structure defined by its walls, monuments, and stable traditions, but a living structure that was changing rapidly. Lawrence Manley sees this duality in the pages of John Stow's *Survey of London:* "If Stow's opening and closing accounts of ritual help to establish, in the manner of a map, a symbolic terrain that inscribes the civic order and its past upon the urban landscape, his personal survey of that contemporary landscape reveals, as do the endlessly varied routes actually walked by a city's population, a mobility and heterogeneity on which no symbolic or ritual system could hope to impose a complete or stable order" ("Of Sites and Rites" 52). Shakespeare's voyages within the city of London provided the basis for the Italian ethos that takes shape on his stage.

2

The Piazza

> Furthermore, the city ought to be planned not only with a view to housing and other essentials; it should also provide pleasant areas and open spaces set aside as ornament and for recreation, away from the cares of civic business: race courses, gardens, ambulatories, swimming pools, and so on.
> —Leon Battista Alberti, *On the Art of Building in Ten Books* 4:101

SHAKESPEARE'S LONDON was not a city of squares or circuses, let alone swimming pools. As the swimmer-poet Byron says in his poem *Beppo*, "For, bating Covent Garden, I can hit on / No place that's called 'Piazza' in Great Britain" (39–40). The architect and set designer Inigo Jones, who brought Italian scenic design to England, developed Covent Garden for the fourth earl of Bedford and created what has been called "his Italianate piazza" (Trease 126), or "London's first formal open space" (Summerson 124), but he did this in 1630–32, long after Shakespeare had departed (Power, "East and West" 178). Nevertheless, there were other spaces within London that Shakespeare could have drawn on to create, by analogy, the piazza or square, the signature urban space of his Italian cities.

We do not know exactly when Shakespeare, like many other young men who were contributing to the dramatic explosion of its population, came to London. Nor from what direction he came. If from the south on Borough High Street past the Bankside district where the Globe theater would one day rise, he would either have walked over the much-celebrated London Bridge or have crossed the river by ferry. From any other direction he would have entered the walled city through one of its gates—Aldgate and Bishopsgate in the east, Moorgate, Cripplegate, and Aldersgate to the north, Newgate and Ludgate to the west. The main arteries of the city ran from east to west (as they still do), between the Tower and the great houses along the river, in what would become the fashionable West End toward Whitehall and Westminster.

Approaching the city from any direction, he would have passed through open fields, many of them to be built over as the city rapidly expanded beyond the confines of walls whose foundations in some areas dated back to the Roman city of Londinium. (They too can still be seen amidst high-rise buildings, below elevated walkways, bordered by bits of green and marked by placards.) And within the walls the urban setting was a mixture of great guildhalls, churches, merchant houses, combined shops and residences, and the tenement blocks that so bothered the London chronicler John Stow. The city contained certain dominant structures—the Tower, St. Paul's, the Guildhall and the Royal Exchange, Grey Friars and Blackfriars, Baynard's Castle along the river, and the Inns of Court. Shakespeare lived in a walled city that contained the equivalent of small villages: the wards, parishes, and precincts that were the administrative and legal centers of daily life. Each of these neighborhoods, so carefully chronicled by Stow, developed its distinctive identity. A city dweller, even if not native born, comes to know the rhythms of urban space as a succession of open vistas and dead ends, blind alleys and the garden spaces that would recall the fields outside the walls—Moorfields, the artillery ground, Spittlefields, and the churches such as St. Giles and, west of the city, St. Martin-in-the-Fields.

When Shakespeare read his sources and found references to Italian cities with their distinctive piazzas, he might have thought of the open space before a church, or guildhall, or inn, a gathering point within the city that shared certain dynamics with an Italian square. These urban spaces would have served as analogues for the foreign settings, as is suggested by Simon Thurley: "The preaching place was formed around 1540 to the north of the royal lodgings in an area formerly occupied by the privy garden. It was a cobbled courtyard surrounded by an antique loggia, in the centre of which was erected a square pulpit with a canopy"

(200). To this one could certainly add the lively atmosphere of London's markets, the freedoms of Cheapside, Newgate, Leadenhall, and Smithfield, and the chaos of St. Paul's church, as represented in Thomas Dekker's pamphlet *The Dead Tearme* (1608): "What damnable bargaines of unmercifull Brokery, and of unmeasureable Usury are there clapt up? . . . and such humming (every mans lippes making a noise, yet not a word to be understoode,) I verily beleeve that I am the Tower of *Babell* newly to be builded up, but presentlie despaire of ever beeing finished because there is in me such a confusion of languages. Thus am I like a common Mart where all commodities (both the good and the bad) are to be bought and solde" (quoted by Agnew 86).

The theater itself provided an apt analogue to the piazza within the urban landscape. The *città ideale* of Italian painting resembles a theatrical set. In the *commedia erudita* the setting of the play, represented scenically in perspective, was often the central space of the very city where the play was performed, as was the case for Machiavelli's *La mandragola* (D'Amico, "Power and Perspective" 5). The interrelationship extends to Renaissance architecture in the noted example of Filippo Brunelleschi's use of perspective in the plans for the Florentine Baptistry, which becomes the center of an urban space seen from the ideal point of view of a citizen-spectator. In architecture, politics, civic pageantry, and theater, the city as stage and the staged city mirror one another. We know that the Roman Colosseum became the symbolic equivalent of the universal city-center, and this identification might transfer to any staging place of similar design, as can be seen in the following description of a cockfight quoted by Simon Thurley: "King Henry the Eighth of that name had had a sumptuous amphitheatre of fine workmanship built, designed like a colosseum and intended exclusively for fights and matches between these little animals [cocks]" (190). In the public amphitheaters that ringed London, the wooden columns painted to resemble marble exploited the identification of the stage and the ancient city (Ruffini 346; D'Amico, "The Treatment of Space" 273). It is in this context that Giovanni Botero in his dedication to *Delle cause delle grandezze delle città* can speak of the city as the theater of human virtues (343).

This equation also worked within the English tradition. Elizabethan royal entries and progresses and the lord mayor's shows transformed

English cities into a form of public theater. David Bergeron underlines the theatrical quality of Elizabeth's first royal entry (January 14, 1559) as revealed in the pamphlet that described the festivities: "Permeating the whole report in the pamphlet is the unmistakable impression that this queen in the golden litter is very much part of the action; she is one of the actors in the total pageant—part of the theatrical experience.... thus it is not surprising that the writer, presumably Mulcaster, adds: 'So that if a man should say well, he could not better tearme the citie of London that time, than a stage wherin was shewed the wonderfull spectacle, of a noble hearted princesse toward her most loving people, and the peoples exceding comfort in beholding so worthy a soveraign' (p. 28)" (14–15). What is the *platea* of medieval theater or the raised stage of an interlude if not the creation of a square within a town, a hall, or an innyard? To the extent that the players succeed in attracting an audience, they become the center of an activity that recreates the vitality of the piazza.

One of the most important attributes of the piazza, or square, then as now, is its inherent theatricality. The city and its theater converge when the city becomes a stage for self-representation (Braudel 381). We know that in London the civic authorities were often at odds with theater. But the rapid increase in the city's population not only provided a ready market for theater but also led to the development of an urban identity that in a sense demanded theater, whether professional or occasional (McCoy 245; Anglo 108). The gates of a city provide a natural frame for processions and entries; the walls and conduits become raised platforms for speeches and the open spaces of churchyards or halls a natural gathering place for the citizen-spectators. Lawrence Manley argues that "the transformation of the city into a sacred space, a physical embodiment of historic destiny and community spirit" was enacted through processions that ritualized time and allowed the city's leaders literally to follow in "the 'steps of the forefathers,' tracing out in a series of processions a highly ordered ritual space" ("Of Sites and Rites" 43). Civic pageantry mediated between the city's past and present, between its traditions and its burgeoning social, political, and commercial interests. Manley says of the lord mayor's shows that in "their overt myth-making, they reflected the forces that were undermining the traditional community—a heightened emphasis on acquisition, mobility, wealth and status, and a deepening symbiosis between London and the centralized, bureaucratic state" (48). The conflict between the city leaders and the professional theatrical companies can be understood as a variation on a fundamental conflict within the city over who would control the process of representing the city to itself and to others.

One result of that conflict was the construction of theaters that ringed the city just beyond the reach of its jurisdiction. The theaters constructed just outside the city walls recreated the dynamic of the walls that remained in many ways the signature of London, as ably described by Professor Manley: "The core of the city remained, however, the area defined by the old walls, which ran from the Tower in the east to the street now known as London Wall in the north, and from there to the Fleet river and Blackfriars in the west. Bounded on its outside by a deep ditch that was gradually being filled in and breached by a series of massive gates opening on to the main routes to the north, London could be sealed shut at night and in times of crisis. Its walls remained the symbol of its power as a world unto itself" (*London* 12). A microcosm of the city, the piazza can be open because it is enclosed, a center of vitality because it regulates exchange.

In the tradition of ancient theater and its Italian imitators, *The Comedy of Errors* represents the events of one day within a central urban space flanked by the city's port and its mart and backed by its houses, those of good and ill repute, houses whose separateness dissolves as the play's action unfolds between the world beyond the city and the focal point of exchange within the city. The city's marts and fairs, inns and prostitutes, masters and servants link the Mediterranean city of Ephesus with Sicilian Syracusa and with Shakespeare's London. East and west, as well as north and south, meet in the city's urban center, aptly represented by its inn, the Centaur, which will reappear as the Sagitarry of *Othello* (1.1.158).

When Shakespeare turns his attention to northern Italy and to the city-states that stretch from Milan in the east to Verona and Venice in the west, he enters a region famous in the Renaissance for theater, learning, business, and politics—for its poets, painters, writers of novellas, its actors and dramatists, its humanists, merchants, and princes (Bartlett 49). He seldom alludes directly to the artistic ferment of the Italian Renaissance (as Ben Jonson does in *Volpone*), but in his plays the piazza or square becomes a center for that lively interchange of opinion and business that animated Renaissance Italy.

The piazza can take the form of an open public space at the center of the city where various paths cross, or it can be a smaller opening on a street "before" a specific house. In the latter instance the more public action that unfolds in the street bears some direct relationship to a private dwelling represented by the facade, with its doors for entrances and exits and an upper gallery (or some practicable theatrical structure on stage) to serve for a window or balcony. The city, as represented on Shakespeare's stage, exploits the dynamic interplay between the sense of enclosure created by the galleries, the facade, and the space under the roofed "heavens," and the dramatic openness of the amphitheater. The square stands within walls that define the city, and it communicates with the outside world through the city gates or through the market and port that control the ebb and flow of commerce.

The city can be walled without being a fortress. Like London, and particularly like the Globe on Bankside, Shakespeare's urban space almost always stands near a real or imagined estuary, a river and port complex that leads to the sea. Alberti underlines the military value of this urban axis when he asserts that "a military road should extend from the harbor into the center of town, with access to several neighborhoods, along which a counterattack may be launched from all sides against any intruding enemy fleet" (*Ten Books* 4:115). In Shakespeare's urban landscape a more welcoming inn typically flanks the port.

Shakespeare's stagecraft thrives on the quick succession of scenes, transitions between open and enclosed spaces that create a complex urban perspective. Because of its geographical position and its history, the theater could be identified with the inn, and with the social and economic currents that drew individuals to the city center. Commenting on the Italian piazza Inigo Jones designed for a masque performed at the Inns of Court in 1634, Stephen Orgel says that "Jones chose not a classical Roman forum, but the center of the life of an Italian Renaissance city-state, the architectural embodiment of republican principles" (*Illusion* 80). The piazza, an open space where all the citizens of the city-state can gather, suggests political principles that one might identify with the republics of Venice or Florence. But the public square might also become the focal point for civic discord and rebellion or serve as the stage for a display of princely, if not tyrannical, power.

Shakespeare's early comedies *The Two Gentlemen of Verona* and *The Taming of the Shrew* open with young men traveling between cities motivated by the desire for education of an academic or more generally courtly nature. The two gentlemen of Verona converse in a space that opens to the port from which Valentine will depart: "My father at the road / Expects my coming, there to see me shipp'd" (1.1.53–54). Within the city love holds the "home-keeping youth" Proteus, who asks to be remembered when Valentine sees "some rare noteworthy object" in his travels (13). The "road" is the generic port of Shakespeare's Italian cities, as much London on the Thames as Verona on the river Adige. Arthur Brooke focuses on the fruitful setting of Verona and its river in the opening lines of his *Romeus and Juliet:* "The fruitfull hilles above, the pleasant vales belowe, / The silver streame with chanell depe, that through the towne doth flow / The store of springes that serve for use, and eke for ease" (ll. 5–7). It is, in a sense, the ease of life in Verona that leads Valentine, unlike Romeo, to set out "to see the wonders of the world abroad" (l. 6). In Milan he will pursue those "studies" that sharpen a young man's wit. Shakespeare introduces the audience to an Italian city-state in the courtly-humanist tradition where fathers "put forth their sons to seek preferment out" (1.3.7) in warfare, courtiership, or academic studies. Antonio believes that his son Proteus "cannot be a perfect man, / Not being tried and tutor'd in the world" (20–21). Young men move between these northern Italian cities not to escape parental authority but to fulfill the good counsel of the fathers, as English gentlemen traveled to northern Italy to complete their education.

Typically Shakespeare does not identify Verona's Piazza Brà or its imposing Roman amphitheater, the Arena, the most famous of those antiquities that Brooke calls "signes of thinges betyde of olde / To fyll the houngry eyes of those that curiously beholde" (9–10). Some years later, Thomas Coryat will report of Verona that "the worthiest and most remarkable of all [its monuments] is the Amphitheater commonly called Arena" (2:19–20). Shakespeare's was not a theater designed to arouse or satisfy this visual curiosity through the use of scenery painted in perspective, though he might have used the verbal cues that Ben Jonson employs in *Volpone* to particularize the sense of place (Praz 153) and for some productions he might have exploited the classical look of the London amphitheaters that caught the attention of Johannes de Witt, who noted in his diary the "wooden columns painted in such excellent imitation of marble that it is able to deceive even the most cunning" (Gurr, *Shakespearean Stage* 132). As de Witt says, "since its form resembles a Roman work, I have made a sketch of it," a sketch subsequently copied by Arend van Buchell. It may be that Shakespeare did not know enough about Verona to make the link between that city's Arena and the classical form embodied in London's amphitheaters. He simply uses the city's central space to characterize Verona as a particularly open place.

J. L. Styan provides an apt summary of the analogous fluidity of theater itself: "The urgent elements of a Shakespeare performance have to do with the structure of scenes, the simultaneous staging of conflicting action, the easy passage from one place to another, the mixing of realistic and symbolic and parodistic styles, the trick of slipping from prose to verse and back again, and many other conventions characteristic of the flexible Elizabethan stage" ("In Search" 204). A dramatist who represents a foreign city has the opportunity to exploit it and to shape whatever preconceptions of that city the audience might bring to a performance. The urge to travel is often aroused by a desire to see those "certaine signes of thinges betyde of olde" that one might have heard of or read about. As is the case with Valentine, one can also hunger for wider experience, something which cannot be satisfied within the walls of one's own city. And for any young man trying to identify with Valentine's freedom to move beyond the imagined city of Verona, the best analogy might have been the freedom to move to a theater outside London, a theater whose actors were particularly skilled at representing movement.

Shakespeare could have expected his audience to identify Verona, if only in the most general sense, with northern Italy, a region generally referred to as Lombardy and known for its fertile plains, its universities, its Renaissance courts, and its merchants. Whatever the audience might have expected, or whatever we expect today, Shakespeare sets the action moving in an open space within a city that invites young men to satisfy their desire for honor and fame by traveling.

Following a theatrical scheme that he will employ with greater subtlety in other plays, he balances the opening exchange between Valentine and Proteus with a game of wordplay between Proteus and Valentine's page Speed, who has proven himself to be a "worthless post" when it comes to delivering a letter from Proteus to Julia. The verbal game of follow the punning leader mirrors the movement of money and of information, of news and letters, within the prototypical city center, where various lines of communication and miscommunication will meet. The extended wordplay set off by the pun on "shipp'd" and "sheep" reinforces the idea that young men and their pages are expected to go abroad. Proteus knows his father would approve of an invitation to join Valentine in Milan and disapprove of the exchange of love letters with Julia (1.3.48).

Women do not enjoy equal access to the piazza, nor its opening to the "road" and a world beyond the city. Julia's love pilgrimage (2.7.9) to Milan in pursuit of Proteus and Silvia's escape from Milan (5.1.9) must be carried out in disguise because even in Shakespeare's Italy young women do not freely move between cities. And the young men who are expected to note the wonders of the world are less free once they step within the court. After discovering that Valentine has exchanged love letters with his daughter, Silvia, the duke of Milan sees the young man as a "base intruder" (3.1.157) who must be banished. As we shall see, that space within the city identified with the court shares certain characteristics with the open square, but access to the innermost courtly precincts will be limited to those of rank. At the farthest symbolic remove from the piazza is the chamber where a woman is "kept severely from resort of men" (3.1.108).

∾

The open space at the center of the Italian city leads to the port, the market, the court, and to those literal and symbolic gates that control access to and egress from the city. The induction to *The Taming of the Shrew* provides a transition to Padua by way of an English tavern that would appear to be outside the walls of a city or town. The lord who returns from hunting to find Christophero Sly dead drunk and asleep outside the tavern prepares to convey Sly to his own estate, which must be close by, for when the lord hears a trumpet sound he identifies it with "some noble gentleman that means / (Travelling some journey) to repose him here" (1.75–76). A servingman enters to inform the lord that the trumpet signals the arrival of a band of traveling players who "offer service to your lordship" (78). The tavern and the estate are on the road, far enough outside a city for players to seek out a place to repose or to perform. The play performed for Sly takes shape within another play, the "practice" the lord devises to amuse himself and tease the drunkard. That device is, as we know, broken, since we never return to the lord's house where Sly has been metamorphosed into a lord in an English version of an Italian *beffa*. The metatheatrical induction functions as a gateway to the Italian city; the open road that leads from a tavern to the chamber within a lord's estate also takes the audience to an open space in Padua.

The public space before the house of Baptista, a gentleman of Padua, is the space of the stage. The frame distances the action and reminds the audience of those devices, available to a prankster or to the players, that create the illusion of place. The lord uses costumes, pictures, distilled waters, sweet aromas, dulcet music, and dialogue to persuade Sly that he has but dreamed his former life and that "he is nothing but a mighty lord" (induction 1.65). Similar theatrical devices might have been employed by the actor Soto, whose performance the lord recalls—"but sure that part / Was aptly fitted and naturally perform'd" (86–87). The apt and natural performance also has a "cunning" power to transform reality, as the stage itself is transformed to a place outside an inn or to a square in Padua. Shakespeare reminds his audience of the complex nature of that cunning when the lord practices on the players by telling them that Sly is a lord, albeit one given to certain "odd behavior," and quite ignorant of the conventions of theater, courtly or public (95). A play that draws on Ariosto's *I suppositi* through Gascoigne's *Supposes* makes the audience aware of the theatrical suppositions that shape our sense of place (Morris 78). We never quite forget London in Padua or the tavern in the lord's "fairest chamber." Sly's world does not disappear, for to cite but one example, when the action of *The Taming of the Shrew* moves to the country house of Petruchio, we slip back into the environs of the tavern and the lord's house, somewhere in the suburbs of London where we might encounter

"Long-lane end" (4.3.185). Though Sly may be forgotten, the audience never loses sight of the theater itself, that English frame for the Italian action. A good dose of English food helps to transform the shrewish Katherina into a more dainty cate (2.1.189). A part of the ongoing joke of the play for the London audience might have been the image of an English Kate letting fly with stools and lutes in the Italian household of old Baptista. The lord of the induction can be identified with the creator of the play, someone who understands how to manipulate our sense of place as we move from the common to the courtly, from the environs of Burton-heath, not far from Stratford, to a setting that contains a couch "Softer and sweeter than the lustful bed / On purpose trimm'd up for Semiramis" (induction 2.38–39).

Elizabethan theater did not use the kind of scenery that might have resembled the "pictures" the lord promises to show Sly (induction 2.49–60), though Shakespeare regularly employs the kind of verbal scene painting used to prepare Christopher for the reunion with his lady, "the fairest creature in the world." Verbal allusions to paintings of seduction and rape, "as lively painted as the deed was done," might have reminded some in the audience of northern Italian artists such as Titian, Giorgione, and Veronese, artists who recreated scenes from classical mythology in a style that deftly imitated nature. Just as Sly never sees the paintings, the audience never sees anything other than an open stage, which it can imagine to be either a chamber or a piazza. And as Sly is transported to a foreign world where he will have to learn everything anew, even what to call his wife, the audience slips from the environs of London to a street in Padua. Sly adjusts to the courtly setting with his native appetite for "a pot o' th' smallest ale" firmly in place. Nor does the play abandon its native taste for bawdy jokes, as when the page, dressed as Sly's wife, puts off his invitation to join him in bed with a medical excuse, to which he responds, "Ay, it stands so that I may hardly tarry so / Long" (induction 2.125–26). The audience knows where it is, somewhere between the wanton pictures of the Italian Renaissance and the bawdy puns of the English theater.

We move from England, where travelers, huntsmen, players, and drunks move outside the city, to "fair Padua, nursery of arts" (1.1.2.), a cultural center which draws students to its famous university. Lucentio, like Valentine in *The Two Gentlemen of Verona*, fits the pattern of a young Italian gentleman who travels from one city to another with his father's "good will." Shakespeare evokes the positive image of fertility and ease with the reference to "fruitful Lombardy, / The pleasant garden of great Italy" (1.1.3–4). Coryat comments on the students from all over Europe who "with great desire flocke together to Padua for good letters sake, as to a fertile nursery, and sweete emporium and mart town of learning" (1:238 and 298). While Valentine leaves Verona to pursue a courtly education in Milan, Lucentio, a merchant's son, leaves Pisa to undertake a more academic "course of learning and ingenious studies" (1.1.9). Though we are informed that Lucentio's father, now dwelling in Pisa, is a Tuscan of the Bentivolii who himself or whose son has been "brought up in Florence," the young man describes his arrival in Padua in terms that would seem more appropriate to a country gentleman entering the big city of London: "Tell me thy mind, for I have Pisa left / And am to Padua come as he that leaves / A shallow plash to plunge him in the deep, / And with society seeks to quench his thirst" (21–24). The audience might not follow the Italian geography very carefully, but it would recognize a young man's eagerness to move from the shallows of a small town to the allure of the big city, where he can take the plunge in experience, if not in that part of philosophy "that treats of happiness." Tranio's response—"No profit grows where is no pleasure ta'en. / In brief, sir, study what you most affect" (39–40)—anticipates the transition from the academic to the theatrical, for the open space of the Italian city presents a group of Paduans whose arrival, though not announced by a trumpet, recalls the players of the induction. As Tranio says, their entrance provides "some show to welcome us to town" (47). The world Lucentio left behind, the Tuscan world of Florence and Pisa, hardly qualifies as a small pond, but the play creates a sense of the Italian city, of whatever size, as a place where the traveler will encounter those public displays that make urban life an entertaining plunge. For Shakespeare the Italian city, whether approached from Pisa or Westminster, becomes the quintessential urban center, with its inviting freedom of access and the opportunity it offers to exchange your old identity for a new one.

Shakespeare's representation of Italian cities draws on both the ideal city, imbued with the spirit of Renaissance harmony, and the more dynamic city, whose vitality spills out from behind the facade onto the open space of the stage. The degree of confusion that erupts will vary from one play to another, as will the extent to which the traveler or spectator finds that chaos either entertaining or disquieting. The opening scene connects the piazza with the house of Baptista, who enters fending off Bianca's suitors, Gremio and Hortensio, with the assertion that Katherina must be married before Bianca can be wooed. The public character of Padua as a center of learning extends to the private household, where Bianca will studiously await her turn on the marriage market: "My books and instruments shall be my company, / On them to look and practice by myself" (1.1.82–83). After she exits, the father makes additional plans to encourage his daughter's delight in "music, instruments, and poetry" by bringing into the household schoolmasters "fit to instruct her youth" (92–95).

Lucentio's first excursion into the liberal arts combines theater and grammar, for he will assume the identity of Cambio, the language teacher, to gain access to Bianca. The piazza of this northern Italian city generates more of the improvised theater one might identify with the commedia dell'arte than it does strictly academic pursuits. Gremio, called pantaloon in the stage direction (47), is assigned the role of the miserly old merchant of the commedia. Not only does the city square welcome foreigners, it draws them in with the spirited public shows and pastimes that cause Lucentio to fix his gaze on Bianca, a young lady who knows how to play the demurely studious daughter. Tranio prefers the show put on by Katherina—"That wench is stark mad or wonderful froward" (69). The central square remains in many ways the stage itself, a place where the rather elaborate joke played by the English lord in the induction will be mirrored in a number of ensuing suppositions. The kind of game that might be seen as peripheral to London life, something identified with vagabond players or a fanciful nobleman who might be the patron of such players, takes center stage in the Italian city. In this sense, Shakespeare represents Italian society as centered on theater. I do not mean that he falls into the modern trap of stereotyping Italians as theatrical because they "talk with their hands," but rather that he exploits a fundamental analogy between the lord of the induction and a society that thrives on the art of supposition. As the play moves from the open piazza to the closed setting of the final game won by Petruchio, we move back to the more fixed hierarchies of rank, gender, and social convention that "supposedly" prevail at home. We prepare to exit the theater.

When Petruchio and his man Grumio enter Padua as visitors from Verona, they immediately adopt the manner of performers, acting out a *lazzo*, or comic set piece of knocking at Hortensio's door. Like Valentine and Lucentio, Petruchio has left home for experience and fortune: "And I have thrust myself into this maze, / Happily to wive and thrive as best I may" (1.2.55–56). While Hortensio attacks the household of Baptista as though it were a fortress—"For in Baptista's keep my treasure is. / He hath the jewel of my life in hold" (118–19)—the literal and figurative treasure represented by Katherina requires something more than the costume that transforms Hortensio into Litio. In Petruchio Shakespeare introduces a performance artist who parodies the *sprezzatura* of Castiglione's ideal courtier. Removed from the sophisticated confines of the court and set to work in the public square, Petruchio appears artfully rude. The piazza serves as a market for education, trade, and marriage, as well as a theater that multiplies roles within its magic circle. The disguised Tranio must produce a false father to back his marriage offer—"I see no reason but suppos'd Lucentio / Must get a father, call'd suppos'd Vincentio; / And that's a wonder" (2.1.407–9). In this world servants become masters and sons beget fathers.

The mingling of the fluid world of the piazza with the more closed world of the household takes a number of forms in the play, none more interesting than the begetting of the supposed Vincentio. The scene that introduces the pedant who will become the supposed father takes place in a space outside Baptista's house—a garden, or loggia adjacent to the street—from which Tranio and Hortensio can observe Lucentio, disguised as the tutor Cambio, reading from and acting out Ovid's *Ars Amandi* with Bianca. In this scene Shakespeare maintains the image of the city-state as open to travelers like the pedant, a Mantuan who stops at Padua on his way to Rome and Tripoli, carrying with him "bills for money by exchange / From Florence" (4.2.89–90). The much-traveled pedant has also been to Pisa and has heard of Vincentio, one of its "grave citizens." The detail assists the proposed disguise, but it also advances the impression that the Italian cities of Tuscany and Lombardy are linked through commercial bills of exchange and through equally important family ties. On the other hand, Tranio convinces the Mantuan pedant to take on the identity of Vincentio because of the supposed friction between Mantua and Padua: "'Tis death for any one in Mantua / To come to Padua. Know you not the cause? / Your ships are stay'd at Venice, and the Duke, / For private quarrel 'twixt your Duke and him, / Hath publish'd and proclaim'd it openly" (4.2.81–85). Shakespeare briefly opens the counterimage of the Italian city-states enclosed within their walls, ruled by dukes whose private quarrels have public consequences. For a moment politics blocks the free movement of students, merchants, and pilgrims.

Something of the same duality appears when the real Vincentio encounters Petruchio and Katherina on the road to Padua (4.5). After some teasing that establishes once and for all Katherina's willingness to agree with whatever Petruchio says, be it that the sun is the moon or the old man a gentlewoman, the newlyweds accompany Vincentio to Padua. Having exited at the end of act 4, Vincentio, Petruchio, and Katherina enter a few lines into the next scene (5.1) before the house of Lucentio, executing a quick transition to what appears a very open city. But when the pedant "looks out of the window" impersonating the father and when Tranio appears in Lucentio's attire, old Vincentio becomes the outsider whose behavior threatens the city and requires that an officer be called: "Thus strangers may be hal'd and abus'd. O monstrous villain!" (5.1.108). The city just as suddenly opens up again when Lucentio explains that he has married Bianca, whereupon the agreeable patriarchs of Pisa and Padua resolve their differences.

∽

> Unlike self-made merchants, who tended to be hard-working, sober, thrifty and cautious, they [city nobles] were violent, flamboyant and quarrelsome; they looked down on everyone else, had an absurdly touchy sense of honour, and their feuds ravaged the towns. Moreover, they invariably congregated together in family groups or clans, the power of which was increased by their amalgamating with each other or absorbing outsiders.
>
> —Mark Girouard, *Cities and People* 38

The open stage as piazza maps an urban space that would have reminded the audience of the social and economic forces that drew many young men, like Shakespeare, to the city of London, forces that caused the city to expand dramatically during the last decades of the sixteenth century (Rappaport 77, 115). Both the city government and the court attempted to control the building that took place within and outside the walls of the city. But London continued to attract young commoners who could learn a trade and become citizens, and nobles who came to study at the Inns or to pursue a career at court (Stone 477). Neither walls nor proclamations could contain London's growth. The open space of the stage drew the city's expanding population to itself, and theater, in turn, became the object of laws that sought to control the time, place, and nature of performance. Within the precinct of that stage, Shakespeare creates an urban landscape centered on the open piazza of the Italian city-state. While movement carries with it the danger of metamorphosis and the threat of exile or imprisonment, the danger can be harnessed, as in Petruchio's strategic role-playing, or defused, as when authority figures, like Baptista and Vincentio, authorize the transformations love hath wrought.

The idealized city square of the Renaissance presents to the viewer geometrically organized space and is meant to serve as a microcosm of the ideal city (de Seta 29). Its monumental structures represent the proportions of classical architecture and of civic order. In the *città ideale* the classical allusions mix with the suggestion of more contemporary urban forms—the city gate, residences with their loggias, and the central fountain. This image of the city created by urban designers and painters merges with the image created on the Italian stage through the use of perspective in scenic design (D'Amico, "Poetic and Theatrical Perspectives" 312).

Did the public theaters in London, with their pillars painted to resemble marble, suggest a similarly monumental organization of space? We know that for royal entries and other civic pageants the open spaces within London were decorated with triumphal arches and with other architectural devices situated at conduits. On these special occasions parts of the city might have resembled the configuration of space that characterized the piazza of the ideal city. These urban scenes created an idealized image of the city and of its governing orders (Bergeron 18–19). Theater can be understood as a place where citizens gather before an image of their city projected through scenery and through the language and action of a play, as in Machiavelli's *La mandragola* (Flaumenhaft 86). Theater becomes as central to the definition of a city such as Florence as its famous Duomo or Palazzo Vecchio. And like the shifting scenes of a progress, open spaces within the city can be identified with different aspects of the city's complex public life, as represented by the market, the port, the temple, the arch, the throne, or the scales of justice.

Shakespeare's language can conjure up anything from a generic center between the market and the port to a more specific public location whose features take shape as the play's dialogue shades in or highlights the architectural features of his stage. Unlike the Renaissance theater that began to develop a fixed perspective scene against which the action of a play moved, Shakespeare lets each scene reflect the perspectives of his characters. In place of the fixed image we have an urban setting that changes shape as the dynamic and often chaotic life of the city drives the action. We have seen how Shakespeare uses the piazza to represent the openness of the Italian city, a characteristic expanded in his treatment of the piazza as market. Within this public arena Shakespeare merges the values of the *città ideale* with the conflicting interests and lifestyles of a diverse citizenry, turning a harmonious center into a jousting place.

The public space of *The Merchant of Venice* takes shape between the port and the mart, with Shylock's house and the courtroom of the ducal palace serving as the two Venetian interiors the play visits, one most private, or alien, and the other aristocratic and public. The piazza is a place of multiple perspectives. Venetian merchants and gentlemen conduct the business of their lives, the trading, masquing, and marrying, very much in the public space where the play begins. Alberti compares the port to "a confining pen, as on a racecourse; it is the starting point of your journey, and also the place to which you retire, once the course has been completed" (*Ten Books* 5:114). The piazza San Marco of Venice is both an enclosed arena and a port opening on the *bacino*, where ships would arrive from the distant places Shakespeare evokes in the opening lines of the play:

Your mind is tossing on the ocean,
There where your argosies with portly sail

> Like signiors and rich burghers on the flood,
> Or as it were the pageants of the sea,
> Do overpeer the petty traffickers
> That cur'sy to them, do them reverence,
> As they fly by them with their woven wings. (1.1.8–14)

Venice was a city whose nobles, or *signiors*, were also merchants. England did not have a noble merchant class, but younger sons of the gentry were making their way into trade in great numbers during the sixteenth century. In his *Survey of London*, John Stow informs us that "merchants of all nations had landing places" along the Thames (41), for London, like Venice, was unique in combining the role of capital city and port (Beier and Finlay 14). Mark Girouard points out the important link between geography and economics within the urban centers of Italy: "The central location of the Italian merchants on the Mediterranean put them in a strong position to dominate the movement of goods from east to west and north to south, and they built on to their geographical advantages by their business methods, which were far in advance of those used by other nations"(23). Monetary exchange links Shakespeare's Venetians who pursue trade with those who devote their time to the "plots and purposes" of love. As Lawrence Stone says of the English nobility, "play within moderation was a suitable pastime for a gentleman, one of whose functions was to live in idleness with elegance and grace" (567), as does Bassanio, "a scholar and a soldier" (1.2.113), who adventures for love and a golden dowry. As Harold Bloom says of the young Venetians in the play, "Everyone is a lot fresher than they were going to be four centuries later in *La Dolce Vita*, but basically they are the same set" (179).

Though Antonio and Bassanio are friends who stand together within the piazza, they also differ. Gratiano criticizes the merchant for being a man who has "too much respect upon the world" (or his investments), to which the melancholy Antonio responds: "I hold the world but as the world, Gratiano, / A stage, where every man must play a part, / And mine a sad one" (1.1.77–79). Gratiano portrays Antonio as one who puts on the mask of "Sir Oracle" in a "willful" manner, to gain a reputation for "wisdom, gravity, profound conceit" (92). Shakespeare may have been aware of the Venetian investment of political and economic capital in the terra firma, that Belmont to which the suitors turn. The Venetians, it was said, sought to cast off the commedia stereotype of the miserly pantaloon, or pantaleone, and to adopt the more liberal style favored by Bassanio: "Theyr former course of life was marchandising: which is now quite left and they looke to landward" (Chambers and Pullan 27). The commedia image of the old miser attaches to Shylock, but the "sad" merchant and the Jew are far more sober than the madcap suitors.

In keeping with Shakespeare's representation of the Italian city as a place of complex exchanges and relationships, the Venetian and the Jew meet in the open, but meet as antagonists: "You call me misbeliever, cut-throat dog, / And spet upon my Jewish gaberdine, / And all for use of that which is mine own" (1.3.111–13). Shakespeare's Venice has no ghetto—Shylock's pun on "use" and "usury" points to his freedom to lend money, to charge interest if he so desires, and to move in an unrestricted manner within the city. But Antonio can just as freely call Shylock a dog and spit on him when they meet.

While Antonio wears the mask of gravity, Gratiano plays the garrulous comedian; for as Lorenzo says, "I must be one of these same dumb wise men, / For Gratiano never lets me speak" (1.1.106–7). Bassanio wants his friend to modify this role in Belmont "lest through thy wild behavior / I be misconst'red in the place I go to" (2.2.187–88). The plans for a masque and the disguising used to effect Jessica's elopement are carried on in the spirit of aristocratic play associated with a form that came to England from Italy. As Enid Welsford points out, the "true character of the masquerie was evidently appreciated by Shakespeare, who in his early plays, where the scene is laid in Italy, makes the masque an impromptu social affair" (102). In addition, the masque brought with it a sense of gallantry and of something risqué, which derived from the fact that the masquers each chose a lady who was entertained with dancing and "*gallant conversation*" (135). Shakespeare might have been aware of the *compagnie della calza* in Venice, fraternal organizations of young patricians who sported distinctive hose (*calza*) and who performed plays on important public and private occasions. Their *momarie* combined aristocratic display with the inversions of everyday values found in the popular spirit of the Venetian carnival (Muraro 334; Zorzi 101–4). And that potentially disruptive spirit comes into the piazza with Gratiano.

We never enter an aristocratic interior to witness a dinner or masque because Shakespeare makes the Venetian piazza a place where private feeling and public roles merge (Ariès and Duby, *Passions* 9). We can see this in Salerio's account of how Bassanio and Antonio parted: "And even there, his eye being big with tears, / Turning his face, he put his hand behind him, / And with affection wondrous sensible / He wrung Bassanio's hand, and so they parted" (2.8.46–49). The theatricality of the scene as portrayed by Salerio should not diminish the sincerity of feeling behind the gestures. The metaphor of an older man pregnant with sorrow over the loss of his friend to marriage might remind an audience of the well- or ill-deserved reputation for homosexuality among Venetian noblemen: "The coiffure [*habitus capitis*] which Venetian women have recently taken to wearing could not be more indecent in the sight of God and men, since by means of this coiffure women conceal their sex and strive to please men by pretending to be men, which is a form of sodomy. ...This vice was openly practiced in Venice without shame; indeed, it had become so habitual that it was more highly regarded than having to do with one's own wife" (Chambers and Pullan 123–24; Michael Shapiro 97–100). In Jonson's *Volpone*, the learned Lady Politic mistakes Peregrine for a prostitute "in man's apparel" (4.2.8) because of her readiness to see Venice as a city of cross-dressing courtesans. Men attracted to prostitutes posing as men might also be attracted to other men; Portia will accuse Bassanio of being a bit too interested in the young doctor of Rome.

The conduct of life in public leads through Bassanio's love and Shylock's bond to the court, where intense personal feeling must defer to, or work around, the international reputation of Venice as a city governed by laws that take precedence over personal alliances. While the Rialto remains open to men who wear very different masks, the household accentuates differences of religion and custom (1.3.33). Venetian merchants and gentlemen can dine together, but Shylock knows that the Christians do not invite him to dine for love (2.5.13). They flatter him, and he will feed on, if not with, them. Like the Christians, he has mixed impulses. He withdraws when he hears that the evening's entertainment will include a masque, yet he foolishly leaves the keys to his sober house with a daughter who thinks the house a hell. But as a man caught up in a complex exchange of interest and feeling, he exhibits behavior that typifies Shakespeare's urbanites. We follow the Venetians of the play in calling Shylock the Jew, rather than the city dweller, the Venetian, or the Italian. Shakespeare's audience might have seen him as someone whose "dimensions, senses, affections, passions" (3.1.60) have been shaped as much by the complex nature of the Venetian piazza as by the unseen synagogue.

In the city appetites are apt to be more keenly aroused and, as Gratiano suggests to the masquers who await Lorenzo, just as quickly satiated (2.6.8–19). Shylock wants to shut out the sounds of the frolicsome Christians in a city famous for its carnival. A port city readily mixes the excitement of travel with the pleasures of dining, masquing, and stealing. From Shakespeare to Byron and beyond, Venice during carnival has been known as a place of "fiddling, feasting, dancing, drinking, masquing, / And other things which may be had for asking" (*Beppo* 7–8). What Shylock calls the "Christian fools with varnish'd faces" steal his daughter in a scene that might be taken straight out of a Venetian commedia dell'arte scenario, for it not only transforms his daughter into a disguised page and a Christian, but makes Shylock the pantaloon mocked in the street (2.8). While the differences that separate Antonio from young men like Lorenzo and Gratiano lead to nothing more than parting jokes or tears, for Shylock the piazza will become something more like the scene of the Venetian war of fists. According to Robert C. Davis, the *guerre dei pugni* transformed the well-known features of the urban landscape of Venice, its bridges, squares, and *campi*, into battlefields: "It is, in short, a Venice full of unexpected connotations and unforeseen heroes: not very much like the Republic of decorum, hierarchy, profit, and social control that most of the world has known for centuries" (6). Our first impression of the characters assembled in Shakespeare's Venetian square fits the traditional image of decorum, with potential differences relegated to asides. But the play provides a glimpse of another kind of energy, what Davis calls "the exaltation of violence over civic peace" (44), which can spill into the streets and squares of the city with the masquing aristocrats and the mocking boys. Shylock suffers most directly from the manifestations of urban misrule, but the discord spreads to Antonio and eventually reaches Belmont when the news arrives of Antonio's low estate (3.2.317). The royal merchant whose public gestures toward his friends epitomize generosity and decorum expresses his contempt for Shylock by spitting on, kicking, and calling Shylock a dog, with no apologies (1.3.126–31).

Shakespeare gives his open stage a Venetian character by identifying the city with merchant ventures, romantic voyages, and masques. The personal relationship between Antonio and Bassanio and the public bond used to finance the expedition to Belmont reflect the mixed public and private role of those Italian families, such as the Bardi, Medici, and Strozzi, who became "the great and famous Italian banking firms of the Middle Ages and early Renaissance" (Girouard 23). The development of business techniques like bills of exchange and double-entry bookkeeping did not diminish the importance of personal connections and family relationships. However, the brief scene in which the "naughty jailer" allows Antonio to "come abroad" (3.3.9–10) juxtaposes the personal level of business with the wider interests of the state (19–21). Unlike the merchant bankers and traders connected by the bonds of friendship and family, Shylock and Antonio are only linked by the legal bond and their residence in Venice. Within Venice, Shylock has been free to charge interest and Antonio to deliver those whose loans were forfeit, or, as Shylock sees it, to play "the fool that lent out money gratis" (3.3.1–3). On the public stage of Venice there are many ways of playing the fool, and Shylock resolves that he will not "be made a soft and dull-ey'd fool / To shake the head, relent, and sigh, and yield / To Christian intercessors" (14–16). He has been called a dog, and now he can use the fangs of the law to bite.

If the market allows strangers to exchange commodities within a protected sphere (Fumerton 179), the legal bond moves Antonio from that open space to a prison, and that displacement, in turn, recalls the kind of confrontation between rival clans, or tribes, that the market was designed to prevent: "He hates our sacred nation, and he rails / Even there where merchants most do congregate / On me, my bargains and my well-won thrift, / Which he calls interest. Cursed be my tribe / If I forgive him!" (1.3.48–52). Venice promoted itself as the marketplace of Europe and the East, an urban space where merchants of different nations and religions could gather to do business (McPherson 62). As Antonio says, "the trade and profit of the city / Consisteth of all nations" (3.3.30–31). Venetian law, in effect, promises to keep the market open, not to confiscate goods for political motives and not to set private interest above the laws. These laws are analogous to the rational, geometric architecture of the *città ideale*. But Antonio and Shylock bifurcate the ideal urban space. Differences of custom and religion create radically different perspectives for the two men: "Mark you this, Bassanio, / The devil can cite Scripture for his purpose. / An evil soul producing holy witness / Is like a villain with a smiling cheek, / A goodly apple rotten at the heart" (1.3.97–101).

Antonio and Shylock are not the merchant strangers who meet within a marketplace where they can agree to put aside their differences and freely exchange goods or services; they are as diametrically opposed as creatures of different species (115–19). The conflicting perspectives seem briefly to come into focus—the Christians invite Shylock to their dinner to celebrate the bond, and the audience crosses the threshold of Shylock's household. Whether the merry bond is but another example of the villain's "smiling cheek" or an offer of "kind" and "kindness" extended not from dog to man but between men, it cannot, as Portia will famously reveal, countermand the seal of citizenship.

In *The Merchant of Venice* we enter a complex urban space, a piazza that magnifies the relative openness of Italian society, while revealing an underlying contradiction between a commercial system based on law and, on the other hand, a system that serves friends and family who share a culture, whether as individuals they are prone to be melancholy, like Antonio, or "something too liberal," like Gratiano. We are told that Shylock's outcries "rais'd the Duke, / Who went with him to search Bassanio's ship" (2.8.4–5). This image of Shylock assisted by the duke counterpoints the public humiliation of the "dog Jew" crying out for his lost daughter and his lost ducats.

Shakespeare's audience, whether at one of the public theaters, or at court, or the Inner Temple, would never have been very far from the Thames River and those ocean thoroughfares plied by argosies or by suitors who cross deserts and seas to visit fair women (2.7.43). Since both forms of commerce thrive on the exchange of information, it is not surprising that among the many urban appetites being fed within the play we find the appetite for news. An exchange of letters and of garments leads to Jessica's elopement (2.5 and 6), while what Solanio calls "the plain highway of talk" carries news of shipwrecks and a daughter's betrayal (3.1.12). Tubal brings news from Genoa of a daughter who has taken to the road, leaving diamonds in her wake and selling her birthright for a monkey: "It was my turkis, I had it of Leah when I was a bachelor. I would not have given it for a wilderness of monkeys" (3.1.121–22). Shylock feels the difference between prodigality and commerce.

The aristocrats do not fear being known as prodigals. The open thoroughfares of pleasure lead away from the city, from Shylock's sober house to a pawnshop in Genoa or a Palladian villa in Belmont. International trade requires a different understanding of reputation. James Shapiro quotes Privy Councillor John Wolley's argument against anti-alien legislation: "This Bill should be ill for London, for the riches and renown of the City cometh by entertaining strangers, and giving liberty unto them. Antwerp and Venice could never have been so rich and famous but by entertaining of strangers, and by that means have gained all the intercourse of the world" (183). Shapiro draws the parallel between Wolley's opinion and the notion that, as Antonio says, to deny the commodity that strangers have with Venice would be to "impeach the justice of the state" (3.3.29). Justice serves the commercial interests of the state by protecting the strangers who have free access to the Venetian piazza. The perspective changes, however, when the action moves from the open piazza to the closed courtroom, where the same judicial system that had protected the trader attacks the alien.

∽

While Shakespeare fills the central space of the Italian comedies with domestic and mercantile activity, he does not usually turn the facade of the stage into a ducal palace from whose window, or balcony, a ruler might overlook the conflicts that break out within the piazza. The ruling authority within his Italian cities more often withdraws to an inner court or hall. His early tragedy *Romeo and Juliet* represents a notable exception to this pattern. In this play, Shakespeare makes the piazza a potentially violent arena that would have recalled the Shrove Tuesday riots, the attacks on aliens living in London, and the behavior of retainers who could turn public space into the stage for an attempted coup. Though historians are reassessing the disorder that existed in Elizabethan-Jacobean London, one view is that the problems of an expanding metropolis were controlled by the royal court, by the city fathers, and by the overlapping local administration of the wards and parish precincts: "Often spontaneous and uncontrolled, disturbances never intentionally challenged authority or even had as their object the attainment of specific, realistic goals" (Rappaport 11).

However, the underworld of London spawned its share of violent conflicts, and the ruling class often lacked the polite grace of Castiglione's ideal courtier. Drawn to London by the increasing centralization of power in the court, noblemen brought their violent confrontations to the streets of the city. Lawrence Stone describes a number of such encounters and traces the government's generally successful policy of containing them (Stone 225, 231, 398). John Stow records "the strong building of stone houses against the invasion of thieves in the night, when no watches were kept" (174). These structures are not quite the medieval tower-palazzi of a city like Florence, but they are protected spaces within or just outside the city's walls. As Ian Archer points out, Londoners thought of themselves as achieving a balance between authority and freedom:

> Some explicitly recognized the peculiarity of London by reference to continental contrasts, albeit with some patriotic hyperbole—thus the anonymous author of a tract defending the city's orphanage custom pointed out that London was governed "not by cruell viceroyes, as is Naples or Millaine, neither by proude Podesta, as be most cities in Italie, or insolent Lieutenants or presidentes, as are sundry Cities in France ... but by a man of trade or a meere merchant, who notwithstanding, during the time of his magistracie, carrieth himself with ... honorable magnificence in his port, and ensigns of estate." (*The Pursuit of Stability* 50)

In his comedies, Shakespeare's rulers, who are neither merchants nor tyrants, typically rule cities whose piazzas may be unruly but are generally peaceful. Gail Paster argues that Shakespeare often tends to "ruralize his comic cities," which lack the "nitty-gritty traces of urban habitation" that he will introduce into a play such as *Measure for Measure* (178).

However, in his tragedy *Romeo and Juliet*, Shakespeare does turn the Italian piazza into an urban battlefield. The chorus-sonnet that opens the play focuses first on the household and then on the "fair" city made "unclean" by an "ancient grudge." The word "ancient" reappears with reference to the patriarchs and their uncivil discord (1.1.92, 104), to the Capulet family's "ancient feast" (1.2.82), and to the "ancient vault" or "receptacle" (4.1.111; 4.3.39) of Capulet's tomb. The word might have suggested the antiquities of Verona, particularly its famous amphitheater, the Arena. But in this play things ancient are not always venerable. The old nurse, the "ancient lady" Mercutio mocks in the public square, becomes "Ancient damnation" (3.5.235), the fiend who has betrayed Juliet's trust. The generally positive identification of Italian cities with the ancient world follows the pattern of the *città ideale*, where architectural symbols of ancient culture—the arch, the temple, and the column—frame the open urban space. If Verona was considered "fair" because adorned with ancient monuments, Shakespeare's version of the city has a contemporary edge to it created by aggressive jokes about thrusting women to the wall and by the explosiveness of the Italianate dueler Tybalt. A destructive force within the city, the ancient feud has eroded the authority of the prince and undermined the social tranquility of the city's public space.

The rigorous study of ancient political wisdom that Machiavelli recommends has, on the other hand, escaped Prince Escalus, for the ruler of Shakespeare's Verona lacks the will or political acumen required to cleanse the city by taking definitive action against the warring factions. Though he describes himself as "moved" (1.1.88), the prince does not get the attention of his subjects with the kind of political theater that Machiavelli described in chapter 7 of his *Prince* when Cesare Borgia left the severed body of Remirro de Orca in the public square of Cesena (de Alvarez 45; D'Amico, "Machiavelli's Borgia" 26). Escalus calls his rebellious subjects "beasts" (1.1.83) but has not learned Machiavelli's lesson of fighting with both the laws that are proper to man and with the force proper to beasts (*The Prince* XVIII; de Alvarez 107).

The city is, perhaps, always divided between its impressive architectural forms and the new or ancient grudges acted out by its unruly citizens. We are not told the cause of the conflict, but in the opening scene

Shakespeare uses the servant-retainers to demonstrate its genesis in the Italian vendetta: "If any man wrong thee, wrong him againe, or else be sure to remember it" (Florio, *Second Frutes* 19). Shylock is not the only one who learns the lesson of revenge out in the city's piazza. Hardly the duelists Mercutio mocks (2.4.19–35), the servants Sampson and Gregory, with their broad swords and "washing" or slashing blows, give the Italian feud English features.

The walls of a city, which should protect its citizens from external threats, seem to exacerbate the conflict by compressing opponents within one space, forcing one group or the other to the wall. Coryat says that the captain's palace in Verona, formerly of the Scaliger's, "looketh towards that goodly walke where there is a great meeting of Gentlemen and merchants twise a day" (2:25). Shakespeare projects into the central meeting place of his Verona more of the quarrelsomeness of the English aristocracy. The privilege drawn from a medieval tradition of military prowess was often reduced to theatrical displays in tourneys and pageants or to rough-and-tumble confrontations between small armies of retainers in London, brawls that might rise to the level of rebellion, as with Essex's attempt in 1598. For Shakespeare's audience, old Capulet's "long sword" might have evoked the medieval origins of the English, if not the Italian, aristocracy (75).

The bifurcation of what should be a unified public space within the city would be signaled by the use of opposing entrances for the two households—the Capulets rushing in through one gate, or portal, that leads, we imagine, to their enclave within the city, and the Montagues from the other. The action of the play never moves to the place of civic authority, the palazzo of Verona's prince. Rather, the "civil" brawl draws Prince Escalus to the public space to confront his rebellious subjects; in him we see a version of the Italian *podestà* figure who was supposed to bring authority to feuding Italian communes (Martines 42, 116). That ideal of civic purity, represented by the fountain that stands at the center of the square, has been defiled by the "bloody hands" and "mistempered weapons" of the opposing clans that produce the "purple fountains issuing from your veins" (1.1.85). Prince Escalus tries to protect the public interest of "our" streets by taking Capulet and later Montague to "old Free-town, our common judgment-place" (102), where he supposedly will subject both households to the authority of the state. The patriarchs do not have any clearly defined political power within the city, though they are obviously prominent members of a noble class whose influence dominates public life through family alliances of the kind that would emerge from the marriage of Juliet to the county Paris.

The action of the play moves between the public square, where citizens are free to bandy insults or arrange assignations, and the household of old Capulet, a citadel within Verona which Romeo and his young friends invade, much as the masquing Venetians invaded Shylock's house. This idea of assault directly echoes the play's opening ("I will take the wall of any man or maid of Montague's") and is repeated in Romeo's lines on the all-too-virtuous Rosaline: "She will not stay the siege of loving terms, / Nor bide th'encounter of assailing eyes, / Nor ope her lap to saint-seducing gold" (1.1.212–14).

The conversation between Lord and Lady Montague and Benvolio, which takes place on a stage still littered with the signs of the brawl, sets Romeo apart from Verona's piazza. If that urban space has become a stage where Tybalt enters with "his sword prepar'd" (109), we catch a glimpse of Romeo in the wings, outside the city walls: "Where, underneath the grove of sycamore / That westward rooteth from this city side, / So early walking did I see your son. / Towards him I made, but he was ware of me, / And stole into the covert of the wood" (1.1.121–25). Even within the household Romeo withdraws from the more public space of the great hall. Old Montague laments that his son steals home at dawn and "private in his chamber pens himself" (138) secret and close (149). Shakespeare initially distances the young man, for better or for worse, from the urban space where men act out roles assigned by ancient grudges. In the role of lover Romeo is not less conventional but far less violent.

The piazza as battleground becomes the appropriately ironic setting for Capulet and Paris to discuss marriage, an institution that should merge public and private interests, as well as public and private spaces within the city. Though Capulet considers his daughter an asset to be given or withheld in accordance with the needs of the clan, he for the moment balances his "will" and his daughter's "choice": "But woo her, gentle Paris, get her heart, / My will to her consent is but a part; / And she agreed, within her scope of choice / Lies my consent and fair according voice" (1.2.16–19). The easy-flowing couplets reflect Capulet's confidence that an accord will be reached. The mood is more in keeping with the spirit of Shakespeare's comedies, though the scene opens with a reminder that in the political arena the old patriarchs of the city only agree when they are "bound" (1–3).

Shakespeare reintroduces the comi-tragic mixture of private grudges and public agreements through Capulet's illiterate servant who carries private invitations that are read in public. The play merges the comic sense of the square of the Italian city as an area open to a wide range of exchanges, from love letters to bawdy jokes, with the tragic sense of the ancient Italian arena as an urban space where nobles, in the guise of fencing gladiators, exhibit their distempered humors. As a theater of love or war, the public space creates the context for performance, of display before an audience of fellow citizens. The agreeably social dimension of Verona links the public square to the public space within the Capulet home, the great hall where the feast will take place. Building on that convergence, Capulet might use his "fair according voice" to move beyond the ancient grudge, for he possesses the authority, as we see when he restrains Tybalt, and perhaps the inclination to play a part in the creation of a spirit of consent in ancient Verona. But that inclination never shapes public policy, and the potentially inclusive spirit of the piazza does not absorb the Capulet household.

Shakespeare takes the essence of the Renaissance city, the opportunity it provides to consort freely with all and sundry in its open square, and makes that the basis of tragedy. In Mercutio he creates a more explosive version of Gratiano, the friend whose "wild behavior" must be tolerated, if not controlled (*The Merchant of Venice* 2.2.187). Shakespeare replaces the *sprezzatura* of Castiglione's courtiers with a strain of English madness that owes more to the queens or sluts of London, via Queen Mab, than to Verona's *piazza brà*. Romeo excuses the bawdy talk of Mercutio, much as Bassanio excuses Gratiano: "A gentleman, nurse, that loves to hear himself talk, and will speak more in a minute than he will stand to in a month" (2.4.147–49). Having been made the object of Mercutio's public mockery, the nurse considers him a "saucy merchant" full of "ropery" and a "Scurvy knave"—clearly not a gentleman. But among the restless gentlemen of Verona, to be "sociable" rather than "fishified" is to be ready for a public game, rather than a private love affair, to be a man who will perform in the square, where reputation stands or falls according to the sharpness of one's wit or one's rapier. Romeo appears to have returned to the fold, to be once again one of the boys, but he moves outside the urban space of Mercutio's sports, drawn toward the extramural space of love, toward the sycamores, gardens, and abbey walls that border the city. Both Tybalt's childlike obsession with the ancient grudge and Mercutio's mercurial temper pull Romeo toward the piazza, where he acts out the role of avenger.

The last scene set in the piazza merges the heat of a Mediterranean summer, the heat of Italian blood ("thou art as hot a Jack in thy mood as any in Italy"), and the Italianate style of dueling that had become popular in England (Yates, *Florio* 133). We are informed that Tybalt, restrained by old Capulet during the feast, has sent Romeo a challenge (2.4.7). Mercutio's speech mocking those who look for public occasions to quarrel is itself a performance that leads directly to the confrontation with Tybalt. The occasion for a quarrel comes, appropriately, from the phrase "Mercutio, thou consortest with Romeo" (3.1.45). Consorting, which for Shakespeare represents the essence of the life of the city square, becomes the occasion for a challenge. Mercutio interprets the word "consortest" as an insult because it makes him a base, public performer—"dost thou make us minstrels?" (3.1.46; Stone 582–83). Benvolio, ever the ineffectual peacemaker, is sensitive to the public setting: "We talk here in the public haunt of men. / Either withdraw unto some private place, / Or reason coldly of your grievances, / Or else depart; here all eyes gaze on us" (50–54).

The force of these aristocratic quarrels cannot be restrained by the prince's edict, which has, as Romeo puts it, "Forbid this bandying in Verona streets" (89), or by Romeo's secret reason for loving Tybalt (the fact that they are now in-laws), any more than it is controlled by Mercutio's own sense of the contradictions inherent in the quarrelsome nature of men. The code of honor drives the public behavior of most aristocratic young men and their retainer-servants, forcing them to react aggressively to any real or imagined insult, and to reject any "vile submission," as Mercutio calls Romeo's response to Tybalt's "villain" (73). Tragically, the heart of the Renaissance city, its open central space, becomes the setting for yet another variation on the ancient grudge. The central space of the *città ideale* can be open and harmonious because the will of its citizens is balanced by consent.

The fatal wounding of Mercutio in the public square precipitates Romeo's revenge, for he has been made to appear effeminate, his "reputation stain'd / With Tybalt's slander" (111–12). The stain of blood returns, as in the first scene, to pollute the city's fountain. The geometric ratios of an idealized civic square reflect a notion of proportion, of balance within the individual and between the citizens and the state's institutions. In this play, Shakespeare reshapes the Italian piazza to create an opposite image of individual humors creating distorted perspectives. Like heat rising from the pavement under a Mediterranean sun, these passions warp the idealized harmony of the *città ideale*. On the open space of Shakespeare's stage, the parries of wit become deadly, the metaphors literal ("Ask for me to-morrow, and you shall find me a grave man" [97–98]). The chaos of the fight and the screams of Lady Capulet once again disrupt the supposed order of the city, while the prince's decision to exile Romeo displaces the tumult but does not begin to create the emotional and intellectual perspective that would be needed to make the city center a place of civic harmony. We are given some hints of a more balanced perspective in old Capulet's ability to see with the eyes of his own youth and to restrain Tybalt during the feast, in his sense of the importance of the event to his household's reputation and to the city at large, in the friar's attempts to use spiritual or natural authority to mitigate extremes, and in Juliet's insistence that she be married to her impetuous lover. But these intentions never converge.

In other chapters I will consider in more detail the relationship between inner spaces and the institutions of the city. In Verona the frustrated Escalus comes into the square to deliver his edicts; in republican Venice we withdraw to a courtroom where the duke must bow to the authority of the law. Shakespeare's urban rulers certainly have the power to exile a Valentine or a Romeo. But the authority of the father, undisputed within the household, does not extend through the prince into the city.

The equation between husband and prince that Shakespeare introduces in Katherina's concluding speech in *The Taming of the Shrew* does not appear in any distinctive way as a feature of his Italian civic centers. Just as the prince had forbid "bandying" in Verona's streets, Katherina recants her former rebelliousness: "My mind hath been as big as one of yours, / My heart as great, my reason haply more, / To bandy word for word and frown for frown" (5.2.170–73). Such looks and such behavior destroy a woman's beauty, making her "like a fountain troubled, / Muddy, ill-seeming, thick, bereft of beauty" (142–43) because, the speech suggests, a wife should obey her husband as a subject obeys a prince. Though the fountain appears in the context of "meads" and "fair buds," it can also be associated with city life, since the relationship between wife and husband, or subject and prince, is represented as a debt paid for a service rendered—the service of governance, or "maintenance," being the provision of something the subject needs, like water. The speech makes the political hierarchy appear natural, as well as socially expedient—"scornful glances" are as damaging to a woman's beauty as frosts to meads or whirlwinds to fair buds. If not wholly unnatural, for winter and storms are a part of the natural world, the glances cost more in frustration than they are worth.

This assumes that the husband and the prince can weather difficulties—"To watch the night in storms, the day in cold" (150). As Lena Orlin points out, effective governance will create in the subject, or woman, a sense of being "indebted beyond the possibility of requital" ("The Performance" 187). But the hierarchy does not assert itself quite so naturally in the Italian cities, where Shakespeare's princes have authority but little effective power. Shakespeare represents the Italian city as a place of comic transformations and tragic confrontations, where men and women of different cities, faiths, social classes, and households encounter one another as friends or foes. We are not asked to imagine the piazza as a space dominated by an architectural symbol of authority, such as a tower (or Palazzo Vecchio). The civic rulers of Shakespeare's Italian cities do not exact the debt of obedience in return for protection from those hostile forces that stand outside the walls of the city. In *Othello*, the city fathers rely on the Moor to provide the military leadership that will secure their households. In the figure of Don Pedro in *Much Ado About Nothing*, Shakespeare combines the military leader who protects the city with the patriarchal overseer who attempts to control the domestic world within its walls (see chapter 8). But Don Pedro remains a surrogate governor not wholly at one with the city. The city squares of the Italian plays are not islands of tranquility buffered from the outside world by strong walls and wise rulers.

∽

If the Illyria of *Twelfth Night* can, with the assistance of the Italian names used in the play, be considered an Adriatic city, the behavior of Duke Orsino in act 5 might prove an exception to the absence of power figures in the piazza, for as he suggests to Feste, the time has come for him to stop playing the fool and start showing his authority. Though set before and closely tied to Olivia's household, act 5, scene 1 has a distinctly public character. The duke has emerged from his lovelorn isolation to confront the cruel fair. When the officers bring in Antonio, the duke recalls not only Antonio's face when he saw it last "besmear'd / As black as Vulcan in the smoke of war" but other details of a sea fight (5.1.52–53). This echo of his military authority becomes more immediate when Orsino identifies Cesario as the "instrument / That screws" him from Olivia's favor. Orsino suddenly casts off the role of passive lover to become, momentarily, the political tyrant whose toughness will equal the cold behavior of the "marble-breasted tyrant" Olivia. He is ready for mischief, ready to kill someone he loves to spite someone he now thinks he hates—"I'll sacrifice the lamb that I do love, / To spite a raven's heart within a dove" (5.1.130–31). No one intercedes, but in the tolerant spirit of comedy, the duke backs off when the priest confirms that Cesario and Olivia are married—"Farewell, and take her, but direct thy feet / Where thou and I (henceforth) may never meet" (168–69). We move from the pagan spirit of those "unauspicious altars" where Orsino has worshipped in the role of languishing lover, and where he seems capable of sacrificing "the lamb" Cesario in the guise of tyrant, to the public institution represented by the priest, whose lines evoke the ceremonial order of the "compact" between Olivia and Sebastian. To pursue the analogy with the *città ideale*, we might argue that though he does not make use of a theatrical set painted in perspective, Shakespeare uses language to create an image of the temple, an institution whose authority keeps the city and its ruler balanced (see chapter 7). We can imagine an open piazza framed by the temple and the arch, icons of spiritual and temporal authority, set in that visual order which mirrors the ideal organization of space and of civic life within Illyria.

On the other hand, the happy ending owes a great deal to Shakespeare's characteristic representation of the Italian piazza as a center of freely flowing action that resists closure. The final transformation of Cesario to Viola hinges on a theatrical change of costume. Viola delays embracing her brother, and being formally united with Orsino, until she can return in what she calls her "maiden weeds." Viola's rather sudden revelation that the captain "upon some action / Is now in durance, at Malvolio's suit" (5.1.275–76) further delays the removal of her "masculine usurp'd attire," since Malvolio later exits vowing revenge "on the whole pack of you" (378). The question of attire unbalances the conclusion, if we are thinking of visual perspective, or sounds a discord if we think of the conclusion as resolving harmonies. But in another sense Shakespeare remains true to the character of his Italian cities when he allows a steward, like the outsider Shylock, to be a spoilsport with legal rights. The ebb and flow of conflict and resolution played out within the piazza will continue. Illyria faces the external threat of shipwrecks and pirates, as well as internal threats to law and social decorum from a volatile ruler and litigious subjects. Malvolio's dream of being married to his mistress accords with the open spirit of the city, though when his imagination takes the next step and opens Olivia's bedroom, the steward projects himself into a space that remains closed to him. But in keeping with his general conception of the Italian city, Shakespeare maintains the fluid atmosphere of Illyria even as the happy ending fixes boundaries. The duke chooses to entreat Malvolio to a peace and to address Viola as Cesario until her final transition from "the Count's servingman" to his "mistress, and his fancy's queen" (5.1.380–88).

As the characters vacate the public space before Olivia's house where this long scene has been played out, Feste's song moves us from the Italian city dominated by its central square suffused with the magic of transformation and metamorphosis, to the city of London with its knaves, thieves, and tosspots, where "the rain it raineth every day." In the Italianate world of Illyria, the controlling hierarchy coexists with a more pagan world of Saturnalia, presided over by the two-faced Janus, a god who sanctions various forms of duality, including the mixing of traditional gender roles. It may have seemed all too apparent to some Puritans that theater itself operates under the auspices of this same pagan god.

In many ways the piazza is the quintessential feature of Shakespeare's city-state. With its potential for encounter and exchange, confusion and discovery, it is a microcosm of the Renaissance city. Shakespeare's open, nonlocalized stage does not require a sharp differentiation between the street and the square; both serve as urban locations where a variety of characters meet. More important is the distinction between a city like Venice, oriented toward the open, central piazza, and the Milan of *The Two Gentlemen of Verona*, or the Sicilia of *The Winter's Tale*, which are oriented toward courtly interiors. In the latter example, though a lord will inform Leontes that Polixenes is "here, in your city" (5.1.186), the audience has experienced Sicilia as a courtly complex with its walls and postern gates, gardens, prison, court, and bedrooms, but not as a city with an open square and busy streets.

Shakespeare's representation of the Italian city varies in accordance with the dramatic character and genre of each play. There is no space between the inner world of Sicilia's jealous fantasies and the outer world of the oracle and of pastoral Bohemia. To deny Leontes his diseased perception is to turn the outer world to nothing: "Why then the world and all that's in't is nothing, / The covering sky is nothing, Bohemia nothing, / My wife is nothing, nor nothing have these nothings, / If this be nothing" (1.2.293–96). Only Paulina's sharp tongue brings the corrective perspectives of the open piazza and the street into the court. In his pastoral tragicomedy, Shakespeare begins the process of regeneration in Bohemia, but generally the potential for renewal derives from the open character of the city itself.

The reversal of this identification of place and genre is instructive. In *Romeo and Juliet* the settings of comedy, the garden, piazza, and bedroom, frame the emergence of a love that struggles to overcome the city's ancient grudge. By foreshadowing tragedy in the garden, by setting the decisive murders in the piazza, and staging the father-daughter confrontation in the bedroom, Shakespeare underlines the tragic mixture of comic form and content, as he does with the "fatal" sonnet that serves as prologue, and with Mercutio's dying puns.

Similarly in *Othello*, the elements of city comedy are given a nasty edge, which points toward the tragedy that will unfold on the island of Cyprus. The mocking from the street of the pantaloon whose daughter has eloped, and the confrontation in the street between the old man and the captain, anticipate the scenes where Othello plays his own tormented role in what he perceives to be the stale city comedy of a wife's betrayal (4.1 and 2).

As Shakespeare developed his own variations on the structure of New Comedy, he was drawn to the Italian city-states because they could be used to represent the potential for a spirited exchange of ideas, goods, and persons within and between urban centers. This potential was present in London, but Shakespeare's development of a comic form that brought Plautus and Terence to the English stage by way of Greene and Lyly (Frye, *Anatomy* 182) required the romantic distancing that Italy provided. Shakespeare was not a city boy, but living and working in London he found the spirit of renewal, what Frye identified as the "green world" (*Natural Perspective* 144), not only in the forest and wood but in the piazzas, streets, and gardens of his Italian city-state.

3
City Streets

THE MAJOR ARTERIES of Shakespeare's London ran from Bishopsgate, Aldgate, and the Tower in the east toward what was to become the more fashionable district outside the walls to the west, beyond Ludgate and Newgate along Fleet Street and the Strand. Streets such as Old Fish-Cannon and Eastcheap would have taken an urban traveler past stately merchant homes, gardens, churches, and large complexes such as Grey Friars, as well as alleys crowded with tenements. The great markets straddled the central Newgate-Aldgate axis of the city (Porter 48), a hive of handicrafts, wholesale and retail trades, with manufacture and various services located close to or beyond the walls. Fernand Braudel says of the city that "it extended like a 'bridgehead to the north.' For it was northwards that the whole network of roads, lanes and alleys ran that connected London to the counties and the rest of England. The major highways, all old Roman roads, ran towards Manchester, Oxford, Dunstable and Cambridge. They were the scene of a bustling throng of carts, carriages, before long stagecoaches and post-horses, by which the London traffic spilled out on to the road network" (552). From the gates in the northern wall, approached through West Smithfield, Moor Fields, the Old Artillery Garden, and Spittlefields, the main streets took a more circuitous route south through the city toward the Thames, London Bridge, and the river crossings to Bankside.

When Shakespeare makes his stage a street within one of his Italian settings, the imagined urban artery typically passes before a house on an axis that leads to a port, or to the gates that open to fields, suburbs, and the open road. Shakespeare does not seek to create a picturesque version of the street life of an Italian city, as he might have done by combing his sources and his experience of London, and as Ben Jonson did to some extent in his *Volpone*. In Shakespeare's Italian settings the street functions as a conduit for movement within the more generic urban landscape.

On special occasions the pageants that were staged in London moved through streets that were transformed into theatrical sets. At points along the way theatrical representations would display the city or the court to itself, defining what it meant to be a citizen and a loyal subject of the queen. These displays sought to fix values that were identified with and embodied in the structures and institutions of the city. But the very transformation of the streets during a period of civic festivity reflects the dynamic energy that made the city a center of change. Nobles, the young sons of gentry, merchants, and laborers were drawn to London. They transformed the city and were transformed by it, for better or for worse (Rappaport 314).

The fixed elements of the public theater, or of any space Shakespeare and his company adopted for a performance, were utilized in various ways to effect the transition between the place of the stage, its geographical and social location near the city of London, and the fictive places recreated within the confines of that theater. As we have seen, Shakespeare imagines an Italian social system that allows gentlemen of known families to move between city-states in search of wives, education, or adventure. The streets of these cities are, therefore, open to those who commute between Verona and Milan, Pisa and Padua, Belmont and Venice. Similarly, getting to Shakespeare's theater itself might have involved a voyage of sorts across the river Thames, or beyond London's walls. Most of the city streets of Shakespeare's Italian settings are near a place of embarkation—a generic river or seaport. As is the case most notably with the infamous seacoast of Bohemia in *The Winter's Tale*, or Milan's seaport in *The Tempest* (1.2.145), the geography of the stage simply replaces "real" geography.

An important function of the street scene in Shakespeare's plays is to draw the audience into the imagined setting, and it is frequently a servant's lines that merge London with the Italian city. Launce, for example, recreates a departure scene that would have made the London audience feel perfectly at home in Verona: "I think Crab my dog be the sourest-natur'd dog that lives: my mother weeping, my father wailing, my sister crying, our maid howling, our cat wringing her hands, and all our house in a great perplexity, yet did not this cruel-hearted cur shed one tear" (*The Two Gentlemen of Verona* 2.3.5–10). For Howard C. Cole, this parody of the "tide of tears" Julia sheds when Proteus catches the tide and departs for Milan burlesques but also supports the main plot ("The 'Full Meaning'" 222–23). When Launce acts out the departure scene, using his shoes, staff, and hat to represent the domestic players (leaving out the hand-wringing cat), he performs a *lazzo* that places him squarely in the tradition of the Italian commedia dell'arte, even as the comic business superimposes London on Verona. After Panthino calls Launce "aboard" to follow his master Valentine, the action shifts to Milan, where Speed picks up the verbal game Launce had left off. We have moved from one Italian city to another but have never left the city of London and its servant-apprentices who took leave of their families, accompanied by the likes of Crab perhaps, to follow a master or to make their fortune in the growing metropolis. The street runs through London, as we see when Launce and Speed meet in Milan and immediately repair to an "alehouse" (2.5.7) while engaging in some verbal play that includes a topical reference to the English "church-ale" festival (57–58), with a nod, perhaps, toward the alehouses located just outside the theater.

Often acting as messengers or go-betweens, the servants are naturally at home in the streets, and their colloquial language, puns, and asides create an equally natural affinity with the audience. The street is, in this sense, a part of the *platea*, as opposed to the more distanced locus of a court or stately interior. And the Italian city streets through which we move in Shakespeare's plays are not exotically dangerous, even for young women. The streets are not identified with the threat of rape and violence that we find, for example, in an Italian play such as *Gl'ingannati* (D'Amico, "The Treatment of Space" 269). Though Julia conceals herself to prevent the "loose encounters of lascivious men" (*The Two Gentlemen of Verona* 2.7.41), the young women who take to the streets disguised as pages, following not only love but a convention of Italian drama (Campbell "The Two Gentlemen of Verona" 56), are not particularly fearful or sentimental. They depart dry-eyed, more in the spirit of Crab than the hand-wringing cat. Jessica blushes to see herself "transformed to a boy" (*The Merchant of Venice* 2.6.39) and Julia does fear that her "unstaid" journey will make her "scandaliz'd," but in Shakespeare's Italian plays the streets are not identified with scandal. When Portia and Nerissa "turn two mincing steps / Into a manly stride," they burlesque the behavior of "bragging Jacks" who boast of their conquests (*The Merchant of Venice* 3.4.60–77), but Shakespeare does not portray the gentlewomen of Belmont as being at risk in their excursion to Venice. Portia's cover story of a monastic visit serves to test male fidelity rather than to protect female reputation. It is only in the forest outside the city that we encounter outlaws of the kind Silvia meets when she pursues Valentine (*The Two Gentlemen of Verona* 5.1.9).

When Shakespeare sets a scene in the street, he does so to underline social and psychological transition. Those characters who are most at home in the street are the city dwellers who make a profession of transition—the clowns, fools, and servants—and those strangers who must make their way into and through the city. The street is home to the city's transient servants, disguised women, strangers, and clowns. And these roles often merge in subtle ways, especially in *Twelfth Night*. The urban space that links the court of Orsino with the house of Olivia has its generic port, where Viola arrives disguised as a servant-eunuch and where Sebastian and Antonio alight in their travels. It has lodgings in its south suburbs, much as London did, and some sights to be seen (though apparently no theaters): "In the south suburbs at the Elephant / Is best to lodge. I will bespeak our diet, / Whiles you beguile the time, and feed your knowledge / With viewing of the town" (3.3.39–42). In its streets, strangers are apt to encounter the clown Feste, whose wanderings outside the household exasperate Olivia (1.5.3). And it is in the street that the servant-fools meet one another, as when Viola/Cesario asks if Feste is Olivia's fool, to which he responds: "No, indeed, sir, the Lady Olivia has no folly. She will keep no fool, sir, till she be married, and fools are as like husbands as pilchers are to herrings, the husband's the bigger. I am indeed not her fool, but her corrupter of words" (3.1.32–36). Feste, among others, has observed Olivia's interest in the young messenger Cesario, who may be playing the fool, or corrupter of more than words with his lady, while also betraying Orsino, the bigger fool, who wants to be Olivia's husband. Folly "does walk about the orb like the sun, it shines every where" (38–39); it moves between Olivia and Orsino, like a go-between, making fools of lords and ladies. For the professional clown, the street provides an escape but also functions as the market for profitable gags and clever begging. It has its risks, for the entertainer must amuse in order to survive, but Shakespeare does not represent the street as a labyrinth. The Italian city-state of Shakespeare's stage combines excitement with a complex sense of order.

Generally free of thugs and pickpockets, when the street is dangerous it is so for characters like Antonio, who have done some offense to the state, or Sir Toby, who receives a hurt from Sebastian after he pushes the fight between Sir Andrew and Cesario a bit too far (5.1.190). Momentarily the street merges with the more violent outposts of Illyria, where Antonio engaged in the "sea-fight 'gainst the Count his galleys" (3.3.26) and where, as we learn later in the play, he reportedly "took the *Phoenix* and her fraught from Candy" and "did the *Tiger* board" (5.1.61–62). But the moment passes, and Shakespeare returns us to streets where wordplay replaces swordplay.

~

The public space before an identified house has a slightly different dramatic character. The house stands within the walls of the city, as the stage stands within the circle of the galleries. In turn, the house, like the city's walls, protects what it encloses. Patriarchs must be careful of their daughters and their ducats, for as Feste sings, "'Gainst knaves and thieves men shut their gate" (*Twelfth Night* 5.1.395). But the house is not, on the other hand, sealed off from the street. To be sure, Shylock carefully shuts up his house (*The Merchant of Venice* 2.5) and Brabantio has to deal with Roderigo haunting about his doors (*Othello* 1.1.96), but the permeability of the domestic barrier would have been familiar to the audience, for it reflects the character of London, where "neighbors were well-informed about each other's behaviour because so much popular sociability took place within the street" (Archer, *The Pursuit of Stability* 76).

The street harbors more "shallow fopp'ry" than outright violence of the kind a sober householder, like Shylock, wants to lock out. Thomas Moisan ("'Knock me'" 278–80) discusses the "gently subversive" disruption, or blurring of hierarchical class distinctions, revealed in the street scene where Petruchio commands his servant Grumio to "knock" at Hortensio's gate—"Knock, sir? Whom should I knock? Is there any man has rebus'd your worship?" (*The Taming of the Shrew* 1.2.6–7). The inversion of the master-servant relationship played out in the street foreshadows the confrontation between Petruchio and Katherina Minola, also known more familiarly as Kate and Katherine. From my perspective, this rough-and-tumble confrontation between master and servant, both of whom are friends to Hortensio, reflects the freedom that Shakespeare projects into the Italian city. It is in the street that Tranio and Lucentio swap identities and that Vincentio finds his identity usurped by the pedant. Shakespeare once again takes a characteristic of the space surrounding his stage, the vibrant and at times chaotic life of the streets and alleys of London, and sharpens the focus when the setting moves to Italy. Servant and master are separated by class and yet tied to one another by custom. Petruchio demonstrates his physical, rather than intellectual, dominance when he ends the exchange by wringing Grumio's ear for not comprehending. The master has power over the servant, but like straight man and comic, master and servant fall into a familiar routine, or *lazzo*. The Italian street scene thus magnifies the performance element of a social relationship that must have been common in London.

The streets are also open to the winds of fortune that move young Italians from one city to another. When Hortensio asks what "happy gale" has blown his friend to Padua from "old Verona," Petruchio answers, "Such wind as scatters young men through the world / To seek their fortunes farther than at home, / Where small experience grows" (1.2.48–52). Since Petruchio travels to "wive and thrive" and to "see the world," Baptista's household provides the perfect match, offering as it does a young woman "With wealth enough, and young and beauteous, / Brought up as best becomes a gentlewoman" (86–87), whose dubious reputation (89–90) will more than satisfy Petruchio's desire for experience.

For those who pursue Bianca, the walls of the house and the authority of the father function as the traditional blocking devices of comedy. For Petruchio, Baptista's household is not a citadel or "keep" (118) that must be attacked from the street. Rather than invading in disguise, as Hortensio and Lucentio will do, Petruchio sets out to overcome Padua's Katherina by bringing the raucous spirit of the street into the house and confronting the woman whose aggressive persona intimidates her family and entertains her neighbors. He becomes the intruder, the confrontational upstart who mirrors the role Kate plays within the house.

Petruchio conquers by abducting his bride from the marriage ceremony and subjecting her to the rigors of the open road. He removes her to his house, a suburban space that she finds as disorderly as the street, where he reverses the "knocking" scene by purposefully misunderstanding his servants. As William Hazlitt remarks, "The whole of his treatment of his wife at home is in the same spirit of ironical attention and inverted gallantry" (343). Petruchio's household also has a distinctly English cast, with its servants named Curtis, Nathaniel, Gregory, and Philip, its bad food, and its cold (4.1). Petruchio's comparison between the taming method he adopts at home and the devices a noble huntsman uses to manage a falcon (4.1.190–96) connects Italy and the England of the induction. Petruchio, as much as the lord of the induction, merges the street outside Baptista's house with the outskirts of London.

Once the action of the play moves back to Padua, the business of the household spills into the street again in the confrontation between Vincentio and the pedant and the public revelation that Lucentio and Bianca have stolen off to be married (4.4, 5.1). In Shakespeare's comedies, the action that develops in the street assists what Frye calls "the removal of a neurosis or blocking point and the restoring of an unbroken current of energy and memory" (*Anatomy* 171). The abundant exchange of energy between Petruchio and Katherina played out in the open balances the game played within Baptista's household, where Lucentio steals Bianca from beneath her father's nose in the guise of a humanist teacher.

The tension between street and household emerges in scenes where a character appears at a window, rather than the door (however that was staged), suggesting a cautious or protective response to someone who calls from the street. The pedant, for example, appears at the window when Vincentio knocks at the door (5.1), insecure in his adopted role as Lucentio's father and fearful that he will be identified as a Mantuan. In other plays, the window provides access, if only auditory, to young women cut off from the street by cautious fathers. Proteus attempts to serenade and seduce Silvia, while Julia looks on: "Now must we to her window, / And give some evening music to her ear" (*The Two Gentlemen of Verona* 4.2.16–17). Valentine has been banished for inadvertently revealing the method he intends to use to "enfranchise" the duke's daughter: "Why then a ladder, quaintly made of cords, / To cast up, with a pair of anchoring hooks, / Would serve to scale another Hero's tow'r, / So bold Leander would adventure it" (3.1.117–20). The bold lover must approach the tower from the street using his grappling hooks rather than the conventional serenade available to the false Proteus.

The pattern of escape and rebellion, which connects the window to the street, generally leads back to the household and the bedroom, back to the city and its traditions, rather than outward in the direction of an open-ended quest. Jessica and Lorenzo wander from Venice but find a home and inheritance in Belmont. The pattern changes as the genre changes; the streets of Verona conduct Romeo and Juliet away from the household and eventually into the tomb.

Lorenzo has no need for a rope-ladder because Shylock leaves a house that, like the merchant houses throughout London, can be imagined to be a two-story structure on the street, not a medieval tower where the daughter can be locked up. Shakespeare establishes this close proximity to the street from within the house when Shylock warns Jessica, ironically, to beware of the masquing that will take place in the city's streets. Though Shakespeare does not include Thomas Coryat's version of urban thugs, the "braves [*bravos*], who at some unlawful times do commit great villainy" (1:413), the play does convey a sense of the potential unruliness of city streets. The masquers Gratiano and Salerio await Lorenzo under a "penthouse," or portico, an architectural structure like the *banche*, or stone benches outside a palazzo that served as an intermediate space between the private house and the public street. The flexibility of Shakespeare's stage allows these quick transitions from the street imagined from within the house to the house seen from the street. The carnival spirit of masquerade invades the house as Jessica puts on the disguise of a page and "in the lovely garnish of a boy" makes her way into the street and then through the canals of Venice "in a gondilo" as Salerio reports (*The Merchant of Venice* 2.8.8).

Like the sport in *Romeo and Juliet*, the masquing ends suddenly (2.6.64–65). While the sober house remains locked in the day-to-day cycle of domestic and commercial affairs, love breaks the house open and quickens the tempo of life in the city. Festivity, like the ancient feast celebrated by Capulet, or the special dinner arranged by Bassanio, has its place within the city. The festive spirit temporarily alters relationships, but the antagonisms that divide the urban world and that thrive in the streets quickly return. Aristocrats who seem to spend much of their time engaged in some form of public play represent a direct threat to a man like Shylock, but they also stand apart from fellow citizens, the merchants, senators, princes, and householders who attend to the everyday business of the city. Sports have their temporal and spatial limits—it is the practical Benvolio who tells Romeo that the time has come to depart ("the sport is at the best" [1.5.119]). But characters such as Mercutio and Gratiano represent a class of aristocrats who do not respect the barriers that separate the street from the household, sober from sportive times and places. A bit rough to be fully identified with Castiglione's courtiers, these city aristocrats are somewhere between prodigals and dreamers, poets and madmen. And it is into their world, the world of the street, that Jessica and Lorenzo disappear to emerge later in a garden in Belmont.

∼

Romeo and Juliet offers what is perhaps the most famous window scene in Shakespeare—the light, which "through yonder window breaks," shines on a garden bordering the street where Romeo leaves his mates behind in more ways than one (2.1, 2). Exhibiting the kind of raucous behavior Shylock feared, the masquers, led by Mercutio, fill the streets of Verona with the free play of insult and sexual innuendo, tokens of comradeship among young men: "This cannot anger him; 'twould anger him / To raise a spirit in his mistress' circle, / Of some strange nature, letting it there stand / Till she had laid it and conjur'd it down" (2.1.23–26). The magic that spills from the window makes the street a very different place for Romeo, though tragically he cannot overcome the street's necromantic spell when driven to avenge Mercutio's murder.

We see that same window from a different perspective when Romeo must use the "poor ropes" (3.2.132) that brought him to Juliet to begin the reverse passage from the bedroom to the garden, the street, and his exile in Mantua—"There is no world without Verona walls, / But purgatory, torture, hell itself" (3.3.17–18). Though Shakespeare's plays were staged in the suburbs of a city that did not share the history of banishment and exile that plagued Italian city-states, his audience could certainly identify with the trauma of being locked out of the city. The street that represents an opening outward for Lorenzo and Jessica becomes a dead end for the banished Romeo, who eventually finds himself on a street in Mantua before the dark space of an apothecary's shop: "I do remember an apothecary—/ And hereabouts 'a dwells—which late I noted / In tatt'red weeds, with overwhelming brows, / Culling of simples; meagre were his looks, / Sharp misery had worn him to the bone" (5.1.37–41).

Shakespeare uses a similar pattern of reveling, love, a window, and a street in *Much Ado About Nothing*, a pattern that narrowly escapes the tragic consequence found in *Romeo and Juliet*. The interplay between the dark street and the seemingly protected world of the wedding recurs in the scheme designed to slander Hero and to satisfy Don John's sick jealousy (2.2.5), for it requires that the waiting-woman Margaret "look out at her lady's chamber-window" dressed as Hero. The prince and Claudio "shall see her chamber-window ent'red, even the night before her wedding day" (3.2.113–14), and the metonymy of entering will stand for her sexual betrayal. Shakespeare does not, however, stage the scene where the men observe the supposed betrayal. Instead he shifts directly to a city street, where members of an English watch discover the conspiracy after it has been performed. Again the street functions as a transitional space between the world of the audience and the imagined setting of the play. In the street the English watch can expose a plot that befuddles the Italian gentles. If we anticipate a transition directly from the interior of Leonato's house to the place where at midnight Claudio will see what he calls "mischief strangely thwarting" (3.2.132), Dogberry's instructions to the watch build up tension before Borachio reveals that the deception has already taken place (3.3.151).

As we listen to Dogberry rehearse the typical urban problems the watch confronts, we are in a world that is, in its way, more secure than Leonato's domain, despite the uncertainty of Dogberry's language. In Messina's streets the watch can "stay" even the prince, provided, of course, the prince be willing (76, 79). We are in a middle ground between the rule of law and the authority of a ruler, just as Messina is the setting for garden revels that evoke an open Mediterranean climate, while also being a place where the villains Conrade and Borachio must seek shelter from the drizzle of a more English night—"Stand thee close then under this penthouse, for it drizzles rain, and I will, like a true drunkard, utter all to thee" (3.3.103–5; Laroque 265).

In the street Borachio reconstructs the betrayal scene: "She leans me out at her mistress' chamber-window, bids me a thousand times good night—I tell this tale vildly, I should first tell thee how the Prince, Claudio, and my master, planted and plac'd and possess'd by my master Don John, saw afar off in the orchard this amiable encounter" (146–52). The narrator does not set the scene, as it would have been set on stage, with the observers introduced first, planted and placed by the dramatist before the ambiguous encounter is played out at the window. The household conceals, while the narration in the street exposes the plot. The numerous scenes of eavesdropping that take place within or near Leonato's house (1.2.9, 1.3.6, 3.1.7, 3.3.151) lead up to this street scene, where the eavesdroppers constitute an audience that mirrors and mimicks the gentles who witnessed Hero's supposed betrayal. While confusion spreads from the "thick-pleach's alley" in the orchard and the arras in a musty room (1.3.59) where servants overhear their betters discovering love and planning games, the open street invites the drunken Borachio to brag, "Therefore know I have earn'd of Don John a thousand ducats" (3.3.107–8). It is also true that nothing short of an obstinate confession will survive the linguistic confusion generated by Dogberry. But it is the watch as audience, as groundlings, that ultimately counters the deeper confusion generated within the household. The movement from the street to the prison and then to Leonato's house (5.1.202) counterpoints the public slandering of Hero in the church and her removal to the tomb. Unlike Verona's Friar Lawrence, Messina's Friar Francis benefits from the unsought assistance of civic functionaries who are very much at home in the street: "What your wisdoms could not discover, these shallow fools have brought to light" (232–33).

~

Characters conversing in the open space of the stage occupy a space that the audience locates, assisted by dialogue, gesture, and props. The sense of place can come quickly, as in plays whose titles or early scenes indicate the city and the urban space within that city where the action unfolds. Lucentio announces that he is in "fair Padua" (*The Taming of the Shrew* 1.1.2), and Petruchio lets us know that he is not only in Padua but before the house of his "approved friend" Hortensio (1.2.1–5). Through dialogue Shakespeare creates a sense of the city named, the Padua of arts or the Venice of commerce. As urban space takes shape in the imagination, it conditions our perspective as much as a scene painted in perspective. By line 92 of the opening scene of *Romeo and Juliet*, we know that we are in Verona, but also that we are in a city whose streets and squares are particularly volatile.

The fact that some settings remain undefined for a time creates tension. In certain instances we may not know whether the facade of the theater represents the exterior of a house or some other important place within the city. We do not know what is within or what will emerge. The title *The Tragedy of Othello, the Moor of Venice*, if it were known, would lead the audience to anticipate a tragic setting within a well-known city. But with or without the title, the opening of the play creates a sense of uneasiness as it picks up the dialogue between Roderigo and Iago in midstream. Unlike the opening of *The Merchant of Venice*, this street scene does not conjure up the Venice of argosies. We overhear a conversation about one Michael Cassio and a Moor, about military promotion and service and "her father," but we do not know what the facade conceals, any more than Brabantio knows the meaning of the "terrible summons" that causes him to appear, as the stage direction indicates, "*above [at a window]*." As Lena Orlin points out, Iago and Roderigo "play to the conventional notion that Brabantio's familial integrity requires the enclosure of his house around its members and (especially for female members) their confinement within" (*Private Matters* 218).

Though props and gesture will have already suggested it, eventually the dialogue tells us specifically that we are in a street, outside a house at night: "Arise, arise! / Awake the snorting citizens with the bell" (89–90). We also know that "her father" is a person of some standing in the community: "My spirits and my place have in their power/ To make this bitter to thee" and, if we missed the play's subtitle, where we are: "This is Venice; / My house is not a grange" (103–6). The dramatic sense of things seen through a half light in garish detail ("your daughter and the Moor are [now] making the beast with two backs") continues throughout this Venetian street scene: "Strike on the tinder, ho! / Give me a taper! Call up all my people! / This accident is not unlike my dream, / Belief of it oppresses me already. / Light, I say, light!" (1.1.140–44). Teresa Faherty has traced the commedia dell'arte analogues in the play, and many scholars have commented on how the play's comic structure turns tragic. Seen from the street, the interplay between Brabantio, the old pantaloon aroused from his bed, and Iago, the Brighella, or wily servant, who torments him from the street, invites laughter, or would if it were not for the nastiness of Iago and the strained dignity of Brabantio.

Act 1, scene 2 of *Othello* is equally unsettling. It is night, on yet another city street, this one before the "house" where Roderigo has promised he can "discover" the Moor and Brabantio's daughter (who has not been named). But this is no lawless city. Shakespeare introduces his audience to a Venice of "great ones," the vaguely Romanized senators who are called "[toged] consuls" by Iago, who also identifies Brabantio as a beloved "magnifico" more powerful than the duke (or doge). To some extent this patriarch recalls the fathers of Shakespeare's Verona, the old clan leaders who, with their retainers, take to the streets to defend their honor and their daughters. Brabantio calls for "my people," "my brother," and seems ready to summon followers from all parts of the city—"At every house I'll call / (I may command at most)" (1.1.180–81). When soldiers and retainers face one another in the street with swords drawn, Venice threatens to become more savage than a "grange" and to contradict the notion that it was most serene, the *serenissma* that could boast a history free of the civil discords that plagued other Italian city-states. But the controlled words of the "extravagant and wheeling stranger" reestablish a sense of decorum: "Keep up your bright swords, for the dew will rust them" (1.2.59).

As the open space of the stage clears, we move from the dark streets of Venice to the council of state, where public and private matters will be debated. The council scene, with its table, lights, and maps, provides a fitting introduction to a consideration of Shakespeare's interiors, since they can be most generally divided between the public and private.

Before entering the interiors, however, I want to consider an important difference between the treatment of city streets in Shakespeare's Italian plays and the erudite comedy of Italy. In Shakespeare's plays characters do not get lost and do not often talk about losing their psychological and moral bearings in the city's streets. A young lover like Romeo can hide from his companions, Feste can wander far enough to annoy his mistress, and Antonio can lose track of Sebastian, but on the whole the city streets of Shakespeare's Italy do not become that urban maze where the danger of getting lost merges with the allure of letting go. Elsewhere I argue that Italian erudite comedy frequently juxtaposes the scenic *prospettiva*, which represents the city as cultural icon of order, and the action of the play, which draws its characters into the urban labyrinth of desire (D'Amico, "The Treatment of Space" 269–73; Roston 214). According to Lauro Martines, "The perfected forms of the imaginary ideal city—grand, symmetrical, proportioned, in fixed optical recession—went forth from a wish for control over the whole environment and from the implicit assumption that this was possible" (275). While the theatrical *prospettiva* recalls the *città ideale*, often in the form of a particular city, such as the Florence of Machiavelli's *La mandragola*, the action that unfolds before that orderly perspective recreates our sense of the city as a confusing maze. The play's action mirrors the inner experience of characters who are often lost within the city's streets, pursued by external threats and driven by internal desires. Just as intellectual historians argue that perspective as an expression of control in painting and theater mirrors political authority in the Renaissance, we might connect Shakespeare's theater with his creation of a fluid urban environment that I identify with the Italian city-state.

Lewis Mumford argues that something of value was lost in the transition from the medieval to the baroque city, from a city such as Venice, with its "cellular unit of planning," to the city of "geometric clarification" (348). The sense of order or disorder, freedom or coercion, depends on the perspective of one who moves through or observes the city: "In fourteenth-century Florence a newly created grid of rectilinear streets opened up many new lots; houses were built to take advantage of the double exposure, to garden and to street. This established a new relation between house and neighborhood: whereas small squares had drawn people together, long, straight streets tended to alienate neighbor from neighbor. At the same time the intimacy of family life was enhanced: the garden assumed new importance, as did the private bedroom" (Ariès and Duby, *Revelations* 173). From one point of view, the walls of a city set a boundary between the civic order within and the lawlessness without (Braudel 492). A city's monuments represent life lived by ideal standards. Once within the walls, however, the traveler who wanders through the streets may encounter the opposite urban landscape of deceit and seduction, something closer to Dante's infernal city of Dis, which shuts out the good and threatens the visitor.

When Sebastian and Antonio arrive in Illyria, they bring with them the perspective of the outsider, a combination of anticipation and guardedness. Sebastian desires to see "the memorials and the things of fame / That do renown this city," while Antonio must be on his guard: "I do not without danger walk these streets" (*Twelfth Night* 3.3.23–25). Both men wander, or "range the town" (4.3.7), and both are psychologically disoriented by what they experience in the city. Sebastian cannot credit the "flood of fortune" he encounters in the strangely amorous Olivia, while Antonio cannot believe that the youth Sebastian will deny him (3.4.347). Sebastian is the very opposite of the alienated stranger; miraculously, he seems to have inherited a secure place within this foreign city as he moves from the street, to the house, and then to the church.

Thus Shakespeare's conception of the Italian city does not extend to the network of alleys that would have neatly fit Protestant warnings about the dangers lurking in Catholic Italy. Shakespeare seems on the whole closer to Coryat: "For surely many Italians are passing courteous and kinde towards strangers... Therefore I will ever magnifie and extoll the Italian for as courteous a man to a stranger as any man whatsoever in Christendome" (2:13; Redmond 125). The subplot of Ben Jonson's *Volpone* develops the analogy between the traveler in the streets of a foreign, potentially hostile city, and the spectator who makes the theatrical voyage to the foreign setting. The dangers of the street are the dangers of a city dominated by variations on the street's mountebanks. Jonson, the poet-dramatist, guides the audience through a maze that extends from the city's streets through its interiors, including the court of law. Because Shakespeare's Italian cities are generally less hostile, there is in his Italian plays a more positive sense of continuity between the street and the interior spaces of the private houses and public edifices that open up to the audience.

4
Interior Spaces

> This man [Federico] among his other deedes praise-worthie, in the hard and sharpe situation of Urbin buylt a Palace, to the opinion of many men, the fairest that was to bee found in all Italie, and so furnished it with all necessarie implementes belonging thereto, that it appeared not a Palace, but a Citie in forme of a Palace.
> —Castiglione, *The Book of the Courtier* 18

CASTIGLIONE DESCRIBES the ducal palace at Urbino as a city in the form of a palace, drawing upon a commonplace of the Renaissance that was applied to lesser dwellings as well. Leon Battista Alberti asks, "If (as the philosophers maintain) the city is like some large house, and the house is in turn like some small city, cannot the various parts of the house be considered miniature buildings?" (*Ten Books* 1:23). In the words of Andrea Palladio, "the city is as it were but a great house, and, on the contrary, a country house is a little city" (Cosgrove, *Palladian Landscape* 84). Whether palace, house, or country villa, the private abode was thought of as the microcosm of the city-state, "the theatre of family life, as the city is the theatre of public life" (84). To what extent is this true of Shakespeare's representation of the private dwellings within his Italian cities?

If the household is a little city, then the governor of that domestic state, the father, can be a benevolent prince or a tyrant. The fathers of comedy, such as Baptista and Leonato, are more benevolent; those of tragedy, like Brabantio and Capulet, are more the tyrants. Othello's speech to the Venetian council recollects the telling of his life's story in the interior of a Venetian palace, in a space close to the more private or withdrawn area of "house affairs" presided over by Desdemona (*Othello* 1.3.147; Orlin, *Private Matters* 217). Alberti makes a sharp distinction between the public responsibilities of the husband and the wife's role as surrogate supervisor of the household (*The Family* 207–8). There is no question as to who is in charge, for the husband not only attends to the outside world of public affairs but is also the keeper of household treasures (209). Brabantio, a leading citizen in a maritime republic famous for its openness to foreign traders, has "oft invited" Othello into his home. Though the father's authority seems to be modeled on a princely rather than a republican form of government, he has raised a daughter who is independent enough to hint at what is in her heart, to act when she must, and to speak her mind before the Venetian council. Within the public sphere of the household, Brabantio and Othello meet as senator and military commander. Only a man of Othello's "fadom," as Iago says (1.1.152), however much a stranger and a Moor, would have been welcomed into the home of a respected magnifico. In Shakespeare's play, the household as microcosm of Venice includes the exotic outsider. It is the very nature of his city and, by analogy, of his own household that causes Brabantio to anticipate his daughter's escape—"This accident is not unlike my dream" (1.1.142). The English audience might have known that Venice was a city open to exotic strangers, as well as to those notorious "mountebanks" whose medicines immediately come to the father's mind when he hears that his daughter has eloped (1.1.171, 1.3.61).

Venice was also famous for its carnival, a period within the year when masked citizens were allowed to take on the identity of strangers. As though experiencing carnival out of season, Brabantio finds that an assumed barrier within his world has been breached (Burke, *The Historical Anthropology* 187). Aristocratic masquing provides a way for outsiders to gain access to a household, as we see in *Romeo and Juliet*, or to cover an escape, as is the case with Jessica's elopement in *The Merchant of Venice*. As protectors of the household, both Shylock, an alien, and Tybalt, an aristocrat, seek to exclude the "varnish'd" or "antic" masks that represent a threat to the cultural sobriety or clannish integrity of the house (Muraro 337). Tybalt rightly fears an intrusion into the more private space within the noble palace, the social and psychological space where the women are to be protected from the Montagues. We know that it was a tradition of the *momarie,* or masque, for gentlemen to disguise themselves as foreigners who could not speak the native tongue and who, therefore, needed a presenter to frame their pantomime (Welsford 100): "And after the Council of Ten had come down ... a very beautiful mummery took place in the courtyard of the Palace, with six principal performers, who danced, dressed very beautifully, with twelve persons dressed as Saracens bearing torches, and they danced various new dances" (Chambers and Pullan 380). Occasions of this kind transform the interior of a noble palace into a theater where nobles disguised as strangers make the alien familiar.

Unlike the aristocratic masquers who for one night of sport take on the appearance of a Turk or Moor, Othello enters the household regularly and more soberly. And unlike the antic who removes his mask when the festive interlude concludes, Othello continues with his tale until invited by Desdemona to woo her (Greenblatt 232–54). Of course, to the father it appears that Othello has concealed witchcraft behind the mask of easy familiarity. The only way Othello can move from the public space of the household, where he is allowed to recount his life's story, to the more exclusive area of the bedroom is to remove himself and Desdemona to an inn. In so doing, he appears to have stolen Brabantio's treasure and to have taken away the secrets that Desdemona, in the role of the wife, should have preserved.

Brabantio apparently expected Othello to play the role of the exotic guest who will entertain but keep his distance. For Desdemona, the Moor becomes a part of the interior life of the household, which he enlivens with his extravagant tales. For the father, Othello has always been an "accident," a respected guest who, it is assumed, will continue his extravagant pilgrimage beyond the city and certainly outside the magnifico's house. A masque ends with ceremonial dancing, the union of the masquers and the ladies of the court. No public ceremony transforms Othello from temporary visitor to an adopted son with a place within the Venetian household (Vitkus 154). From the point of view of some in Shakespeare's audience, Brabantio might be the commedia pantaloon, a fool who should have known better than to let any man, let alone a Moor, spend time with his daughter inside the house (Faherty 190). Or he might appear a more sympathetic figure, closer to the English audience in his reaction to the complex inclusiveness of his own city. The play makes any spectator uneasy about a city that includes street rogues like Iago and Roderigo.

On the other hand, it is the relatively open, republican character of Venice that gives Brabantio direct access to the duke. Could a prominent Londoner have moved as quickly to a council chamber as Brabantio does? Outside his palazzo, Brabantio is the respected citizen, one among equals in a republic, though his daughter's "escape" will teach him to be a tyrant as a father (1.3.195–98). Brabantio resents the outsider for stealing his daughter and the daughter for taking away the man who graced the interior, imparting to it the exotic variety Coryat observes in Piazza San Marco (1:314, 318). Once the privy areas of the house have been opened, the dream of some vulgar intrusion follows, and Brabantio awakens to the nightmare reality of Iago and Roderigo shouting obscenities outside his window. Othello's fear of Desdemona opening a private space, "a corner in the thing I love / For others' uses" (*Othello* 3.3.272–73), mirrors the father's nightmare. Prompted by Iago, Othello concludes that his race, his military training, and his age ("the vale of years") lock him out of a courtly chamber where his wife "sings, plays, and dances" (see chapter 5). Though Othello knows that his tales had for a time controlled the household, he has no power over this more removed chamber of his imagination, the product of Iago's insinuations and the poisonous myths of "delicate creatures" whose appetites make them whores behind closed doors.

Thus tormented, Othello plays the customer who visits Desdemona, while Emilia plays the bawd who will "shut the door," who "keeps the gate of hell," and must "turn the key" (4.2.28, 92, 96). Tragically, Othello separates the place of virtuous "house affairs" from the hidden chamber of Venetian artifice (Mahler 53). Of course, if the Venetian household had not been in some sense open in the first place, Othello would never have been drawn into this world of tricky, Veronese-like interiors, where he will kill his wife not in his chamber but in "thy bed, lust-stain'd" (5.1.36). And it is Othello who must finally unlock the door to Emilia after he draws the curtains of the bed where Desdemona lies dead (5.2.104).

We do not know what props Shakespeare's company might have used to create a sense of the interior of an Italian household, or palazzo. However, we do have an interesting speech from *The Taming of the Shrew* where the old merchant Gremio, involved in a bidding war for the hand of Bianca, details his possessions:

> First, as you know, my house within the city
> Is richly furnished with plate and gold,
> Basins and ewers to lave her dainty hands;
> My hangings all of Tyrian tapestry;
> In ivory coffers I have stuff'd my crowns;
> In cypress chests my arras counterpoints,
> Costly apparel, tents, and canopies,
> Fine linen, Turkey cushions boss'd with pearl,
> Valens of Venice gold in needle-work;
> Pewter and brass, and all things that belongs
> To house or house-keeping. (2.1.346–56)

The speech mirrors the Albertian household that contains a variety of treasures. A stage decorated with some version of "Tyrian tapestry," "Turkey cushions boss'd with pearl," and the decorative gold associated with Venice might suggest that the house Desdemona keeps also mirrors the exotic world of Brabantio's guest. A painting such as Holbein's *The Ambassadors* tells us that rich interiors could be found at the English court or within the household of an English merchant. This perspective reduces the distance between Othello's "history" and the "house affairs" and brings the Venetian setting closer to interiors that would have been familiar to some of the English audience.

Othello's life experience prepares him for his service against the Turk, which will secure the riches that make "house-keeping" in cities like Venice a form of international economics. As a microcosm of the city-state, Shakespeare's Italian household functions within a system of social and economic exchange. While Brabantio may feel his household has been invaded, the politic Venetians must use Othello to secure the trade routes that allow riches to circulate within their empire. And on Cyprus Othello becomes the jealous householder belatedly shutting the bedroom door after Iago superimposes his own chamber, where Cassio dreams of his encounter with Desdemona, on the marriage chamber and tricks the eavesdropping Othello into almost seeing his betrayal: "Now he tells how she pluck'd him to my chamber" (4.1.141). Cassio becomes one of the Venetian "chamberers" skilled in the "soft parts of conversation" (3.3.264–65). The subtle arts of these courtiers negate Othello's occupation, which he identifies with those ear-piercing sounds of glorious war that are silenced by "her stolen hours of lust" (3.3.338, 350–56).

These distortions transform the chamber into a brothel—"I took you for that cunning whore of Venice" (4.2.89)—the wife into a camp follower. We know that public theaters and houses of prostitution shared a neighborhood in Bankside and that Venice was famous for its courtesans, women whose professional skills and dubious reputations blurred the roles of female courtier, professional performer, and prostitute (Coryat 1:386; Molmenti 330, 351; Jardine, "'Why Should He'" 30; and Olivieri 99). As Margaret Rosenthal maintains, it was at times the public role of the woman who attempted to represent herself as an honest poet that caused her to be attacked: "What most concerned governmental authorities was the blurring of social and class boundaries provoked by the courtesan's 'unruly' presence in Venetian public life" (17, 59).

Desdemona's rhetorical composure before the Venetian council impresses but also runs counter to the image of the *donzella immaculata* (immaculate maiden) who ought to be more strictly controlled. The self-assertive Desdemona of the council chamber moves from the household to a public stage with perhaps too much ease, at least for her father. Witchcraft transforms the quiet daughter into a bad dream and reappears in the courtesanlike arts Othello identifies with a chamber where a woman is "free of speech." When in the *Ragionamento . . . la ultima giornata*, Aretino's prostitute-courtesan Nanna asserts that the arts she teaches far surpass magical practices, she plays on the common identification between sexual power and necromancy (Olivieri 96–98; Aretino 251). Behavior that shocks a father or disturbs a husband can only be explained in terms of potions or of sexual arts that the men cannot lock up—"Sir, she can turn, and turn; and yet go on / And turn again" (4.1.253–54). Here the capacity for exchange becomes threatening.

The fact that it might have been difficult to distinguish the courtesan from the gentlewoman might have troubled the English audience and did trouble the Venetian Senate: "There are now excessive numbers of whores in this our city; they have put aside all modesty and shame, and go about openly in the streets and churches, and furthermore are so well dressed and adorned that on many occasions our noble and citizen women have been confused with them, the good with the bad, and not only by foreigners but also by those who live here, because there is no difference of dress" (Chambers and Pullan 127). Othello thinks of Desdemona as a woman who can act the public role of virtuous wife while playing a very different role in secret: "This is a subtile whore, / A closet lock and key of villainous secrets; / And yet she'll kneel and pray; I have seen her do't" (4.2.21–23).

This fascination with "common" women who combine courtliness with forbidden delights appears in Thomas Coryat's account of his visit to a Venetian courtesan: "And to the end shee may minister unto thee the stronger temptations to come to her lure, shee will shew thee her chamber of recreation, where thou shalt see all manner of pleasing objects, as many faire painted coffers wherewith it is garnished round about, a curious milke-white canopy of needle worke, a silke quilt embrodered with gold: and generally all her bedding sweetly perfumed" (1:405). Here the rich furnishings enhance the erotic "recreation" that will take place in the sweetly perfumed bed, or would do so if Coryat were not merely a witness.

In Othello's imagination a courtly chamber where his wife sings and dances gradually merges with this image of the courtesan's "chamber of recreation," which is what his chamber becomes in his absence, when his wife becomes a whore and his place is filled by Cassio. The ocular paradox that torments Othello is that his wife only changes when he cannot see her. By a kind of witchcraft his presence makes her seem virtuous, so that even when he plays the customer, she continues to appear fair. At the tragic moment when Desdemona prepares the wedding sheets for her deathbed, unwilling to believe there are women who "abuse their husbands / In such gross kind" (4.3.62–63), Shakespeare restores the image of the naïvely virtuous wife who guards the treasures of the bedroom, including her body, but cannot protect herself from her husband.

~

For the jealous husband or suspicious father, the household most resembles a citadel that must be protected. Shylock tries to secure his daughter, his wealth, and his distinctive religious traditions against hostile neighbors. As Gail Paster remarks, Shylock constructs "a city within a city, a city apart" (196):

> Lock up my doors, and when you hear the drum
> And the vile squealing of the wry-neck'd fife,
> Clamber not you up to the casements then,
> Nor thrust your head into the public street
> To gaze on Christian fools with varnish'd faces;
> But stop my house's ears, I mean my casements;
> Let not the sound of shallow fopp'ry enter
> My sober house. (*The Merchant of Venice* 2.5.29–36)

The lines echo Alberti's warning: "We should avoid having windows and doors open out, where thieves or (for that matter) neighbors may be of nuisance, watching and finding out what is being said or done inside. The Egyptians built all their private houses with no windows looking out" (*Ten Books* 5:119–20). Shakespeare does not represent the Italian house constructed around an inner courtyard; his citizens seem to live in the streets or in some version of a city residence centered on a semipublic banqueting hall open to the street.

The great hall of the Capulet clan, the equivalent of the piazza within the urban microcosm of the household, has the potential to be inclusive, as we see in Capulet's response to the young masquers: "Welcome, gentlemen! I have seen the day / That I have worn a visor and could tell / A whispering tale in a fair lady's ear" (*Romeo and Juliet* 1.5.21–23). It is thirty years since Capulet has worn a mask, danced, and played the lover, but the recollection suggests that he can identify with the masquers and with the spirit of play that they bring into the household. For the irascible Tybalt, however, the house will always be a citadel and the "intrusion" a challenge to the "stock and honor" of his kin (1.5.58). For a moment Capulet makes the great hall a place where the "ancient grudge" must be suspended, though his reaction to Tybalt also foreshadows the behavior of a patriarch whose authority within the household cannot be challenged, whether by the boy Tybalt or the girl Juliet.

The expansiveness of the public stage would have helped to create a sense of the hall as an extension of the city's piazza, offsetting the counterimage of the house as fortress closed within its walls and its prickly code of honor. When Romeo and Juliet meet, they create a private world set off by their dancelike movements, by the sonnet they speak, and by the gestures of touching hands and kissing (Welsford 135). Romeo becomes a pilgrim who has journeyed to the holy land of Juliet's lips, a privileged place outside the household and the city. But the masquelike interlude ends when the nurse identifies Juliet—"Is she a Capulet?"—and when Benvolio signals that the time of play has passed—"Away, be gone, the sport is at the best" (1.5.117–19). We return to the household as fortress, where scaling walls can prove fatal, as Juliet reminds Romeo from her window: "And the place death, considering who thou art, / If any of my kinsmen find thee here" (2.2.64–65). Jutting into the skyline like the palace towers of San Gemignano, this household challenges the image of Italian city-states and Italian houses set in a nurturing, garden landscape. In place of an open economy, where ideas and goods circulate freely, we have the walled city whose dominant inner space eventually becomes the tomb.

In the theater of the Capulet household, Shakespeare makes the bedroom the setting for private exchanges, though none of the house affairs conducted there can be separated from the public arena. The intimacy of the bedroom prepares Juliet for her entrance on the public stage of marriage, and in that same private space she must confront her father when she dares to rebel. Whether physically present on stage or imagined, a bed should dominate the room where Juliet is prepared for adulthood, with the nurse's recollection of her husband's joke: "'Yea,' quoth he, 'dost thou fall upon thy face? / Thou wilt fall backward when thou hast more wit, / Wilt thou not, Jule?' and by my holidam, / The pretty wretch left crying and said, 'Ay'" (1.3.41–44). The bedroom opens on both the garden of delight and the garden of the fall. If the nurse's lines on weaning Juliet, "sitting in the sun under the dove-house wall," evoke an image of Italian warmth and sensuality, the wormwood and the earthquake are there to remind the audience of the fact that the earthly paradise cannot escape the bitter laws of a fallen world.

The "pretty wretch" who proposes marriage to Romeo and calls upon "love-performing night" to curtain off the bed so that Romeo can "leap to these arms untalk'd of and unseen" (3.2.7) quickly outstrips the social education provided by Lady Capulet and the nurse. Juliet does not make the anticipated journey via the city's streets from her own bedroom to the church and thence to the bedroom of a husband. Romeo comes to her bedroom; she only moves from that room, which she tries to control, to the friar's cell and to the tomb. Within the house she travels a vast distance from the early scene with her mother and the nurse to the scene in that "same" room where she takes the potion (4.3). The interiors are decorated by language. If Shakespeare uses the nurse's recollections to infuse the bedroom with the sunlight of a garden and the playful, if naïve, optimism of a family secure within its traditions and social codes, during Juliet's last night the bedroom takes on the claustrophobic character of the tomb she is about to enter.

If in one conception of the Italian household the father protects the treasures and secrets of his house with the authority of a prince, in *Romeo and Juliet* Shakespeare shows how other forces within Italian society promise or threaten to transform the house from a citadel contained within the protective circle of its walls to a more open urban residence. The open architectural features of the Renaissance palazzo, such as the loggia and the garden, provide the setting for poetry, theater, and courtly dialogue. The initial dialogue between the lovers in the garden introduces forms of exchange that are boundless and dreamlike; its poetry opens perspectives that redefine one's place within the household and the city. And it is that poetry which can give the interior a very particular character in the imagination, as when the bedroom at dawn opens to a garden with its nightingale and pomegranate tree.

The staging of scenes 4 and 5 in act 3 underlines the close proximity of the space where Capulet and Paris discuss plans for a public ceremony and the space where the lovers consummate their secret marriage: "Sir Paris, I will make a desperate tender / Of my child's love. I think she will [be] rul'd / In all respects by me; nay more, I doubt it not. / Wife, go you to her ere you go to bed" (3.4.12–15). The authority of the patriarch extends from the great hall of his residence to his daughter's bedroom, where he sends his wife as emissary. From one point of view, Capulet breaks Alberti's distinction between a royal and a private household when he begins to behave like a tyrant. Carpaccio's *Saint Ursula* panel provides an interesting point of comparison. We see the king leaning on a bed, contemplating the demands his daughter enumerates, and in another panel the daughter in her bed when she is visited by a divine messenger (Zorzi 30–36, 114). It is quite another matter for Juliet, with only the shadowy support of the friar, to shift the center of power within the Capulet household. In the parting scene between the lovers, Juliet commands the *locus amoenus*, which extends from the interior of the house into the garden, but that transitional space becomes a graveyard foreshadowing the final meeting in the tomb: "O God, I have an ill-divining soul! / Methinks I see thee now, thou art so low, / As one dead in the bottom of a tomb" (3.5.54–56). With the entrance of Lady Capulet, followed by her agitated husband, Shakespeare imaginatively alters the setting from a bedroom that opens on a garden to an undefined place within the household where a "decree" stands between father and daughter like a wall. Though the garden outside the bedroom can be identified with the orchard outside the friar's cell, the secrets of nature cannot release Juliet from the bedroom.

Shakespeare gives us the tragic side of that equation between duty and service that had informed Katherina's speech to the wives in act 5, scene 2 of *The Taming of the Shrew*. When the daughter's duty does not match the father's care, she can be exiled from the house as surely as Romeo was exiled from the city: "And you be mine, I'll give you to my friend; / And you be not, hang, beg, starve, die in the streets, / For by my soul, I'll ne'er acknowledge thee, / Nor what is mine shall never do thee good" (*Romeo and Juliet* 3.5.191–94). Driven from the protection of the household, the daughter will find herself not in a garden but in the open fields: "Graze where you will, you shall not house with me." We move between the public space of the house, where the reconciliation between Juliet and Capulet requires preparation for the public ceremony of marriage, and the private space, where the bedroom becomes a tomb, first in Juliet's imagination (4.3) and then in the very public lamentations of her family (4.5). Juliet had identified the consummation of her love with a metaphorical place apart from the household, a place where she would determine the laws of exchange—"O, I have bought the mansion of a love, / But not possess'd it, and though I am sold, / Not yet enjoy'd" (3.2.26–28). But the ancient grudge blocks any consideration of the kind of escape that released Jessica from the father's "mansion."

The patriarch's supervision of what circulates within the household and from the house into the street is less strict in Shakespeare's comedies, though *The Taming of the Shrew* ends with Katherina the bride delivering a set speech on the hierarchy of values that places the wife under the control of her husband. The banquet held at the house of the foreign groom Lucentio, not the citizen-father Baptista (5.2.8), celebrates reconciliation within and between households: "At last, though long, our jarring notes agree, / And time it is, when raging war is [done], / To smile at scapes and perils overblown" (1–3), though the "jarring notes" return in the jibes exchanged between the "quick-witted folks" who make up the extended wedding party. The wager proposed by Petruchio to test the obedience of the wives marks yet another transition from the private phase of wooing to the public institution of marriage. The hall within Lucentio's house becomes a theater where the wives, who have exited, will be called upon to perform in accordance with the rules of marriage, rather than romance. Unlike Jessica and Lorenzo, who flee the house and the city to make their way beyond the reach of civic or parental authority, or Romeo and Juliet, who follow the friar's more radical attempt to create a refuge from the "jarring notes" and "raging war" of Verona, Lucentio and Bianca create their own marriage but stay within the city and the house. They first go secretly to church and then gain the consent of the fathers. Though Petruchio appears to have triumphed, everyone assumes the "jarring notes" caused by Katherina's shrewishness will persist in the bedroom. But the wager marks a point where values will be fixed and further exchange stopped; the "scapes and perils" of wooing-as-warfare give way to the extended peace of marital bliss.

Katherina's speech on the institution of marriage not only clinches the wager but demonstrates that the shrew was itself a role she will now remove, like her cap, though it will always be debated whether she does so to reveal the true self that had been obscured within the father's household or to put on another role that will allow her to function within the household she enters as wife. The point has often been made that Petruchio resembles a director who assigns the role that his wife will act out within the public space of the banquet hall.

Shakespeare's audience would have been familiar with the civic role performed by prominent households within the parishes of London. The hall within a house was a stage where important community values could be inculcated. The banquet scene frames Katherina's conventional representation of the husband as prince, the authorized guardian of order and the protector of the softer, more nurturing wife. As prince, the husband directs his energies outward, while the wife "li'st warm at home, secure and safe" (5.2.151). The metatheatrical character of the scene can be used to undercut the speech, as in the Franco Zeffirelli film where the persona of the actress Elizabeth Taylor winking through Katherina reminds the audience that the jarring notes of her relationship with Richard Burton are far from over and that peace, if there is any, will be on her terms. The wink says that this is a game women have to play in a society whose public rules are designed by men.

The setting of the speech reminds the audience that within the household and the city nature and custom meet in complex ways. If the wife who is not obedient to her husband's "honest will" is "but a foul contending rebel" (158–59), what is she if the will is not honest, if the prince is a tyrant? The Italian cities of Shakespeare's plays are not dominated by particularly strong princes. Are we to conclude that the plays are self-defeating homilies, warnings against the kind of dramatic energy that comes to life in these imagined cities but which would not be present if we lived in a world of ideally just husbands and ideally obedient wives? When Katherina agrees to call the sun the moon, Petruchio concludes: "Well, forward, forward, thus the bowl should run, / And not unluckily against the bias" (4.5.24–25). The metaphor makes obedience as natural as the movement of a bowl following the laws of physics, but it would also remind the audience of a game in which human skill influences the forward motion.

The hierarchical social structure in Katherina's final speech is like the architectural order of the Italian *prospettiva*. It may have been intended to echo the induction, where pictures "painted as the deed was done" are used to arouse and beguile Christopher Sly when he is transported to the interior of the lord's house and awakened in the bedroom. The dining chamber in Lucentio's house becomes the setting for Kate's version of the marital *città ideale*, whose public and private buildings reflect the kind of political order that excludes contending rebels, along with dishonest commands. Those who join in the spirit of the banquet within a house where peace reigns do not forget the city's other face, where the shifting of names, roles, and professions brings the spirit of the play closer to the improvisational skill of the commedia dell'arte. And that instructive duality need not be eliminated by means of a clever directorial wink.

~

There are a number of instances in Shakespeare's Italian settings where the audience perceives a young woman's bedroom as a prison rather than a warm and secure refuge from the tempests of the outside world. In her discussion of Shakespeare's use of language to evoke place, Judith Dundas observes that single words are the norm to indicate place; "hence any deviation in the form of an adjective, a metaphor, or any slight amplification by attributes will have the effect of sudden illumination no matter how trite the word combination may be" (339). The evocation of place in one scene may shape the audience's imaginative understanding of the relationship between place and character in a subsequent scene. For example, when the duke traps Valentine by pretending to need advice about how to win a woman who is kept under lock and key, he describes a chamber "aloft" that can only be reached with the assistance of a rope-ladder, the very device Valentine has concealed under his cloak and that he intends to use to reach Silvia (*The Two Gentlemen of Verona* 3.1.111–36). When Silvia appears at her window to plan her escape with Sir Elgamour, her lines evoke the analogous image of a bedroom as prison, seen from the point of view of the imprisoned lady. She must escape from her father's anger and the unholy match with Proteus—"But think upon my grief, a lady's grief, / And on the justice of my flying hence" (4.3.28–29). A similar evocation occurs when Capulet portrays his disobedient daughter as a whore who will be dragged from her room, or prison, to the church, which ironically becomes her scaffold—"Or I will drag thee on a hurdle thither" (*Romeo and Juliet* 3.5.155). When the house has become a prison or a hell, as it is for Jessica (*The Merchant of Venice* 2.3.2), the young ladies of comedy must escape. Silvia moves from the household via Friar Patrick's cell (5.1), while Juliet, abandoned by her mother and the nurse, must embark on a more inward journey when she takes the potion and contemplates awaking in the tomb.

A private room within the household can also serve as the setting for intimate exchanges. In *Twelfth Night* when Cesario/Viola tells the story of a sister who died for love, the chamber that had been populated by Orsino's servants becomes a place where the duke can set aside the roles he plays and reflect on someone else's life (2.4). Similarly Viola, as Cesario the saucy page, and Olivia, the mourning sister, perform on the public stage of the household and then remove their masks when Viola asks that the room be cleared for a more private colloquy: "What I am, and what I would, are as secret as maidenhead: to your ears, divinity; to any other's, profanation" (1.5.215–17). Viola intends to examine her rival more closely but is drawn into an increasingly intimate exchange that grows out of the secret of their shared maidenhood.

Thus the bedroom, which can be an extension of the Italian garden, an earthly paradise within the household, or a prison within the fortress governed by a patriarch, also functions as a nucleus within Shakespeare's Italian society for intimate exchanges of identity. Pictures and mirrors would seem appropriate props, as when Julia, disguised as Sebastian, answers Silvia's question about the effect of Proteus's betrayal on his former love:

> She hath been fairer, madam, than she is:
> When she did think my master lov'd her well,
> She, in my judgment, was as fair as you;
> But since she did neglect her looking-glass,
> And threw her sun-expelling mask away,
> The air hath starv'd the roses in her cheeks,
> And pinch'd the lily-tincture of her face,
> That now she is become as black as I. (*The Two Gentlemen of Verona* 4.4.149–56)

Does Julia in her role as Sebastian appear darker because she has abandoned not only her looking glass but the protective mask, and perhaps cosmetics which make women fair? The recollection of Sebastian playing Ariadne "trimm'd in Madam Julia's gown" and the picture of Silvia that Julia studies contribute to our sense of multiple perspectives in this chamber where young women reflect on the nature of beauty and love. In addition to providing a space where the more public roles can be set aside or examined, the inner chamber serves as preparation for the journey outward and for the inner transformation that characters undergo in Shakespeare's comedies. Julia looks for counsel and assistance from Lucetta as she prepares for her pilgrimage disguised as a vain, fantastic youth (2.7.47), and when Nerissa and Portia step aside to prepare their disguise as young men, their private chamber becomes a dressing room where they can reflect on the comic intricacies of disguise and social role-playing (3.4.57–84).

Shakespeare frequently counterpoints scenes of inner transformation and outward disguise, using a private interior to frame both. He contrasts the private space shared by the two young women in *The Merchant of Venice* with the casket scenes, which have the ceremonial character of international diplomacy. With the arrival of Bassanio at the gate of the villa, the public act of choosing, which has been scripted by the father, confronts the daughter's private affection: "One half of me is yours, the other half yours—/ Mine own, I would say; but if mine, then yours, / And so all yours. O, these naughty times / Puts bars between the owners and their rights!" (3.2.16–19). Though Portia controls the household, she is also the princess Hesione trapped within her father's will (56). After Bassanio acts out the public role of the redeemer, Portia begins a conversion of what is hers to her "lord, her governor, her king" (165). The line echoes Katherina's characterization of a husband as "thy lord, thy king, thy governor" (*The Taming of the Shrew* 5.2.138). Portia gives "this fair mansion," her servants, and her golden self to Bassanio with a ring and a condition—"Which when you part from, lose, or give away, / Let it presage the ruin of your love / And be my vantage to exclaim on you" (172–74). But Antonio's letter interrupts the ceremony before Portia can complete the role of the "unlesson'd girl" who must abdicate her position as "queen" of herself and her mansion. Neither in her control of the household nor in her performance as Balthazar, the doctor of Rome, does Portia appear at all unlessoned. In act 5 Portia completes the transfer by restoring the ring via Antonio, but we cannot circle back to the point where Portia speaks in the role of the woman who surrenders all authority within the household to her new husband. Portia's private musings on the nature of masculinity and her public performance in Venice add to our sense of a character of great complexity, while her lord and governor remains much the same.

There are many sources of anxiety within Shakespeare's Italian households. Launce recounts how Crab betrayed his master among "three or four gentleman-like dogs, under the Duke's table," where he did not remain a short "pissing while, but all the chamber smelt him" (*The Two Gentlemen of Verona* 4.4.17–20), and does so just before the intimate exchange between Julia and Silvia with its learned allusion to "Ariadne passioning / For Theseus' perjury" (167–68). Launce, who conjures up what must have been a familiar mixture of courtly table manners and currish behavior at various levels within a household, takes a whipping for the incorrigible Crab: "Nay, I remember the trick you serv'd me, when I took my leave of Madam Silvia. Did not I bid thee still mark me, and do as I do? When didst thou see me heave up my leg and make water against a gentlewoman's farthingale? Didst thou ever see me do such a trick?" (34–39). Having a strange dog ruin her farthingale is not the worst indignity a young woman must endure within the sometimes crude world of the court. The dog that was supposed to be given as a gift was, we learn, a lapdog, more suitable for the erotic intentions of Proteus: "Ay, sir, the other squirrel was stol'n from me by the hangman's boys in the market-place" (55–56). This evocation of a decidedly uncourtly banquet exemplifies Shakespeare's poetic representation of place, which can encompass gross indignities as well as more subtle, but no less painful, forms of betrayal and dishonesty.

In *Twelfth Night* the madness of love and the misbehavior of her household provide a dual challenge for Olivia in her role as *padrona di casa*. The unauthorized absence of Feste, the drunkenness of Sir Toby, the very presence of Sir Andrew, the infatuation Olivia experiences after her first interview with Viola, and the gulling of Malvolio spread disorder from room to room within the interior of the Illyrian palazzo. Conflict between the festive spirit of carnival and Malvolio's notion of decorum has formed the basis of a number of studies of this play. Geoffrey Bullough provides an interesting passage from Sir Nicholas L'Estrange's *Merry Passages and Jests* which reflects a similar contest between dignity and disquiet taking place within Elizabeth's court: "The Knolls, in

Queen Elizabeths time, had his lodging at Court, where some of the Ladyes & Mayds of Honour us'd to friske & hey about in the next roome, to his extreame disquiete a nights. . . . at last he getts one to bolt theire owne backe doore . . . stripps off his shirt, and so with a payre of spectacles on his nose, & Aretine in his hand, comes marching in at a posterne doore of his owne chamber" (Bullough 2:372). Using Pietro Aretino, the satirist of courtesans and courtly excess, the irate Knolls "fac'd them" for the better part of an hour while he literally controlled the interior. Malvolio, however, departs from the standard of polite decorum that even the tolerant Olivia requires and must look for his revenge, if he is to find it, outside the house.

The private room can also contain quieter, if no less spirited, forms of indulgence. The secret and the sexual find a place within the interiors Shakespeare evokes in his Italian plays. When Malvolio pictures himself coming from a daybed where he left Olivia sleeping, Sir Toby erupts with "Fire and brimstone!" (2.5.50). Olivia's "Let the garden door be shut" leads in its own way to a version of hell, when she is clearly ready to give herself to Cesario—"A fiend like thee might bear my soul to hell" (3.4.217). However, Olivia's desire does not cause her completely to abandon her sense of decorum, as Sebastian reasons when he says that if she were mad, "she could not sway her house, command her followers, / Take and give back affairs, and their dispatch, / With such a smooth, discreet, and stable bearing / As I perceive she does" (4.3.17–20).

Shakespeare's representation of the Italian household does not contain a scene that was common in Italian erudite comedy—an accomplished or intended sexual encounter within a bedroom. In *Gl'ingannati*, an analogue, if not an indirect source, for *Twelfth Night* (Salingar, *Traditions* 238), Isabella enjoys the masculinity of the twin Fabrizio before marriage (4.5). It is generally assumed that *The Taming of the Shrew* draws on George Gascoigne's *Supposes*, a translation of Ludovico Ariosto's *I suppositi*, a play that opens with Polinesta revealing that she has secretly been sleeping with Erostrato, a young man who has taken up residence within the household disguised as the servant Dulippo. And there are many other instances that one might cite, including the invasion of Lucrezia's bedroom by Callimaco in Machiavelli's *La mandragola* (4.9–10), the doubling of the assignation in Giovan Maria Cecchi's

L'assiuolo (5.2), the use of three bedroom plots in *L'Allessandro* of Allesandro Piccolomini, and the various approaches to a *camera terrena* (2.9) or *camera scura* (4.4) that enliven Bernardo Dovizi da Bibbiena's *La Calandria*. For Jackson I. Cope, this bedroom activity constitutes a subgenre of Renaissance comedy (4).

But with Shakespeare, whether it is Bianca and Lucentio, Romeo and Juliet, or Sebastian and Olivia, the lovers stop at a friar's cell or convenient chantry before they go to bed. Significantly, the scene that comes closest to this familiar topos of Italian comedy occurs in *Much Ado About Nothing* as a triggering device for the tragicomic attack on Hero by the villain Don John (3.2.113–14). Whether drawn from Italian comedy, from the novella tradition, or from Plautine comedy, the scene Borachio recounts is both convoluted—he woos Margaret "by the name of Hero" at her "mistress' chamber-window"—and a rather tame version of this Italianate topos. Shakespeare seems to go out of his way to distance his plays from the versions of seduction, rape, and sexual confusion that abound in Italian comedy. The violent response to Hero appearing to talk with a man at her window (4.1.91) can be understood in a number of ways. The plays do not try to meet assumptions about Italian sexual license that Shakespeare's audience might have brought to the theater, whether those assumptions were drawn from literature or accounts of life in Italy. This may be so because Shakespeare thinks of Italy, especially the Italy of his comedies, as an open but not a profligate society. Or it may be that he needed to exercise restraint with regard to what could be represented on his stage.

When the entrance to the bedroom is in some way forced or faked, the dramatic tone becomes decidedly serious, as in *Measure for Measure*, *All's Well That Ends Well*, and *Cymbeline*. In the first two plays the bed trick cancels a purposed act of rape or sexual betrayal, but with none of the carnival spirit that we find in the Italian plays. In the moral geography of Shakespeare's settings, Vienna is the darker city. Angelo forces Isabella to enter his room in the middle of the night (4.1.35) and derives no pleasure from the brief encounter that ensues (4.4.20). There is nothing particularly funny about Bertram's attempted seduction of Diana, which is set in Florence and has more to do with military "rapes and ravishments" (4.3.251) than with the varieties of sexual play that one finds in Italian erudite comedy. Like many of the lovers of the Italian plays, Bertram is to knock at Diana's chamber window at midnight, but he does not conquer her maiden bed (4.2.53–57) because control of the interior of the widow's household has passed to Helena, who turns the room into a trap for her reluctant husband. And Jachimo's stealthy intrusion into Imogen's bedroom is portrayed as a violation of her image and of her spirit.

The intimate colloquy between the countess and Helena (*All's Well That Ends Well* 1.3) recurs in the scenes in the widow's house in Florence where Helena takes up lodging as a pilgrim. There she dines in private and invites the widow and Diana to join her—"and to requite you further, / I will bestow some precepts of this virgin / Worthy the note" (3.5.99–101). The private interior of the house becomes a place for more plotting than precepts as Helena attempts to fulfill the mocking challenge offered by Bertram's letter: "When thou canst get the ring upon my finger, which never shall come off, and show me a child begotten of thy body that I am father to, then call me husband; but in such a 'then' I write a 'never'" (3.2.57–60). Though Helena has managed to control the interior of the widow's house, as well as the bed Bertram thought he had conquered, the silent midnight encounter produces no sexual pleasure: "But O, strange men, / That can such sweet use make of what they hate, / When saucy trusting of the cozen'd thoughts / Defiles the pitchy night; so lust doth play / With what it loathes for that which is away—" (4.4.21–25). Shakespeare evokes a *camera scura*, a dark room of lust and betrayal where a man blindly makes love to a woman he hates while dreaming of one he desires.

It is possible that Shakespeare's representation of the bedroom and its relationship to the house and the city was shaped by his stage, particularly the upper stage or some equivalent that would suit the representation of the house as a citadel, with the daughter, a valued possession, locked in a room overlooking a street, garden, or courtyard. In Italian comedy, the spirit of carnival extends from the bedroom to the city streets, where lovers become man and wife or find a way to enjoy the carnival of illicit sex on a regular basis, as we see at the conclusion of *La mandragola* and *L'assiuolo*. The sexual encounter is usually recounted from the point of view of the male lover or described by an eavesdropping servant. Helena's lines provide a very different perspective on what takes place in the dark room and evoke a different psychological interior, with none of the comic descriptions of squeaking beds and panting lovers.

The nature of the Italian set design, with its contrast between the street where the action unfolds and the houses whose interiors are closed off by the scene itself, may have contributed to the dramatic representation of sex as something that most assuredly happens *behind* the doors or windows of the scene. Theater architecture was not deterministic, but it certainly mirrored other elements, such as the patterns established by Plautus and Terence, as well as the general spirit of conflict between comic excess and social order. Similarly, Shakespeare's open interiors develop from a characteristic of his stage, a theatrical feature used to articulate his conception of life within the Italian city. Shakespeare introduces patriarchs who guard their treasures, and their daughters, but who do not seal off the family from the outside world. Whether it is Baptista bringing tutors into the household to instruct Bianca, Brabantio oft inviting Othello, Capulet tolerating the masquers, or Shylock leaving the keys with his daughter, we find a consistent pattern of opening the interior, though regrets soon follow. Life would not move as freely between the interior of the house, the street, and the piazza if Shakespeare did not imagine the Italian city-state as open to exchange on various levels, despite the barriers represented by the walls of the house and the city. We know that Italian cities in fact controlled their gates much more carefully (Ferrone 51). A staple of Italian comedy, the customs official, does not appear in Shakespeare's Italy.

The *prospettiva* of Italian comedy typically represents the audience's city, "your" city as Machiavelli says in his prologue to *La mandragola*. In addition to the visual identification of the city with the scene, Italian comedy provides context for the action through references to well-known historical events, such as the sack of Rome. Proverbial expressions and slang, as well as references to notorious personages and to noted fools, add to the realistic texture of these plays, reinforcing the identification established between the set—the city represented in perspective—and the world of the audience. Annibal Caro's *I Straccioni*, for example, builds urban history and geography into the action of a play. This kind of theater particularizes the public character of the city, while the bedroom remains a generic dark space behind the scene. The sexual energy barely contained within the bedroom balances the various recognitions and miraculous discoveries that extend the symbolic geography of the Italian plays out into the Mediterranean, into a world of loss, wandering, and renewal. The happy ending brings together these three strains of comedy—the sexual energy of the bedroom, the dangers and adventures identified with movement outside the city (if no farther than the baths outside Florence), and the concluding moment when your city, a city recreated in a specific historical and social context, becomes the ideal city.

Shakespeare, as we have seen, does not attempt to identify monuments or to give his Italian cities a specific historical context. When the language of the plays establishes a direct connection with the audience, it is usually a clown who shifts the context to England. When an interior space frames a more intimate monologue or dialogue, the experience is distanced by the less colloquial style of Shakespeare's verse. In his discussion of Shakespeare's adaptation of the double plot found in "modern versions of Roman comedy in Italian," Leo Salingar identifies Shakespeare's ability to give his characters an inner life, a capacity to "observe themselves passing into a new phase," as part of "a more fundamental innovation which in its general effect distinguishes Shakespeare's plays from all previous comedies" (*Traditions* 221–22). Shakespeare uses the interior of the household to frame this "capacity for introspection" (222), drawing the audience closer to the inner world of his characters, while also setting that world apart from the more familiar language of the clowns and the generic incidents that animate the comedy of family life in England and Italy.

5
The Court

> A royal palace should be sited in the city center, should be of easy access, and should be gracefully decorated, elegant, and refined, rather than ostentatious. But that of a tyrant, being a fortress rather than a house, should be positioned where it is neither inside nor outside the city.
> —Leon Battista Alberti, *On the Art of Building in Ten Books*, 5:121

WE DO NOT KNOW what props Shakespeare may have used to create the sense of interiors richly decorated with grotesques in the Italian style, or if, indeed, he did so (Thurley 88; Summerson 52). A courtly interior of this kind might have been created for *The Winter's Tale*, act 5, scene 3. Though Paulina welcomes the court party to her "poor house," where Perdita will view the statue of her mother, Leontes tells us that they have passed through a "gallery" that offers "many singularities" to the view (10–13). This is the kind of passageway in a noble house that would contain rich furnishings, maps, tapestries, and other rare objects. The gallery serves as a preparation for the unveiling of the statue, which "excels what ever yet you look'd upon, / Or hand of man hath done" (16–17) and is, therefore, kept apart. The room that contains the statue is very much a theater, with a curtain that can be drawn to discover the work of "that rare Italian master, Julio Romano" (5.2.97), an artist identified in England with the use of decorative grotesques.

As we have seen, the interior of a house can be a microcosm of the city, enclosing within its walls the dynamics of harmony and conflict, orderly government and rebellion. Interior spaces—the great hall, watching

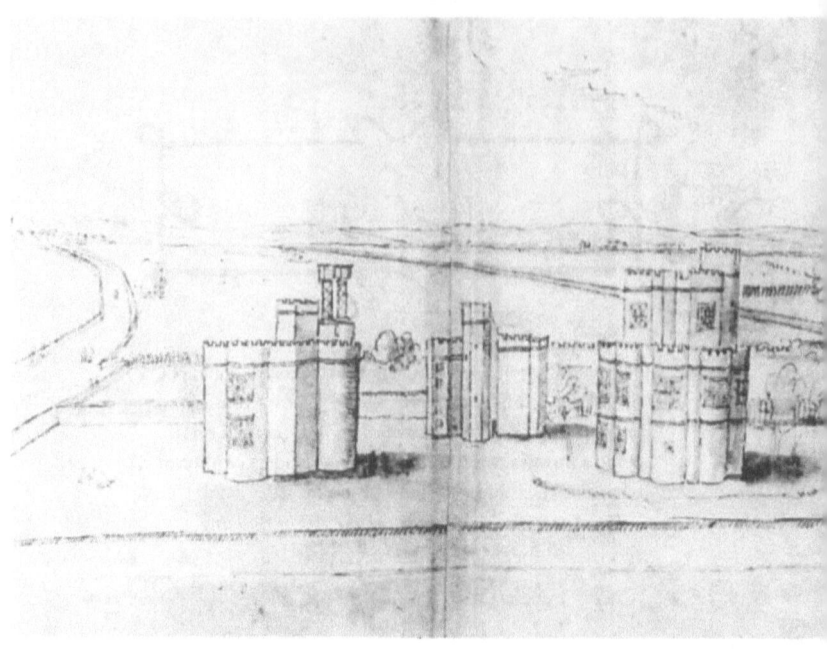

1. *Hampton Court Palace, a View from the North (Centre)* by A. Van de Wyngaerde. Reproduced with the permission of Ashmolean Museum, Oxford.

chamber, guard chamber, presence chamber, gallery, closet, and chapel—controlled the array of courtiers and servants who populated the court (Thurley 113–43). As Lauro Martines remarks: "At its strictest, a court was the space and personnel around a prince, as he made laws, received ambassadors, dispatched letters, gave commands ... took his meals, entertained, and proceeded through the streets. ... The most brutal and obvious manifestation of the prince's power was his residence in the city: a fortress designed to withstand riot, revolution, or war" (221). The size and richness of an interior, the value of its paintings, tapestries, playing cards, earthenware vessels, silks, wedding chests, and engraved arms expressed the power and prestige of the ruler. And the theatrical nature of this display provided a bridge between court and theater, between the most exclusive center of prestige and the common stage (Thurley 207, 88).

Since the court was, by definition, an exclusive space within the Italian city-state, the signature institution of Italy's Mantua, Urbino, Ferrara,

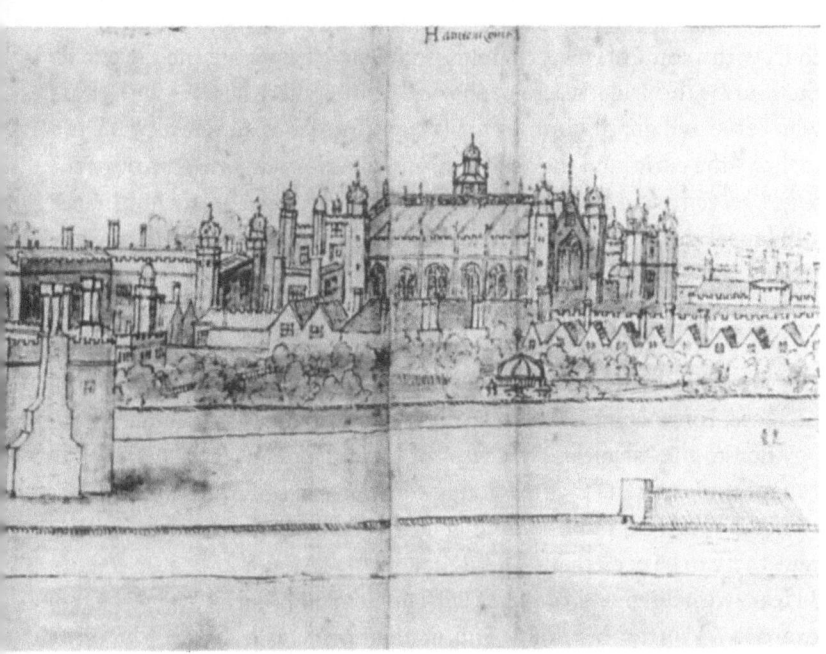

and Rome would seem to be at odds with my conception of Shakespeare's Italy. Shakespeare, however, invents courts that are as welcoming to outsiders as his piazzas are to visiting scholars and merchants. In *Romeo and Juliet* the Italian city comes to life as a collection of households, each governed by a patriarch. Rather than presiding over the city from a rich and powerful court, Prince Escalus is, as we have seen, represented as something closer to the *podestà*, a rather ineffective mayor. *Much Ado About Nothing* merges the courtliness of a city-state, the Messina governed by Leonato, with the broader authority Don Pedro brings to the city from his triumph in the wars. The Sicilia of *The Winter's Tale* is an undefined region outside the walls of a court that turns in upon itself. The courtliness of Messina, though it projects a sense of exclusiveness with its inside jokes and games, is generally open. The extremes of inclusion and exclusion make the court of Leontes potentially tragic.

Though in the courts of the Renaissance the prince's word was law, Shakespeare's version of the courtly setting typically links the political court with a court of law. A complex mixture of the private and the public, the court is the "ruler's actual, physical home, where he lives with those who serve and guard him," but it is also the seat of administration and justice, "the *curia*, and the abode of functionaries, law-officers, courtiers, pages, servants and soldiers, each with a direct personal link to him, in the still feudal chain" (Bertelli 9). The often ambiguous relationship between public and private interests made the court notorious for its slippery footing.

In an early play such as *The Two Gentlemen of Verona*, Shakespeare creates a loosely defined court that attracts young men in search of experience. For Valentine, Milan is a place of "wonders" that stands in opposition to the "shapeless idleness" of life at home in Verona. The word "shapeless" suggests that the young courtier will be formed by his experience at court. Panthino recommends that Antonio dispatch his son Proteus there to be perfected: "There shall he practice tilts and tournaments, / Hear sweet discourse, converse with noblemen, / And be in eye of every exercise / Worthy his youth and nobleness of birth" (1.3.30–33). The apparently inconsistent references to the "Emperor's court" (1.3.38, 2.4.76) suggest that Shakespeare instinctively imagined the political dimension of a court as extending beyond the walls of a city-state, though the only military excursion outside the city takes us no farther than the forest. The power of the court and the link between that power and the private household of the ruler, represented by an inner chamber, emerge when the duke responds to Valentine's intention to "enfranchise" Silvia from her father's control: "Wilt thou reach stars, because they shine on thee? / Go, base intruder, overweening slave, / Bestow thy fawning smiles on equal mates, / And think my patience (more than thy desert) / Is privilege for thy departure hence" (3.1.156–60). In the hierarchical order of the court, a young man such as Valentine must look to "mates" (a term that suggests his social inferiority) for social and romantic intercourse.

Scenes in Shakespeare's Italian courts are structured around one-to-one personal encounters and typically take place, or are reported to have taken place, in a banquet chamber, a bedroom, or a private *cubiculum* identified with the political power and social prestige of the ruler. Within

Milan we see nothing of the courtly education alluded to by Panthino—no jousts or conversations between courtiers in a public setting. Scenes of that kind Shakespeare reserves for his English history plays. Perhaps reflecting English impressions of the splendid but smaller Italian courts of Mantua and Urbino, Shakespeare accentuates the openness and intimacy of the court, where proximity to the body of the prince was, in fact, much more carefully monitored (Thurley 125). The name Proteus has often been identified with the changing nature of one man's personality, but it also relates to the word "shapeless" and to the fluidity of the court in *The Two Gentlemen of Verona*. Betrayed by its deceptively open character, Valentine gets a lesson in courtly rhetoric from the duke, who first sets him up with an account of Silvia's "peevish" resistance to a proposed match with Sir Thurio and then draws him on by revealing his supposed plan to "take a wife, / And turn her [Silvia] out to who will take her in" (3.1.76–77). Portraying himself as an older man whose "aged eloquence" gets him nowhere with a "coy" lady of Milan, the duke cleverly makes Valentine his "tutor," and the naïve young man obliges with advice on how to woo by using the tongue to flatter and lie: "Though ne'er so black, say they have angels' faces" (103). The audience would certainly appreciate the dramatic irony of young Valentine, who we assume is not lying to Silvia about her complexion, offering worldly advice to a seasoned courtier like the duke, who conceals his autocratic power behind the cloak of civility, as Valentine conceals the rope-ladder beneath his cloak.

The duke's invented tale of frustrated wooing mirrors the political principle he eventually reveals to young Valentine, that power controls access to even the most remote chamber, "far from the ground, / And built so shelving that one cannot climb it" (3.1.114–15). On the other hand, the duke is no tyrant. The fictionalized account he creates of himself as a ruler who will not use his power to force a young woman foreshadows the forgiving strain he reveals in act 5. Shakespeare does not portray the court as a place of sinister influences and dark corners to which the innocents are drawn and where they might be corrupted. Julia arrives in disguise, Valentine devises his own plan to steal Silvia away, and Proteus flourishes in villainy, but none of them becomes shifty as a result of the influence of the court in Milan. Shakespeare's young courtiers move with the currents of society into a world where roles do change—Proteus says his love for Julia "like a waxen image 'gainst a fire / Bears no impression of the thing it was" (2.4.201–2) and that a picture of Silvia has "dazzled" his "reason's light." But the culture that encourages the journey from Verona to Milan as part of an educational process must eventually accommodate Valentine the lover, as well as Proteus the manipulator. Shakespeare does not exploit the verticality of the stage, the upper areas or the balcony, to emphasize the authority of the Italian duke as both the governor of a city-state and as a figure whose military power extends beyond the walls of the city. The perspective of the play remains more horizontal, in keeping with the movement to a forest of wonders where the social and political hierarchy will be temporarily inverted before the social order is restored.

Shakespeare thinks of the Italian court as a complex world separate from but adjacent to an urban center. Directly after he entraps Valentine, we see the Duke in turn tricked by Proteus. The Duke's plan to use the foolish Thurio to cure his daughter's melancholy after the banishment of Valentine mirrors and reverses the fiction he used to entrap Valentine, for his daughter is a courtly lady who withdraws rather than being "kept severely from resort of men" (3.1.107) and he, as father, now wants Silvia to experience the kind of courtly wooing that might "make the girl forget / The love of Valentine" (29–30) and love his "friend" Thurio. In this project he enlists the aid of Proteus as counselor in love and as "direction-giver" to Thurio (3.2.89). Shakespeare sets up a complex and funny interplay between the Duke's courtly notion that "the force of heaven-bred poesy" will temper his daughter's feelings and a more worldly version of seduction that resembles the technique Valentine had recommended to the Duke in the previous scene (3.1.102–3). Proteus will "weed her love from Valentine" and Thurio recommends that "as you unwind her love from him, / Lest it should ravel and be good to none, / You must provide to bottom it on me" (3.2.49–53). The word "bottom" draws attention to the folly and perhaps physical absurdity of Thurio as lover and the audience knows Proteus to be the clever courtier who will let nothing unravel in the pursuit of self-interest. The idea of dishonestly entangling, rather than persuading Silvia, returns when Proteus criticizes Thurio for not being aggressive enough as a courtly lover: "You must lay lime to tangle her desires / By wailful sonnets" (68–69). Women at court, even the Duke's daughter, must be trapped with the right combination of flattery and poetry. Showing off what the Duke calls the "discipline" of the courtly lover, Proteus picks up the reference to "heaven-bred poesy" and launches into a description of the suffering a man must go through to succeed as lover and poet:

> Write till your ink be dry, and with your tears
> Moist it again, and frame some feeling line
> That may discover such integrity:
> For Orpheus' lute was strung with poets' sinews,
> Whose golden touch could soften steel and stones,
> Make tigers tame, and huge leviathans
> Forsake unsounded deeps to dance on sands. (74–80)

Proteus describes the falseness that only he practices in his mocking account of the histrionic suffering of the poet/lover, whose ink must be watered with real tears to produce a convincing, if strained impression of integrity. There is little room for Orphic ecstasy in a world where poetry serves to persuade, to lime, or to entertain, as Proteus entertains the unsuspecting Duke with his Ovidian learning. The slightly comic image of dancing leviathans continues in the mocking tone of Proteus's recommendation that Thurio follow the "dire-lamenting elegies" with a little night music at his "lady's chamber-window," where a consort of musicians can "Tune a deploring dump" that should win, or as Proteus says "inherit her," alluding to the authority of the father that underwrites the poetic wooing.

Shakespeare uses the scene to satirize the poetic pretensions of courtly lovers and to reduce the class-conscious Duke to something of a citizen-father tricked by the wily Proteus whose clever put-on makes him, in this scene, more of a comedian than a lover or a villain. Thurio's suggestion that they should "into the city presently / To sort some gentlemen well skill'd in music" reminds the audience of the relationship between the court, with its false rhetoric of "heaven-bred poesy," and a nearby urban center. When Proteus says that "the night's dead silence / Will well become" Thurio's "sweet-complaining grievance" he has no idea that his performance outside Silvia's window after Thurio and the musicians have exited will be witnessed by Julia in her role as Sebastian. But newly arrived in Milan, she has been immediately taken by the Host to see the gentleman she inquired after and to hear some music that might cheer her up, for she, like Silvia, appears "allycholly" (4.2.27). She finds Proteus's attempt to entangle Silvia thoroughly out of tune, though the demonstration of courtly poetry and betrayal puts the Host to sleep.

Shakespeare links the court with the common-sense perspective of the city in other ways that will prove a healthy corrective to the false strains of Proteus. The Host informs Julia that Launce has been sent for a dog that his master will present to Silvia, the same dog that we will learn is stolen from Launce (4.4.56). Leaving market matters behind, Proteus will turn from the "foolish lout" Launce to a youth who shows "good bringing up, fortune, and truth" (69), unaware that the well-bred Sebastian will do him greater harm than Launce's dog when the go-between Sebastian reminds Silvia of the betrayed Julia.

Here as elsewhere in Shakespeare's comedies, the young women share the corrective perspective of the world outside the court, the world of the Host, the clowns, and the musicians. Silvia has no difficulty seeing through the idolatry of Proteus, a man who would worship her picture and who sends her false words and false tokens (4.4.120–40). Sebastian's recollection of his acting in "pageants of delight" playing "the woman's part" costumed in "Madam Julia's gown" (158–63) suggests a city, rather than a courtly performance. As someone who is both deeply involved and yet can stand aside to reflect on the role she plays and the roles she sees played out around her, Julia is closely related to the various meanings of the word "shadow" that are at work in her exchanges with Proteus and Silvia (4.2, 4.4), meanings that revolve around the painted image of Silvia, Julia's desire to imitate or act Silvia's part, as well as the insubstantial nature of Proteus's blind idolatry. This is the first of many plays in which Shakespeare will mix courtly shadows, the disguises and duplicity adopted either for advantage or protection, with the education resulting from the varied perspectives that only the city seems to provide.

The Two Gentlemen of Verona does not include a dialogue between the society at court and a standard of justice by which the court and its ruler can be judged. The only reference to a court of law comes from the outlaws who have been banished for breaking the law but who Valentine feels can be redeemed: "They are reformed, civil, full of good, / And fit for great employment, worthy lord" (5.4.156–57). The forest becomes at best an impromptu courtroom where the duke pardons the exiles, even the outlaw who in his "mood" stabbed a gentleman "unto the heart" (4.1.49).

We do not expect to find a princely court in Shakespeare's Venice, that most serene republic, though *The Merchant of Venice* includes the social courtliness of Belmont. But in keeping with the city's well-cultivated image, Shakespeare highlights the court of law. In *Othello* social courtliness appears in what Othello imagines about Desdemona and Venetian society, while legal matters are prominently featured in the war-room meeting of the duke and senators, which doubles as a judicial hearing (Oz 203) to examine Brabantio's accusation that his daughter is "abus'd, stol'n from me, and corrupted / By spells and medicines bought of mountebanks" (1.3.60–61). When Othello identifies his wife's social graces with courtliness and deception (3.3.183), one is reminded of Lord Gaspar's comments on the female courtier in Castiglione's *The Book of the Courtier*: "I will that this woman have a sight in letters, in muiscke, in drawing, or painting, and skilfull in dauncing, and in devising sports and pastimes, accompanying with that discrete sober moode, and with the giving a good opinion of herself, the other principles also that have beene taught the Courtier" (Castiglione 195). Gaspar carefully balances a woman's ability to entertain with its apparent opposite, the "sober moode" and the "stayednesse, noblenesse of courage, temperance, strength of minde, wisedom and the other vertures, a man would thinke belonged not to entertaine, yet will I have her endowed with them all." Even after he has begun to lose all faith in Desdemona, there is a moment when Othello recalls to mind the woman who combined domestic virtue—"So delicate with her needle!"—with the courtly virtues—"an admirable musician! O, she will sing the savageness out of a bear. Of so high and plenteous wit and invention!" But absent his faith, these attributes merely confirm Iago's cynical conclusion—"She's the worse for all this" (4.1.187–91). Imagined from the outside, courtliness signifies looseness, an ability to arouse rather than soothe the savageness of men like Cassio, whose lack of sobriety completes the picture of a profligate Italian courtier being served by a subtle Venetian courtesan.

Portia presides over a courtly villa, somewhere between the island of Shakespeare's source and a landed estate on the mainland east of Venice, an area famous for its Palladian villas (McPherson 57). The suitors are drawn to a theatrical setting, where they must perform before spectators who will witness their triumph or failure, just as if they had been engaged in a tournament or joust (Lombardo 145). Music, a procession, rich carpets, the caskets set center stage, and the costumes, particularly Morocco's, would serve to merge courtly Belmont with Whitehall.

On the other hand, the court-chamber where Shylock presses his case against Antonio doubles as a place of formal accusation and as an urban space where the Venetians gather as an informal family that excludes the alien Shylock (Oz 81). United by customs, by taste, and by religion, Shakespeare's Venetians are comically restrained by their laws and their mercantile self-interest. It is the will of Portia's father that Belmont be open to any of the Jasons who wish to sail there in search of the golden fleece of marriage. Similarly, Venetian law opens the city to all who wish to trade there. Venice is a city without walls or a gate, a city surrounded by an element that protects its citizens from invasion while providing the outlet for commerce. Shylock's daughter has escaped or been abducted from his house; Portia happily closes the door on the likes of Morocco and Arragon; and the court would like to shut out Shylock but cannot. In Venice Shakespeare creates the most paradoxical mixture of the open port and the walled citadel. Portia would like to choose her husband and the Venetians would like to deny Shylock, but these private impulses are circumscribed by the authority of a father's will and the peculiar nature of the city's laws. The legal precedent that Shakespeare introduces codifies what I consider the dominant characteristic of his Italian city-states, whose identity seems to depend on a social and economic mandate to include strangers.

With the entrance of Portia as Balthazar, "a young and learned doctor of Rome," sent by the equally learned doctor Bellario of Padua, Shakespeare connects Belmont and Venice with important centers of courtly and intellectual life in Italy. In this imagined Italian society, merchants, soldiers, and doctors of the law move from one city to another, making their entrances and exits accompanied by letters of recommendation. In keeping with an imagined fluidity within and between cities that would have set Shakespeare's Italy apart from the more traditional aspects of English life, a young Roman doctor enters the court and then takes center stage to dominate the proceedings in Venice.

The court setting developed in *The Merchant of Venice* offers some instructive points of contrast with *The Winter's Tale*. Though the duke, like Leontes, acts as presiding judge, the status of Venice as a commercial republic alters the balance of power within the courtroom. While Leontes functions as both presiding judge and accuser, the Venetian duke plays the reluctant enforcer of a legal precedent that threatens the native son Antonio. Balthazar moves easily from one city to another, but the book of law, when combined with the "inhuman" character of Shylock, creates a block reflected in the disposition of the scene, with Shylock and his book and scales on one side of the table and all of the Venetians on the other. Shylock becomes the defendant required to answer for his inhuman intention to exact the penalty, his due by law, "which is a pound of this poor merchant's flesh" (4.1.23), or to demonstrate in public that he only appears to be inhuman.

A court of law is a space within the urban community, like the theater, where the unwritten laws of a society shape the written charters. The duke's appeal to Shylock makes an implicit distinction between those who show mercy and those who are outsiders, for Antonio's losses would, he asserts, "pluck commiseration" even from "stubborn Turks, and Tartars never train'd / To offices of tender courtesy" (30–32). The walls of the city enclose those who have been educated, or trained in courtesy. Showing mercy, it is implied, would demonstrate that Shylock, like his daughter, is "a gentle, and no Jew" (2.6.51). However, the behavior of the young nobles in this and other Italian plays is not very gentle, as Gratiano demonstrates with an exhibition of the "wild behavior" that

Bassanio asked him to curb in Belmont (compare 2.2.187 and 4.1.128). But those gathered in the courtroom assume that their place inside the cultural walls of the city distinguishes them from those outsiders who are rough and stubborn. This distinction can be interpreted as an invitation or a test—those who deserve to be included within the family of the state must demonstrate that they can be "gentle." The play has taken us inside Shylock's household and introduced us to his sober husbandry, to values that would have been shared by some in the audience who might have been suspicious of nobles whose "courtliness" translates to profligate masques and a hereditary right to wild behavior (Salingar "The Idea" 176). The audience would not expect the book of law that supports Shylock to condone Jessica's disguise and her elopement. The courtroom is linked in other ways with the household, Shylock's house that has been broken into, as well as Portia's "mansion," which cannot pass to Bassanio until his ties to Antonio have been broken or redefined. The loss of Jessica fuels Shylock's ungentle behavior, and a combination of Portia's love and self-interest moves her to intervene in the court.

If Portia enters the court knowing how she will interpret the letter of the law and how she will use her trump card—Shylock's status as "alien" (4.1.349)—her opening appeal for mercy can be seen as another test for Shylock or as a test for the Venetians. Men dominate the public space of Venice, much as they do Shakespeare's Verona and Padua. They leave home—a house or a city—in search of love, education, marriage, adventure, and fortune. The households and cities are controlled by those who have already made their way as fathers or merchants, the Antonios and Baptistas and Brabantios. The energy released by this movement through and between cities creates much of the dramatic life of the plays. The young women who are drawn into these currents must use factors, as Juliet uses the nurse, or disguise. Portia, like Olivia, is mistress of her own household, though not entirely of her fate, and she shares with Julia and Viola the determination to move into and through a city disguised as a young man. As mistress of the villa located on the mainland and as an enterprising Italian willing to shift her identity, Portia combines the interests of an aristocratic ruling class that will remain firmly in place and the adventuresome spirit that brought a new energy to the intellectual, artistic, and economic world of Italy. In the context of the court at

Belmont and the courtroom in Venice, Portia embodies the fluidity of Shakespeare's Italy. And yet it is Portia's control of both realms that defines limits.

Portia moves out into the world to assist a dear friend, or "bosom lover" of her lord, but as she intervenes to save Antonio, she also circumscribes his emotional claims. Antonio's courtroom farewell reveals the courtly style with which a noble merchant responds to a death sentence. But the speech is also directed to Portia: "Commend me to your honorable wife, / Tell her the process of Antonio's end, / Say how I lov'd you, speak me fair in death; / And when the tale is told, bid her be judge / Whether Bassanio had not once a love" (4.1.273–77). This speech invites the wife into the circle of friends trained in codes of love and courtesy and at the same time tests her ability to judge the tale itself.

Shakespeare merges the Venetian aristocracy with the English to create the sense of "companions" who enjoy the privileges of wealth, education, and mutual esteem. They can lose their money, as many of them did in the sixteenth century, and they can expand their circle through marriage, even by marrying young women like Jessica and Portia, who might be rather different in their background but who bring gold, beauty, and considerable wit. The courtly values that determine who is yoked together and who left apart cannot be defined by a city's charters; at certain critical junctures the law seems as stubborn and rough as some alien Tartar when it will not bend to the assumed privilege of the inner circle. In England the power of the law was turned against this class when its interests were at odds with the reigning monarch. And within Shakespeare's Venice the laws reflect mercantile values, which the aristocrats have begun to abandon in favor of landed interests. Portia's famous appeal to Shylock for mercy shifts the political perspective from the Venetian republic, with its presiding duke controlled by the city's laws, to the "throned monarch," whose "sceptre shows the force of temporal power," a power which some in England felt was as far above the law and the nobility as mercy is said to be above this "sceptred sway" (4.1.189–93).

Within the play Portia, a woman from outside the city, negotiates the competing interests of the written bond and the unwritten codes that bind companions to one another. By playing at being a doctor of the law, and moving to the alien world of Venetian noblemen, Portia releases

Antonio and her husband from a bond. However, the giving of the rings draws the courtroom back to courtly Belmont, where the transfer of authority to Bassanio had been suspended. In one sense, the circularity of the play limits what I have identified as the spirit of Shakespeare's Italy, for Portia's intervention in the courtroom excludes Shylock and draws Antonio back to Belmont, where he is both included in the worldly ceremony as a ring bearer and left out of the circle of wedded couples. In the spirit of open exchange, Portia returns the ring to Bassanio by way of Antonio, who becomes the best man, or *compare dell'anello*, as well as a substitute for the missing father. Last in a series of fluid adjustments, the marriage ceremony combines elements of the court and of the courtroom, unwritten codes and written laws.

∼

In addition to exhibiting some magnificence, we would expect the courtly setting that we encounter in Shakespeare's Italian plays to mirror typical courtly pastimes, as in *Twelfth Night*, where conversation at Duke Orsino's court focuses on the complex pleasures of love, music, and the hunt. We imagine an interior adjacent to a bower—"Away before me to sweet beds of flow'rs, / Love-thoughts lie rich when canopied with bow'rs" (1.1.39–40)—a protected, if not self-indulgent, world open to skilled artists. Complementing the visual effects Shakespeare may have employed to suggest a rich courtly interior, music transforms the stage into the kind of room where Viola might serve Orsino as "an eunuch" who can speak to him in "many sorts of music" (1.2.56–58). As Cesario, she does not perform that role exactly, but the young servant's company pleases the giddy duke as much as the "old and antique" songs he prefers to the "light airs" that fit the "brisk and giddy-paced times" of contemporary Illyria (2.4.3–6).

In her mixed role as entertainer, servant, and courtier, Viola instructs rather than indulges Orsino. We know that power and influence at court were measured by physical proximity to the ruler, to the body of the prince, and to the privy chambers. As Lauro Martines points out, this direct contact was mediated by ritual, "a tribute paid in gestures," while publicly "power itself was also expressed through ritual and thus magnified" (235). Shakespeare represents Orsino's court as a place where easy intimacy, rather than formal ritual, signals the favor Cesario enjoys—honest dialogue replaces the common trade in flattery and courtly favor (1.4.1–8). Following the spirit, if not the letter, of Castiglione, Shakespeare represents the court as a place where the skillful courtier can use the ability to please as a means to a higher end, the enlightenment of a prince or duke.

Those who enter Orsino's court do so to serve, not to seek experience or education. In each of the courtly settings there are servants and masters (Jardine, *Reading* 72). If we can extend the courtly atmosphere of *Twelfth Night* to Olivia's household, Malvolio can be seen as a legalistic household servant who begins by enforcing a standard of decorum that would protect Olivia's interests, but who then allows himself to be drawn into the less clearly defined social courtliness that proves his downfall. His competition with the professional fool parallels this movement, for he first puts down Feste (1.5.83) and then becomes a performer in spite of himself in his yellow stockings. Feste transgresses, in Malvolio's opinion, when the clown engages Olivia in a catechism that proves her to be a fool for mourning the death of a brother she believes to be in heaven. Feste manages to defend his unauthorized "absence" (1.5.4) while entertaining and instructing Olivia. Cesario and Feste are both rewarded for challenging, rather than protecting, the lord or lady of the court.

Like professional musicians or actors, Cesario and Feste enjoy a considerable freedom of movement, a freedom which typifies Shakespeare's Italy and counters the anxiety regarding vagrants that existed in Elizabethan society. As David Underdown puts it, "A society held together by the cement of the household required that everyone have a parent or master" (*Revel* 36). We know that professional actors could find themselves grouped with sturdy beggars. Without the protection of their livery, the actors were in a legal and social no-man's-land between the city and the court, where they might be alternately persecuted and protected. However, in the world of Shakespeare's Illyria, the professional clown prospers by knowing how to shift perspectives in a challenging and yet entertaining way. The successful servant, like the courtier, would have to be capable of using some version of that grace which Castiglione calls *sprezzatura*, exploiting the ambivalence of social codes while negotiating the ruler's absolute power.

In addition to the movement between residences, there is vertical movement within Illyria—Malvolio aspires, Sir Toby declines, and Maria rises. Viola's influence emanates from the very interior of the court and of the duke's emotions, where the stranger is in tune with the subtleties of music and of love—"It gives a very echo to the seat / Where Love is thron'd" (2.4.21–22). Maria takes over a part of Olivia's domestic court when she stage-manages the *beffa* that transforms Malvolio into a seeming madman. She does this out of spite or simply to exercise the abundant wit bottled up in her diminutive person. We cannot say that Malvolio learns anything from the catechism he must endure at the hands of Sir Topas the curate. Punishment and retribution dominate the trick organized by the servants and played out in a section of the household that becomes a parody of both the court, where Malvolio enters with his ridiculous costume and postures, like a mad courtier, and of a court of law, where Malvolio must undergo a mock judicial hearing conducted by Sir Topas.

The Verona of *Romeo and Juliet* has its Prince Escalus, but the fact that we never enter a court or a place of government within the city reflects the problematic nature of this prince's control over the powerful families who rule the streets. The absence of a clearly defined court plays a slightly different role in *Much Ado About Nothing*. Though called the "governor" of Messina, Leonato clearly defers to the superior authority of Don Pedro, a prince of Arragon modeled on the viceroys who ruled over the Kingdom of the Two Sicilies. Leonato's house is in one sense Don Pedro's temporary court, and in another an official place of residence from which Leonato governs the city, as we see when the watch reports to him. During the festive interlude between war and marriage, Don Pedro establishes his authority over the courtly games devised to pass the time in Messina. The tricks played on Beatrice and Benedick are versions of courtly education, dialogues set up to force the wits to see themselves as others, supposedly, see them. This ambulatory court, where a degree of formality mixes with the fun of improvisation, tests character.

As Shakespeare moves toward the problem comedies, we find the Italianate spirit of exchange producing more tension and confusion. The young military man Claudio, like Bertram in *All's Well That Ends Well*, seems to need more guidance. Twice Claudio allows his insecurity and jealousy to create a false image of others—of his friend Don Pedro and of Hero (compare 2.1.174ff. and 3.3.156). Because the court is everywhere and nowhere during the period of revels, Claudio does not know what or whom to trust.

On the other hand, Beatrice and Benedick negotiate the transition from war to peace by mocking the shifts in fashion and language that take place when the soldier becomes a lover. Showing the value of intellect and wit in a courtly environment where the codes are not clearly defined, Beatrice can joke about marriage with Don Pedro; she knows how to play with the man while not losing sight of the authority he bears—"Your Grace is too costly to wear every day" (2.1.328–29). In Beatrice we find the essence of Shakespeare's version of Italian courtliness—the verbal dexterity of "Lady Tongue," the ability to play or accept being played upon by witty associates, the presence of something like Castiglione's sense of a moral compass that allows one to navigate through the shifting currents of a world that merges legal codes, religious precepts, and social standards in complex ways.

Court and courtroom merge when the religious marriage ceremony becomes a judicial proceeding with Don Pedro and Claudio functioning as witnesses for the prosecution and as judges. As everyone attempts to "read" Hero, Beatrice simply draws the line—"O, on my soul, my cousin is belied!" (4.1.146). Her sense of what Hero is, not what she appears, anticipates the more threatening problem faced by Hermione in *The Winter's Tale* in a court of law dominated by Leontes. The spirited give-and-take, which creates new combinations within Italian society, also causes weaker individuals to recoil from the changes they fear, as Claudio desires and yet fears the transition from the military camp to the still alien world of marriage. The fluidity that animates Shakespeare's Italian cities has its potentially destructive side, a dangerous extension of the trick played on Malvolio and a reminder of the pain suffered by Shylock when the Venetian aristocrats transform his daughter into a page, a

Christian, a profligate, and something of a philosopher. Institutions such as courts of law, and the church, help to set a limit on the more disturbing transformations. And a character such as Beatrice does her part when she shifts from the playful cousin to the woman who defends Hero's honor.

Considering what might have drawn Shakespeare to Messina and Sicilia as the setting for two of his Italian plays, Alan Hager draws attention to the Norman conquest of the islands of England and Sicily and the influence of Lombard jurists in both of those societies (97). When a breach of the public peace has been discovered, Leonato, the governor of Messina, is sought out by those pedantic faithfuls Dogberry and Verges (Melchiori 105). But it is only after Borachio has made his public confession to Don Pedro that Leonato asserts his authority as governor, though the stipulation he sets up for penance serves the friar's scheme more than civil law (5.1.230–292).

For all their playfulness, however, the scenes involving the watch reflect the practices of a duly constituted group of citizens who have the legal authority to patrol the streets and, within the limits of their common sense, to enforce the laws of an urban community. They arrest malefactors, record evidence, and report to higher authorities. When Dogberry, to instruct his charges, reviews the eventualities that might arise in the streets at night, he asserts that "if you meet the Prince in the night, you may stay him" (3.3.75–76). He responds to Verges's doubts by offering a compromise position that the watch can stay the prince if he, or for that matter any man, be willing, "for indeed the watch ought to offend no man, and it is an offense to stay a man against his will" (80–82). The court contained within the walls of Leonato's house operates according to flexible, and at times dangerously undefined, codes. Outside the house we encounter evidence of a legal code, and it is in keeping with that code that the watch does indeed "stay" Borachio and Conrade against their will and in doing so commits no offense. Leonato is the governor of Messina, but Don Pedro is a prince of Arragon implicated, however indirectly, in the scheme contrived by his bastard brother Don John.

Men like Don Pedro bring with them the love of revels and the political power of the court, a power which sets them above the laws enforced in the city's streets. The prince uses his authority to promote the marriage of Claudio and Hero, but the confusion that results from his plan to woo for Claudio at the first night's revels suggests that if he were to choose to "break with" Hero and her father for himself, no one would oppose him (1.1.309; compare 1.2.11 and 2.1.174). But the prince's subordinate, and in theory the prince himself, can be stayed by the watch.

The play contains a hint of the potential for conflict between the courtly-military code of honor and those urban custodians of the law who maintain public order. When Hero is publicly disgraced and slandered, the appropriate response, as Beatrice sees it, is to kill Claudio—"O God, that I were a man! I would eat his heart in the market-place" (4.1.306–7). One wonders what Dogberry would make of such vengeful behavior in the streets of Messina. Benedick translates this desire for violent retribution into the more courtly terms of the challenge, which he delivers, "in earnest" (5.1.145), shortly before the watch appears with Borachio and Conrade. We have seen the same split between public authority and the aristocratic customs of the duel in *Romeo and Juliet*, but there is, unfortunately, no bumbling police force in Verona to make arrests, take evidence, and proceed to court. In the comedies Shakespeare maps cities where authority is rather evenly dispersed between the court, courts of law, the household, and the church. Within Messina the witty, though sometimes blind, courtiers will interact with the well-meaning, though verbally challenged, watch, and the friar will enter with his own version of a play to help set court and city right. A stage that can quickly change from court chamber to street allows Shakespeare to create an urban space around the courtly center of Messina that is open without being chaotic, full of play and of sudden reversals.

In *The Winter's Tale* we are introduced to the courtly world of Sicilia, a place somewhere in time and space between the Italian Kingdom of the Two Sicilies, and the ancient Sicily identified with Greece via the oracle on the isle of "Delphos" consulted by the Greeks Cleomines and Dion. We know that Shakespeare altered his main source, Robert Greene's *Pandosto*, making Sicilia rather than Bohemia the courtly focus of jealousy and tyranny. Roger Warren tells us that the director Peter Hall argued that "Shakespeare saw Sicilia as a country of hot passions rather than as the home of literary pastoral." As a result, Hall's "initial image was of a 'very sultry' Sicilia, contrasted with the fresh green of Warwickshire for Bohemia" (Warren 95).

However, the opening of the play sets a more courtly than passionate tone. The personal visitation of one king, Polixenes of Bohemia, to his childhood friend Leontes of Sicilia cannot be separated from policy, a fact conveyed in Camillo's very courtly language: "Since their more mature dignities and royal necessities made separation of their society, their encounters (though not personal) hath been royally attorney'd with interchange of gifts, letters, loving embassies, that they have seem'd to be together, though absent; shook hands, as over a vast; and embrac'd as it were from the ends of oppos'd winds" (1.1.24–31). The public embassies, "royally attorney'd," merge space and time by means of the handshake, the personal gesture which ratifies the alliance legally established by attorneys and sage counselors.

In his representation of the court, Shakespeare combines the *sprezzatura* of Castiglione's *The Book of the Courtier*, the arbitrary power of the Greek tyrants of Sicily, and the legal tradition brought to the island and to its Norman rulers by the Lombard jurists. This combination fits the mixed genre of tragicomedy. As Robert Henke points out: "If genres constituted different interpretive frames on the world, mixed genres enabled 'dialogues,' as it were, between genres and the different points of view they represent" ("Dramaturgy" 201). The freedom or liberality of life inside the court, where ladies, as in Castiglione's dialogue, not only mingle with men but play a dominant role in the dialogues, becomes a threat to Leontes:

> This entertainment
> May a free face put on, derive a liberty
> From heartiness, from bounty, fertile bosom,
> And well become the agent; 't may—I grant.
> But to be paddling palms and pinching fingers,
> As now they are, and making practic'd smiles,
> As in a looking-glass; and then to sigh, as 'twere
> The mort o' th' deer—O, that is entertainment
> My bosom likes not, nor my brows! (1.2.111–19)

The courtly entertainment that graced noble residences would have included free exchanges of speech between men and women, discrete touching and, perhaps, some of the kissing for which the English women were noted (Einstein 224), and the presentation of self that ranged from the honest construction practiced by Castiglione's courtiers to the deceptive playacting suggested by Leontes in his reference to "practic'd smiles, / As in a looking-glass." The civilized surface may conceal a wife's sexual betrayal, which Leontes portrays as the invasion of the unsuspecting cuckold's property, "his pond fish'd by his neighbor—by / Sir Smile, his neighbor" or a house whose gates can be opened (1.2.195–96; Fortier 582). Leontes's state of mind may reflect a more general English uneasiness about Castiglione's *sprezzatura*, a word which Hoby translates as "recklesnesse" in a passage dealing with masking (Burke, *The Fortunes* 70): "Because to be in a maske bringeth with it a certaine libertie and licence, that a man may among other things take upon him the forme of that he hath better skill in, and use best studie and precisenesse about the principall drift of the matter wherein he will shew himself, and a certaine recklesnesse about that is not of importance, which augmenteth the grace of the thing" (Castiglione 99). Hoby translates *sprezzatura* as "recklesnesse" in the sense of being gracefully offhand, but the negative connotation of the word echoes the ambiguity of the courtier's position at court. The distinction between art and deceit, an important subject within Castiglione's dialogue (132), disappears in Leontes's interior monologue, which portrays courtly arts as a cover for sexual and political betrayal, an invasion of the court as fortress: "It will let in and out the enemy, / With bag and baggage" (1.2.205–6).

Leontes wants to identify his wife's body with a space that he rules and should defend from some enemy (Roberts 161). However, the simple distinction between friend and foe dissolves when Sir Smile, an old friend, uses courtly play to undermine Leontes's defenses. While we know that access to the center of power at court was carefully controlled, within the courtly interior itself the boundaries are much more fluid. Courtly grace by its very nature resists the definition and strict control of legal codes, just as a prince's power may stand above written laws.

When Leontes expresses his fears to Camillo, his trusted counselor, Shakespeare dramatizes a problem that Castiglione takes up in book 4. The ethical direction of a courtier's life saves *sprezzatura* from becoming affected servility, because the purpose of courtly grace is to draw a prince to justice and goodness (Castiglione 261–74; Cox 51). To preserve his own reputation for goodness, the courtier must withdraw from the service of any lord whose commands are dishonest or shameful (112). Camillo follows the model of the virtuous courtier who attempts to lead his prince to virtue (249–67). However, he quickly encounters a problem discussed by Castiglione's interlocutors: can virtue be taught? The problem is particularly dramatic because the powerful Leontes identifies his betrayal with the whispering, leaning, kissing, laughing, "horsing foot on foot," and skulking in corners that are both "nothing" and signs of infidelity to a man who reads them with a diseased mind. Far from being able to instruct, Camillo must either agree or be taken for a "gross lout" and a "temporizer" (1.2.301–2).

Unable to instruct Leontes, Camillo decides to flee the court with Polixenes, and their flight, ironically, becomes tangible evidence of the nothing that so torments Leontes, a political echo of the sexual whispering: "Your followers I will whisper to the business, / And will by twos and threes at several posterns / Clear them o' th' city" (1.2.437–39). Camillo is not portrayed as a courtly temporizer—he will not kill Polixenes, though unlike Paulina he will not risk his life to save Hermione.

In distinguishing the good courtier from the bad, Castiglione's Lord Octavian likens the courtiers who use their graces to corrupt a prince to those who "doe infect with deadly poyson, not one vessel whereof one man alone drinketh, but the common fountaine that all the people resorteth to" (Castiglione 266). The poisoning of Leontes comes from the venom of his own paranoia: "I have drunk, and seen the spider. / Camillo was his help in this, his pandar. / There is a plot against my life, my crown; / All's true that is mistrusted" (2.1.45–48). In Shakespeare's representation of the Italian court, the power concentrated in the person of the ruler is certainly something to be feared when the king mistrusts truth. But Shakespeare introduces some dimension of the law into his courts to temper absolutism. Though Leontes can dominate the trial of Hermione, he must eventually bow to natural law and to the superior power of the oracle.

Leontes typifies the rulers of Shakespeare's Italian courts, as distinct from the historical courts of Italy, in not appearing to be a military man. The tragicomedy of his confrontation with Paulina and the babe revolves around the intermingling of his terrible threats and his relative weakness. He threatens to burn or brain the child and then sends Antigonus to expose it. He would like to take revenge on the "harlot king" but turns instead on his wife. Polixenes is "quite beyond mine arm ... but she / I can hook to me" (2.3.4–7). There is a conspicuous absence of military *virtù* in Shakespeare's Italy; we must look to the England of the history plays or to the tragedies for courts dominated by soldiers.

Shakespeare makes the Italian court the setting for a form of education that goes beyond the accomplishments that might adorn a courtier. He uses the court to frame the movement from self-absorbed blindness to self-awareness that we see in Leontes and to a lesser degree in Orsino. Shakespeare certainly satirizes courtly affectation, but he seems more interested in personal transformation. The distant oracle brings the unstated message of self-knowledge to Sicilia, and that message comes in one form or another to most of Shakespeare's courtiers. Whether it is Beatrice and Benedick seeing themselves as others see them, or Leontes undergoing his sixteen years of self-examination under Paulina's tutelage, at its best the court provides the opportunity for a change of heart or for redemption.

The brief glimpse we are afforded of the Roman court in *Cymbeline* provides another example of courtly education in the ways of the world. In Rome the young Posthumus encounters the "accomplish'd courtier" Jachimo, whose envy shows through his courtly style of speech (1.4.92). Jachimo sets out to challenge and then to deceive the much-praised but naïve Briton. Our negative impression of Rome is tempered by the avuncular role played by Posthumus's host Philario, but an allusion to the notoriously corrupt Roman court appears in the story Jachimo manufactures to seduce Imogen. Shakespeare evokes what the 1611 translator of Sebastian Serlio's *Five Books of Architecture* calls "the most famous Antiquityes of Rome, Italy" (3:4 fol.1), as well as the degeneration of the once great city, when Jachimo wonders how Posthumus can turn from Imogen to a Roman prostitute and "slaver with lips as common as the stairs / That mount the Capitol" (1.6.105–6). The stairs that lead to the Campidoglio, the architectural and political heart of Rome, become the common haunt of prostitutes. Imogen rebuffs the stranger by reminding him of the difference between a "Romish stew" and her father's court (1.6.152). Of course there may be little to choose between the

Italian who invades her bedroom and Cloten, who arrives outside her window with music designed to "penetrate" her (2.3.12). Shakespeare blurs the historical focus in the play so that his Rome is both the Rome of "great Augustus" and the Rome of sixteenth-century stews. The painful journey toward self-knowledge initiated in Rome leads Posthumus back to his native Britain. While the Jachimo who delivers a lengthy confession in act 5 speaks of his "Italian brain," he has ceased to be a Roman in all but name. As the "Italian fiend" or "lesser villain" in the concluding morality play, he is closer to the English vice than to the Italian courtier (5.5.196, 210, and 219).

The court as a center of privilege and power within the city and courtliness as a sign of special social grace occasion the most complex fears of intrusion and exclusion. The court is by its nature an exclusive domain within the city-state from which a Valentine, a Posthumus, or the infant Perdita can be exiled. But Shakespeare conceives of the Italian court and its ruler as part of the city. Isolation produces the love longing of Orsino or the more dangerous jealousy of Leontes. And it is the intervention of someone from the outside, a Viola or a Paulina, that leads to a healthier interaction with a world outside the court. In Shakespeare's Italy, the political court, as well as the courtly household, is open to visitors—the young courtier, the suitor, or the old friend. The tyrannical power to banish or destroy the outsider, whether an upstart courtier like Valentine or an infant like Perdita, reflects the absolute power that existed within the famous courtly dynasties of Renaissance Italy. Within Shakespeare's representation of the Italian court, this power is mitigated by the presence of the law, in one form or another, and by a form of dialogue that saves the court or its ruler from the dangers of claustrophobia.

6
The Garden

THE GARDEN CAN BE thought of as an open space adjacent to a household within the city's walls or as part of a country villa, what Palladio calls "the sole and chief recreation of a villa" (2:46; Mumford 286). The garden belongs within the city because it is nature measured and cultivated; like the walls of the city, it creates a barrier between civilized life and an outside world that can be savage and hostile (Frugoni 112). A villa and garden can also stand just outside the walls but in close proximity to the urban center. For Alberti, the "suburban hortus" is a type of private building "that combines the dignity of a city house with the delight of a villa." Permitting visits to the city, it adds the healthy prospect of "meadows full of flowers, sunny lawns, cool and shady groves, limpid springs, streams, and pools" (*Ten Books* 9:294–95).

Italy itself was often identified as a garden. Shakespeare evokes this image in the opening of *The Taming of the Shrew* when Lucentio says, "I am arriv'd for fruitful Lombardy, / The pleasant garden of great Italy" (1.1.3–4). William Thomas in *The History of Italy* observes that all "the gentlemen and other that are wealthy dwell in the walled cities and towns" (14), but adds that in summer they enjoy country houses "where under the fresh arbors, hedges, and boughs, amongst the delicate fruits, they triumph in as much pleasure as may be imagined" (15). Coryat frequently returns to the theme of fertility and gardens, as in his comments on Mantua—"For they have such store of gardens about the Citie, that I

2. *The Gardener's Labyrinth* by Thomas Hill, London, 1594. Reproduced with the permission of the Huntington Library, San Marino, California.

thinke London which both for frequencie of people, and multitude of howses doth thrise exceed it, is not better furnished with gardens" (1:264). And in Verona he recounts that an Italian "showed me his garden, which is a second Paradise, and a passing delectable place of solace, beautified with curious knots, fruites of divers sorts and two rowes of lofty Cyrpresse trees"(2:36). And it was Italy, the *locus amoenus,* whose gardens provided the model for English prodigy houses, which "needed gardens to echo their new style, and inevitably it was to Italian Renaissance forms that garden designers looked" (Hunt 6). Like the theater, the garden could be seen as a microcosm of the city, as John Evelyn notes in his description of the Villa Borghesi in Rome (1644): "I walked to Villa Burghesi, which is an house and ample Gardens on Mons Pincius, yet somewhat without the Citty-Wales; circumscrib'd by another wall full of small turrets and banqueting houses, which makes it appeare at a distance like a little Towne, within it is an Elysium of delight" (Hunt 62).

The garden as *hortus conclusus* is a natural theater, the setting for music, poetry, and dialogue, the pastimes of an urban elite. As London became more crowded, some great houses were broken up into smaller dwellings and green spaces replaced by tenements, a change in the urban landscape which perhaps made the evocation of the garden world of Italy all the more attractive (Stow 338, 376; Stone 395). As Bruce R. Smith remarks, "As places for erotic encounters, gardens had plenty to recommend them: the Fall of Man in Genesis, the licence of pastoral poetry, the respites in blissful bowers of romantic epic, and the exigencies of early modern social life" (107).

Shakespeare identifies the garden with pleasure and with what one might call the lessons of desire. Lucentio arrives in fruitful Lombardy, moved by his desire "to see fair Padua, nursery of arts" (1.1.1–2), and immediately falls in love. He contrives to pursue Bianca, rather than his university studies, and disguised as the tutor Cambio, he instructs his student in a garden adjacent to Baptista's house. When Baptista wishes to discuss the business of marriage with Petruchio, they "walk a little in the orchard" (2.1.111). Petruchio remains in the orchard preparing for his first encounter with Katherina in terms that may have been designed to suggest the outdoor setting: "Say that she rail, why then I'll tell her plain / She sings as sweetly as a nightingale; / Say that she frown, I'll say she looks as clear / As morning roses newly wash'd with dew" (2.1.170–73). The orchard would suit his contention that the countermeasures he employs encourage the natural bent of a young woman whose crookedness results from nurture rather than nature: "Why does the world report that Kate doth limp? / O sland'rous world! Kate like the hazel-twig / Is straight and slender, and as brown in hue / As hazel-nuts, and sweeter than the kernels" (252–55). As is often the case in Shakespeare's plays, the setting does not so much frame the dialogue as take shape in one's imagination as a result of the dialogue. The natural setting evoked by Petruchio is somewhere between the city garden and the rougher landscape of the open fields, for Shakespeare represents Petruchio as a man who understands the hunt: "Another way I have to man my haggard, / To make her come, and know her keeper's call" (4.1.193–94).

Shakespeare links act 4, scenes 1 and 2 in a number of ways. Hortensio echoes Petruchio's line when he decides to abandon his pursuit of Bianca and accept the wealthy widow, "which hath as long lov'd me / As I have lov'd this proud disdainful haggard" (4.2.38–39). The orchard seems an appropriate place for Hortensio and Tranio to discover the games played by Lucentio/Cambio and Bianca, as the lovers "kiss and court" (27). Petruchio's description of the method he will use to "kill a wife with kindness" recurs when Hortensio concludes, "Kindness in women, not their beauteous looks, / Shall win my love" (41–42). The verbal echoes match the many layers of supposition at play in the garden. Hortensio reveals his true identity and exits, leaving Tranio to go on playing the lover in the role of his master, Lucentio, as he delivers the news: "Mistress Bianca, bless you with such grace / As 'longeth to a lover's blessed case! / Nay, I have ta'en you napping, gentle love, / And have forsworn you with Hortensio" (44–47). The lovers are not concerned that they have been caught napping, if not in *flagrante.*

Shakespeare then merges the place where the lovers play at "The Art of Love" with a street where they can extend their game of suppositions and use the opportune arrival of a pedant to undertake the role of father to Tranio's Lucentio. If we set the scene within a *locus amoenus* near the house, the pedant must be spied coming down a hill (60–61) on a road that passes near the garden wall, a treatment of urban geography that would fit Shakespeare's notion of the Italian house as private and yet uniquely open, even to someone like the pedant, a mixture of pilgrim, businessman, and tourist. Shakespeare's stage allows a quick transition from Petruchio's house, and his exposition of the taming method he will employ, to the garden outside Baptista's house, which in turn merges with a road that will take the pedant on to Rome and Tripoli.

The complex relationship between nature and nurture, the garden and the household, love and social roles built up in these scenes may have contributed to the seeming implausibility of Tranio being aware of Petruchio's "taming school" (55–58), to which we return as soon as the pedant is enlisted to play old Vincentio. It is not so much a question of faulty revision, as it is the dramatist's sense that the garden, the locus of pleasure and of secret games within the city, counterpoints the setting of Petruchio's reign as animal tamer and ringmaster: "Thus have I politicly begun my reign" (4.1.188).

When the action shifts from the garden back to Petruchio's house, we see Kate in a locus that is "politicly" stripped of the most basic amenities. Unlike her sister, Kate will be sorely tried within and outside the house. In her speech to the wives in act 5 of the play, the triumphantly tamed Katherina draws the garden, via the imagery of nature and the fountain, into a larger system of social and political relationships and for the moment brings the various suppositions about what it means to be man, woman, husband, and wife to a natural, or at least comedic, close. On the other hand, the Bianca of the garden remains a bird who continues to shift her bush (5.2.46).

There is a suggestion that the dialogue between Julia and Lucetta in act 1, scene 2 of *The Two Gentlemen of Verona* takes place in a garden, to judge from Julia's reaction after she has rather ostentatiously torn up a letter from Proteus: "Be calm, good wind, blow not a word away / Till I have found each letter in the letter" (115–16). Julia's plans for her love pilgrimage to Milan might also be set in a garden that functions as a transitional space between the household and the city's walls (2.7.83). The exchange of letters, rings, and vows makes the garden in many ways the Italy of Shakespeare's cities, because it is a setting that heightens the potential for transformation.

Some members of the audience may have recalled the mixture of art and nature that typified the formal garden, as distinct from the orchard.

The arched hedges and alleys of a formal garden provide convenient hiding places near the house (Roberts 123). In *Romeo and Juliet* the opportunity for concealment accelerates desire. Romeo overhears Juliet's private "counsel" (2.2.53) from the midst of an orchard: "Lady, by yonder blessed moon I vow, / That tips with silver all these fruit-tree tops—" (107–8). The rigid structures of the city, "high and hard to climb" (63), are for a moment transformed by the figurative power of the rose (43). The tragic form, of course, works yet another transformation when Romeo enters the orchard from within the Capulet household (3.5.41–42). Romeo descends into an orchard that loses its life-giving qualities: "Methinks I see thee now, thou art so low, / As one dead in the bottom of a tomb" (55–56). Though its walls mark the boundary of an urban space defended by Juliet's kinsmen (2.2.65) and of a fate the lovers cannot alter, for a time it serves as a natural landscape where the lovers can rename themselves, exchange vows, and quicken nature's maturation: "This bud of love, by summer's ripening breath, / May prove a beauteous flow'r when next we meet" (121–22).

The audience attending a performance of the play would have passed orchards and kitchen gardens like the one where Friar Lawrence fills his osier cage "with baleful weeds and precious-juiced flowers. / The earth that's nature's mother is her tomb; / What is her burying grave, that is her womb; / And from her womb children of divers kind / We sucking on her natural bosom find" (2.3.8–12). This orchard adjacent to a religious house might have reminded Shakespeare's audience of St. Bartholomew's Priory, Grey Friars Monastery, or Bethlehem Hospital, transitional spaces, like the theater itself, geographically at or near the city's walls, and historically between the Catholic past and the Anglican present. It is to this world that Romeo turns in search of "holy physic." While Friar Lawrence's knowledge of the orchard and of human nature looks toward the city and the reconciliation of the two feuding households (91–92), his authority also extends beyond the city to that "world without Verona walls" (3.3.17) to which Romeo is banished.

The natural virtues identified with the orchard cannot be separated from the mixed character of means and ends: "Virtue itself turns vice, being misapplied, / And vice sometime by action dignified" (2.3.21–22). Honor misapplied becomes the vice that threatens to destroy Verona. The orchard, the cell, the church, and the tomb constitute a social and geographical axis that might serve to transform the city, if the friar could turn the vice of a clandestine affair into the virtue of reconciliation. His attempt to extract some "powerful grace" from love to cure the ills of the city-state gives this representative of the Catholic church, and of the mendicant orders that became particularly active within Italian cities, an important, though ambiguous, role to play in Shakespeare's Verona. The city itself, as potentially rich and life-giving as the garden, is overrun by citizens who are as likely to exchange virtue for vice as to transform ancient customs into something productive. The ambiguity of womb and tomb connects the orchard outside the bedroom with the "yew tree" and the vault where Juliet lies at the play's conclusion, when the audience sees the open stage as both a garden perfumed with the honey of Juliet's breath and as the "[palace] of dim night" (5.3.93–107), a sinister *locus amoenus* where Death keeps Juliet as his paramour.

∼

The formal garden with its arches and hedges has an obvious metatheatrical quality that suits the staged scene designed to precipitate a transformation. In *Much Ado About Nothing* and *Twelfth Night* Shakespeare exploits the geography of the stage to create a sense of the formal garden as a place where individuals retire to converse and to be overheard conversing: "The Prince and Count Claudio, walking in a thick-pleach'd alley in mine orchard, were thus much overheard by a man of mine. The Prince discover'd to Claudio that he lov'd my niece your daughter, and meant to acknowledge it this night in a dance" (1.2.8–13). For Don Pedro and Don John, the garden and the city of Messina are places of passage, the setting for revelry and games, well or ill intentioned. For Leonato and Hero, the exchanges that take place in the garden will profoundly alter life within the city. Claudio, Beatrice, and Benedick are players who, for different reasons, resist the changes that begin within the garden. The temptation to exchange one life for another, one identity for another, brings with it the fear of mockery and betrayal.

Don Pedro considers the garden and the wedding set within it no more than a stopping-off place, "I do but stay till your marriage be consummate, and then go I toward Arragon" (3.2.1–2); for Claudio and Benedick, it frames the transition from the military man to the married man. And while Hero plays her role as the perceptive critic of Beatrice in the garden, her lines foreshadow the necromantic reversal that she will experience when Claudio turns on her: "I never yet saw man, / How wise, how noble, young, how rarely featur'd, / But she would spell him backward" (3.1.59–61).

The garden stimulates the latent affections of Beatrice and Benedick, releasing them from the skirmish of wit in which someone must have the last word or bite: "Hero and Margaret have by this play'd their parts with Beatrice, and then the two bears will not bite one another when they meet" (3.2.76–79). Claudio says this, ironically, just before Don John enters to play his part in the device that will cause Claudio to attack Hero. Like the stage itself, the garden can be a place of games that remove everyday masks or a place where one can be baited into believing a destructive lie. As Beatrice points out, the garden seems to enhance the orange of Claudio's "jealous complexion" (2.1.295).

In *Twelfth Night* the garden becomes something of a battlefield for control of the household and of Olivia, with Maria setting an entertaining ambush. The formal garden with its "box-tree" that will conceal Sir Toby, Sir Andrew, and Fabian emerges in the lines Maria delivers before she baits the trap with the letter: "Get ye all three into the box-tree; Malvolio's coming down this walk. He has been yonder i' the sun practicing behavior to his own shadow this half hour. Observe him, for the love of mockery; for I know this letter will make a contemplative idiot of him. Close, in the name of jesting!" (2.5.15–20). The garden accelerates the chemistry at work within the victim's imagination. Malvolio dreams of a union that will raise him from steward to kinsman, from servant to master of the household. Frequent references to the hunt underline the social competition being played out and merge the garden with the forest, anticipating the less playful conflicts that erupt when Antonio interrupts the mock duel staged between Cesario and Sir Andrew and when Sebastian assaults Sir Toby.

Whether positioned behind the stage pillars or some prop suggesting a hedge, the audience of tricksters watches as Malvolio is drawn from the sunshine of his imagination to the boxlike maze contained within the letter. Anyone at all familiar with the formal gardens of a great house, of the kind we can imagine Olivia to inhabit, would certainly enjoy the image of Malvolio following cupid into this labyrinth of innuendo.

Olivia, of course, has also caught the plague of love (1.5.295) from Orsino's messenger Cesario. Their second meeting takes place after the gulling of Malvolio and can be set in the garden, though the scene begins in an undefined space before the house where Viola encounters Feste and asks, "Is thy lady within?" (3.1.48). Feste suggests that they are both Lady Olivia's fools or corrupters, since Olivia has made her interest in the young man quite clear. When invited to enter, Viola moves toward a gate between the garden and the house, for the entrance of Olivia and her gentlewoman, presumably from the house, interrupts her progress—"I will answer you with gait and entrance—but we are prevented" (82–83). Olivia wants another private audience with Cesario: "Let the garden door be shut, and leave me to my hearing" (92–93).

At this point we are in the garden. Though Cesario would have approached the house from the street rather than the garden, whose gate closes it off from the outside world, the fluid character of Shakespeare's staging allows for this easy transition from an undefined space outside the house to the protected confines of a garden, where Lady Olivia can pursue her private desires. The privacy of the garden accelerates the transition from polite forms—the gesture of Olivia taking Cesario's hand, or the compliment tinged with flirtation of Cesario calling himself the lady's servant—to the open avowal of love. Only Viola knows that Cesario's "last enchantment" was produced, like many garden tricks, by a combination of artifice and nature. As Cesario, she plays a role, but the love for Orsino that gives life to her performance encourages Olivia to exchange her mourning for affection: "a cypress, not a bosom, / Hides my heart. So let me hear you speak" (121–22). Olivia, as much as Malvolio, is lost in a labyrinth, but as Sebastian says later in the play, "Nature to her bias drew in that" (5.1.260). Shakespeare employs a metaphor that combines the green of the garden with the artifice of a game to explain how desire has guided Olivia through the maze to Sebastian's arms.

Although the garden of Shakespeare's Italian settings constitutes something of a world apart, it is never entirely cut off from the household and the city. The clock that calls the lady of the house back to the proprieties of time and place forces her to release Cesario (3.1.128–34)—"There lies your way, due west." To this, Viola responds, "Then westward-ho," imitating the cry of watermen on the Thames. The garden, like the theater, is a place of enchantment and disguise from which Viola would like to be released; "westward-ho" takes her away from the importunate Olivia, takes her and the audience in the direction of the world outside the garden and the theater.

Illyria is an urban space that certainly faces the sea and a port. While Orsino directs his opening thoughts to the hunt, Viola comes from those same salt waves she calls "fresh in love" when she hears her brother Sebastian named (3.4.384). The erotic enchantment that for a time transforms Olivia's garden into a place of confusion comes from the sea, as does the twin who can keep Olivia's bias from deviating too far from nature or custom.

The sudden appearance of Antonio in the garden, which has now become a stage for the mock duel between Viola and Sir Andrew, is never explained. The last we hear of Antonio he is off to the "Elephant," an inn that Shakespeare locates in "the south suburbs" of Illyria, like the London suburbs of Bankside and Southwark where the Globe and the Rose theaters were located. It is as though Antonio, who, we learn later, "did range the town" seeking Sebastian (4.3.7), stumbles upon the theater-as-garden.

By this point the garden, despite its gate, has become a very public place, for Antonio's intervention creates a disturbance that attracts the duke's officers, whereupon the garden merges with the street. When the first officer reports to Orsino outside Olivia's house, he says, "Here in the streets, desperate of shame and state, / In private brabble did we apprehend him" (5.1.64–65). The spell created within the garden begins to dissipate as the events staged there collide with the reality of the streets. Before the officers drag Antonio away, he names Sebastian and provides Viola with the clue that leads out of the maze. Like Orsino in act 5, Olivia emerges from the enchantment of the garden and signals that the games are over as she takes charge of her household and banishes her uncle, an "ungracious wretch /Fit for the mountains and the barbarous caves, / Where manners ne'er were preach'd!" (4.1.47–49).

When Sebastian enters, Shakespeare evokes the last of the enchantment before the lovers make their transition from a world of seeming madness to the more stable institutions of the church. If delivered at the Globe, Sebastian's opening line in act 4, scene 3—"This is the air, that is the glorious sun"—would merge the garden world of Illyria with whatever sun London could offer. The theater is a place of wonder that often defies common sense, but it is not entirely a place of madness. Shakespeare takes us from the open space of the garden to the "chantry," where the seeming madness of romance will enliven the institution of marriage. When Sebastian tries to make sense of Olivia's behavior, he turns to the house and the conduct of affairs there for evidence of her mental stability: "She could not sway her house, command her followers, / Take and give back affairs, and their dispatch, / With such a smooth, discreet, and stable bearing / As I perceive she does" (4.3.17–20). This businesslike side of Olivia shows when she enters with her quickly organized marriage plans, for she is eager to catch the elusive Cesario and to save herself from the dishonor that had lurked in the garden: "What shall you ask of me that I'll deny, / That honor, sav'd, may upon asking give?" (3.4.211–12).

On the other hand, while Olivia and Sebastian move from the light of day to be united "underneath that consecrated roof" of the church, Malvolio undergoes a reverse transformation, held in darkness and tormented by the false curate Sir Topas (4.2). The dangers of the garden and of the fall are as much a part of Illyria and England as they were of Italy, but those dangers are overcome within the conventions of a happy ending that leads the lovers, if not Malvolio, from the near madness of the garden to the church. Early in the play the audience might harbor some doubts about the gardens of Illyria from Viola's remark to the captain that "nature with a beauteous wall / Doth oft close in pollution" (1.2.48–49). She refers to the outward wall of physical appearance, which sometimes hides character flaws. Confident that the captain's appearance does not belie his character, Viola asks for his assistance in her own covering, or disguise. Ultimately, the audience sees some danger, and some rough sport, behind the wall, but it does not spy any pollution in the Illyrian garden.

∽

The music that concludes *Twelfth Night* washes like rain over the garden, the streets, the ducal palace, and the house of Olivia. There is, of course, a great deal of music in the play, but none of it is performed in the garden, as is the case in *Much Ado About Nothing*, where "sigh no more, ladies, sigh no more" sets the scene for the tricking of Benedick (2.3.62). In *The Merchant of Venice*, falling in love is not an affair of the garden, but in that play Shakespeare uses music and the garden to examine a different kind of exchange between earthly and heavenly realms.

Belmont might have suggested to Shakespeare's audience a villa, perhaps even Palladian, with its park-gate not far from "the common ferry / Which trades to Venice" (3.4.53–54). When Portia and Nerissa prepare to depart for Venice in disguise, Portia's concluding lines allude to the space outside the house: "But come, I'll tell thee all my whole device / When I am in my coach, which stays for us / At the park-gate; and therefore haste away, / For we must measure twenty miles to-day" (81–84). Denis Cosgrove says of the typical Palladian villa that a "large, often elaborate entrance, sometimes with elaborate wrought iron gates, gave access from the public highway, while a simpler gate led from the back of the courtyard into the fields" (*Palladian Landscape* 94). While she supposedly fulfills "a secret vow / To live in prayer and contemplation" in a monastery "two miles off," Portia commits "the husbandry and manage" of her house into Lorenzo's hands, "until my lord's return" (3.4.24–31). The word "husbandry" fits the definition of a villa as a "productive rural estate organized around a collection of agricultural and residential buildings" (*Palladian Landscape* 94), and the imagined proximity to a monastery fills in the Italian landscape with a religious institution that had disappeared from the English countryside.

Aside from the "common ferry," a probable allusion to Fusina at the mouth of the Brenta, and the monastery, Shakespeare does not particularize the setting of the Italian villa (Hodge 106), nor does he lean on the specifically Catholic identity. He sets the villa with its garden in a generalized landscape that would fit England as well as Italy; the clown Launcelot insists on the divisions between Christians and Jews, or masters and servants, rather than Catholics and Protestants. Portia's lines in act 3 effect the transition from Belmont to the Venetian court, as does the following scene in which we encounter Jessica, Lorenzo, and Launcelot enjoying their *villegiatura*.

In the garden Shakespeare explores the comic and poetic condition of dwelling between worlds. Launcelot warns the newly converted Jessica that she may well be damned for the sins of her father, or her Jewish heritage, unless she be saved by "a kind of bastard hope" that she is not Shylock's daughter, which damns her with the Charybdis of her mother's infidelity (3.5.1–17; Moisan, "'Knock me'" 284). That she has been converted to Christianity is no less blameworthy, for "this making of Christians will raise the price of hogs" (23). Like Feste, who moves between houses in *Twelfth Night*, Launcelot survives because he knows when and how to change masters. He teases Jessica and Lorenzo because they too are between worlds, having left Venice and taken up temporary residence in Belmont. The clown is a theatrical double. The Launcelot who jokes with his father (2.2) comes from London's streets, while Gobbo derives his Italian name (hunchback) and something of his improvised clowning from the Italian tradition (Oz 186). Lorenzo, left in control of the household, enjoys no more success than any of Shakespeare's masters at backing a servant-clown into a verbal corner. Lorenzo describes Launcelot as a commedia dell'arte performer who "hath planted in his memory / An army of good words" (66–67) or set pieces of comic business, the *lazzi* which he can draw upon to war against his social superiors. Such clowns know how to "defy the matter" in ways that entertain some and annoy others—Malvolio is not amused when Olivia tolerates the clown Feste's impertinence. Lorenzo's limited authority provides Launcelot with all the occasion he needs to begin subverting commands.

While the house encloses and defines relationships, the street and the garden invite verbal improvisation and games. In some ways the scene outside the villa anticipates and parodies the opening of act 5, where we are introduced to a more poetic treatment of being between worlds. This first garden scene also anticipates the triumph of Portia, a woman who uses the clown's skill with a "tricksy word" within the legal world of Venice and within the garden.

Lorenzo ends his praise of Portia by suggesting, jokingly, that as Bassanio has in Portia an incomparable wife, so Jessica has in Lorenzo an equally incomparable husband. They are to continue that more personal discussion at dinner—"let it serve for table-talk." And for all his criticism of fools, Lorenzo ends with his own pun, "Then howsome'er thou speak'st, 'mong other things I shall digest it" (3.5.88–89). After the excitement of the courtroom scene in Venice (4.1), we return to the garden, where Lorenzo and Jessica enter, modulating their table-talk to the beautiful outdoor setting that we are to imagine adjacent to the great house.

The moonlit night and the stillness remind Lorenzo of the moment when Troilus "mounted the Troyan walls, / And sigh'd his soul toward the Grecian tents, / Where Cressid lay that night" (5.1.4–6). Shakespeare does not often go out of his way to identify the Italian settings with Renaissance humanism and with the rediscovery of the ancient works of history and literature that issued from the presses of men such as Aldus Manutius of Venice (Lane 311, 316). The learned lovers recline on a bank in the soft Mediterranean stillness and look up at the stars, while listening to music. The scene painting is, of course, done with poetry that describes "how the floor of heaven / Is thick inlaid with patens of bright gold" (58–59), allowing the audience to imagine the heavenly harmony of those orbs. The actors look up at the afternoon sky, or the painted heavens above the stage, while various spectators associate the garden with anything from the beer gardens of Southwark, to Elysium, Eden, and the Medici villa of Careggi, where Marsilio Ficino translated Plato and Plotinus.

We see something of this complex interrelationship of traditions in a letter from John Evelyn to Sir Thomas Brown (1657):

> Our drift is a noble, princely, and universal Elysium, capable of all the amoenities that can naturally be introduced into Gardens of pleasure, and such as may stand in competition with all the august designes and stories of this nature, either of antient or moderne times.... How Caves, Grotts, Mounts, and irregular ornaments of Gardens do contribute to contemplative and Philosophical Enthusiasms; How Elysium, Antrum, Nemus, Paradysus, Hortus, Lucus, &c., signifie all of them rem sacram et divinam; for these expedients do influence the soule and spirits of man, and prepare them for converse with good

Angells; besides which, they contribute to the lesse abstracted pleasures, phylosophy naturall and longevitie. (Hunt 58)

In act 5 of *The Merchant of Venice,* Shakespeare evokes a similar combination of philosophy and those less abstract pleasures an English audience might identify with a Renaissance villa. Though Venice itself was better known for the printing of humanist texts than for philosophical inquiry, the general atmosphere of courtly dialogue, informed and yet not stiffly academic, fits the setting. The Neoplatonic dichotomy of heavenly harmonies heard by a soul imprisoned within the body's "muddy vesture of decay" recalls Bembo's speech on love from Castiglione's *The Book of the Courtier* (308). The topic of musical harmony in the cosmos also fits the villas of the Venetian terra firma, where, as Denis Cosgrove remarks, "Palladio applied this belief in the enduring structure and motion of the created cosmos to his building through the mathematics of musical consonances incorporated in their dimensions" (*Palladian Landscape* 228).

But we move from the philosophical and classical allusions (Diana and Orpheus) to the more local example of a herd of colts whose "mad bounds" can be quieted by "a trumpet sound," from the ideal of a harmonious correspondence between microcosm and macrocosm to recollections of the fall. When Bassanio wins Portia, she seems to stand at the center of a harmonious landscape, the Palladian world of Belmont, where the "sweet power of music" (79–88) reconciles differences. But some inherent deafness to the music of the spheres inevitably intrudes. The musical interlude enhances the specifically Venetian and the more generally Italian Renaissance setting of act 5 but moves between the contingent world of the audience and the dream of distant places, such as a garden where the painter Titian served as host: "We spent the time looking at the lifelike figures in the excellent pictures which fill the house and in discussing the real beauty and charm of the garden. . . . the sea teemed with gondolas adorned with beautiful women and resounded with the varied harmony of voice and musical instruments which accompanied our delightful supper until midnight" (Priscianese 1540, in Chambers and Pullan 180). No English garden will be quite like this alluring *hortus,* or like the one that the theatrical poet "did feign," which is to say that there are many forms of separation present in the complexities of this scene—the tragic tales of lovers, the Jewish daughter who steals away from her father to marry an unthrift Christian, the division that persists between the body and the soul.

With Portia's return, Shakespeare returns the audience to the more familiar garden that might include the crow and the lark, the nightingale and the wren. The gradations of time and space are modulated poetically, from the bright moonlight and deep night that shows the stars, to the moment when the moon no longer shines and, as a result, a candle burning in the hall beckons Portia: "How far that little candle throws his beams! / So shines a good deed in a naughty world" (5.1.90–91). As Portia reflects on relativity in a fallen world, she draws close enough to hear the music: "A substitute shines brightly as a king / Until a king be by, and then his state / Empties itself, as doth an inland brook / Into the main of waters. Music, hark!" (94–97). The reference to a king, rather than a duke or doge, keeps the setting midway between Italy and England, as does the "inland brook" whose sound comes from the world of the audience. Portia, approaching her villa from the outside, is surprised that the music of the house sounds "sweeter than by day." The "respect" created by the altered point of view changes her perspective, just as the audience shifts between the music of distant Belmont and the mundane, daylight sounds of the crow and the goose to which Portia alludes.

Lorenzo recognizes Portia by her voice: "He knows me as the blind man knows the cuckoo / By the bad voice!" (112–13). Portia grounds the garden scene in the comic perspective, which derives laughter from the human condition, our "muddy vesture of decay." Her lines continue the play on bird songs and anticipate the game Portia sets up regarding marital fidelity (the cuckoo's bad voice). As she gives instructions that their excursion should be kept in the dark, a tucket announces the arrival of Bassanio from Venice.

At this point Portia indicates to the audience that it is dawn: "This night methinks is but the daylight sick, / It looks a little paler. 'Tis a day, / Such as the day is when the sun is hid " (124–26). When Bassanio picks up this line for his welcome-back compliment, we are in something close to the full light of day, and Portia is in full swing with her jokes about a "light" wife and a "heavy" husband. As a female courtier, she turns the garden into a place of wit, with some of it rather sharp, as when she threatens to deny the doctor who had the ring from Bassanio nothing, "not my body nor my husband's bed" (228). The game draws on the more sinister connotations of the fall, or of the garden as a place of illicit pleasure, before it finally becomes the setting for a public conversion that takes the audience back to the transfer of authority from Portia to Bassanio that began in act 3, scene 2.

With Antonio offering his body once again to be bound for his friend, Portia makes him the intermediary who returns the ring to Bassanio. The action remains suspended between the garden and a return to the house where the marriage will be consummated and the contract completed. When Portia calls on Lorenzo to witness that she left the house soon after Bassanio, she says, "I have not yet / Enter'd my house. Antonio, you are welcome" (272–73). It would be wrong to make too much of "my" rather than "our" house (compare 139), but we are still in a dawning half light, and until the marriage is consummated, the house remains hers. "It is almost morning," says Portia, who promises in a rather legalistic way to answer everything "upon inter'gatories" once they have entered the house.

Then Gratiano reverts to his liberal, skipping style of speech (compare 2.2.185–89) with his "first inter'gatory" whether Nerissa would rather wait until the next night or go straight to bed: "But were the day come, I should wish it dark / Till I were couching with the doctor's clerk" (5.1.304–5). Since the doctor's clerk appeared to be "a little scrubbed boy" (162), Gratiano jokes about sodomy while promising to safeguard his wife's sex, her "ring," and the ring that represents his fidelity. Shakespeare does not give us a simple dichotomy between a scene rich in the evocative language of Italian humanism and a conclusion that reverts to the English world of men who are cuckolds before they have deserved it (265). Portia's response, "Speak not so grossly," recalls the soul and the body that "doth grossly close it in" (65). The Italian garden is a place of natural beauty and of artifice, one that includes poetic allusion to Orpheus, as well as Gratiano's jokes.

∼

We have moved from the garden as an area of exchange within the Italian city-state, to the garden setting of Belmont, a villa that stands at some distance from the city. The relationship with the city changes as Shakespeare moves the garden outside the city's walls. The garden on Cyprus where Desdemona entertains Cassio and agrees to be the "solicitor" in his "cause" should be the *locus amoenus* that offers pleasure and refreshment after the threat of war (3.3). Instead it becomes a place of sinister exchange, where Iago, inverting the good intentions of Friar Lawrence, will "plant nettles or sow lettuce" (1.3.321) in his efforts to destroy Othello. Iago uses images drawn from the garden to goad Othello's jealous passion and to frame his portrait of Desdemona as the "super-subtle Venetian." The heroines of tragedy do not use the garden setting to adopt disguises or knowingly engage in play. Juliet's "farewell compliment" initiates a stripping away of masks and names. Desdemona's intention to make an unvarnished plea on behalf of Cassio becomes, ironically, the basis for Iago's insinuation that she is a woman of subtle disguises who "did deceive her father" and has deceived Othello.

The Italian garden, as represented by Shakespeare, mediates between private and public worlds. While it is walled in and adjacent to the house, its gates and prospects open on a road or street. To restore Cassio to his public role Desdemona will use the "grace or power" she has to move Othello at home where "his bed shall seem a school, his board a shrift" (3.3.24). The mixture of the courtly and the legalistic, the private and public comes through in Desdemona's language: "Therefore be merry, Cassio, / For thy solicitor shall rather die / Than give thy cause away" (26–28). These legalistic terms will be echoed in the opening of act 5, scene 2: "It is the cause, it is the cause, my soul." When Desdemona enters to call Othello in to dinner with the "generous islanders," she plays a role that connects the garden with her domestic duties and recalls the Venetian household where Othello "came a-wooing" with Cassio, the trusted companion who took the general's part when, as Desdemona says, "I have spoke of you dispraisingly" (3.3.72).

However, when she drops the handkerchief, the trifle "light as air" begins the transformation of the garden into a stage where Iago can project the distorted image of Desdemona's rank lust. Cassio's sudden flight suggests an illicit intrusion into the garden, or fountain, that becomes, for the jealous man, his wife's body and soul: "The fountain from the which my current runs / Or else dries up: to be discarded thence!" (4.2.59–60). Venice with its canals, as much as London with its Thames and its Fleet, was a city of water, but then, as now, opposing images derive from the condition of water, flowing or stagnant. Othello's image of the polluted fountain, "a cestern for foul toads / To knot and gender in" (61–62), is the source of his characterization of Iago as an honest man who "hates the slime / That sticks on filthy deeds" (5.2.148–49).

A similar opposition appears in *The Winter's Tale* at the court of Leontes, where the garden image of innocence—evoked when Polixenes says, "We were as twinn'd lambs that did frisk i' th' sun" (1.2.66)—suddenly dissolves, and the noble Hermione becomes, in Leontes's mind, "as rank as any flax-wench that puts to / Before her troth-plight" (277–78). The image of a rank garden merges with the jealous husband's fear that his wife's body, his property, has been violated (192–96). The image of the garden pond, in turn, merges with the city under siege, which can be undermined: "No barricado for a belly" (204).

Pastoral Bohemia is a world apart from the garden within Shakespeare's Italian city-states, or the garden beside a Palladian villa, but in this country setting we see many features of the garden reshaped and heightened. Like a comic heroine, Perdita does play at disguise as part of the harvest festival, but she is uneasy about being "most goddess-like prank'd up" (4.4.10). The various exchanges of identity and costume swerve toward a tragic confrontation between father and son, only to be saved by the first of the many marvels of the play's comic resolution, the fortuitous mixture of honesty and deception that moves the action back to Sicilia, where Leontes is granted a return to the lost garden of innocence through the recovery of Perdita: "Welcome hither, / As is the spring to th' earth" (5.1.151–52). This garden space of the imagination can only be entered through the good offices of faith and art, in a chapel where magic brings a statue to life and redeems sixteen years of loss. Surpassing Shakespeare's good and evil gardeners, Friar Lawrence and Iago, Paulina works with "great creating Nature" to fulfill the secret purposes of the gods. The sterility of jealousy gives way to the recuperative sustenance of a fertile garden.

7
The Temple

WHETHER WE THINK of the paintings of an ideal city, maps of Italian city-states, the stage settings for Italian plays, or the view of a city such as London, a dome or spire often dominates the urban perspective. The open piazza of the ideal city is enclosed by architectural features that define what a city should be, and no city is without its temple. Greek, Etruscan, or Roman, the ancient city that Italian humanists studied and imitated was an urban community held together by its religion. More than the market, the port, or even the political and military features of the city, its temple was what made the city a community (Ehrenberg 74; de Coulanges 138). An architectural signature, the dome or bell tower of a duomo or basilica was the visible sign of the spiritual forces that gave a city its identity. The centrality of the temple itself and of those who understood its power within the community could not be questioned, though questions might be raised, as we see in Machiavelli's *La mandragola*, about the uses of that power.

For many of Shakespeare's contemporaries, the attractions of exploring ancient ruins or pursuing humanist studies in Italy was offset by the dangers of Catholicism. Friar Lawrence in *Romeo and Juliet* and Friar Francis in *Much Ado About Nothing* are identified with places of worship that draw the urban community together around the institution of marriage, as one might expect in comedies and domestic tragedies. Shakespeare does not, however, ask his audience to imagine a city dominated by a temple or a society dominated by the church. In this sense the religious institutions represented in these plays seem closer to the English parish than to the Roman basilica. Shakespeare emphasizes religious service to the community rather than the temporal power of the church.

In some plays marriage as a resolution of conflict is perfunctory. *The Two Gentlemen of Verona* concludes in the forest, at some distance from priest and church (5.4.170–74). Of the characters who marry without the father's direct approval, like Othello and Desdemona, or simply elope, like Jessica and Lorenzo, only Bianca and Lucentio go to a priest: "Take you assurance of her, *cum privilegio ad imprimendum solum;* to th' church take the priest, clerk, and some sufficient honest witnesses" (*The Taming of the Shrew*, 4.4.92–95). As glossed by Margreta de Grazia, Biondello's lines suggest that "Lucentio should impress Bianca with his inseminating imprint before she loses to another man's mark the whiteness or virginity proclaimed by her immaculate page-like name" (78).

If the marriage ceremony is a necessary expedient that prepares the way for a public reconciliation with the indulgent fathers (5.1.112), Petruchio has used the ceremony, as described by Gremio, as another of the assaults on convention designed to mirror Katherina's unconventional behavior and to release her from the role of the shrew:

> Tut, she's a lamb, a dove, a fool to him!
> I'll tell you, Sir Lucentio: when the priest
> Should ask if Katherine should be his wife,
> "Ay, by gogs-wouns," quoth he, and swore so loud,
> That all amaz'd the priest let fall the book,
> And as he stoop'd again to take it up,
> This mad-brain'd bridegroom took him such a cuff
> That down fell priest and book, and book and priest.
> "Now take them up," quoth he, "if any list." (3.2.157–65)

The "clamorous smack" of a kiss that makes the church echo concludes the unconventional ceremony. Shakespeare frequently creates the impression of a place of worship conveniently at hand, though not all marriages are as suddenly improvised as Biondello's example of "a wench married in an afternoon as she went to the garden for parsley to stuff a rabbit" (4.4.99–101). When Biondello says that he has been instructed

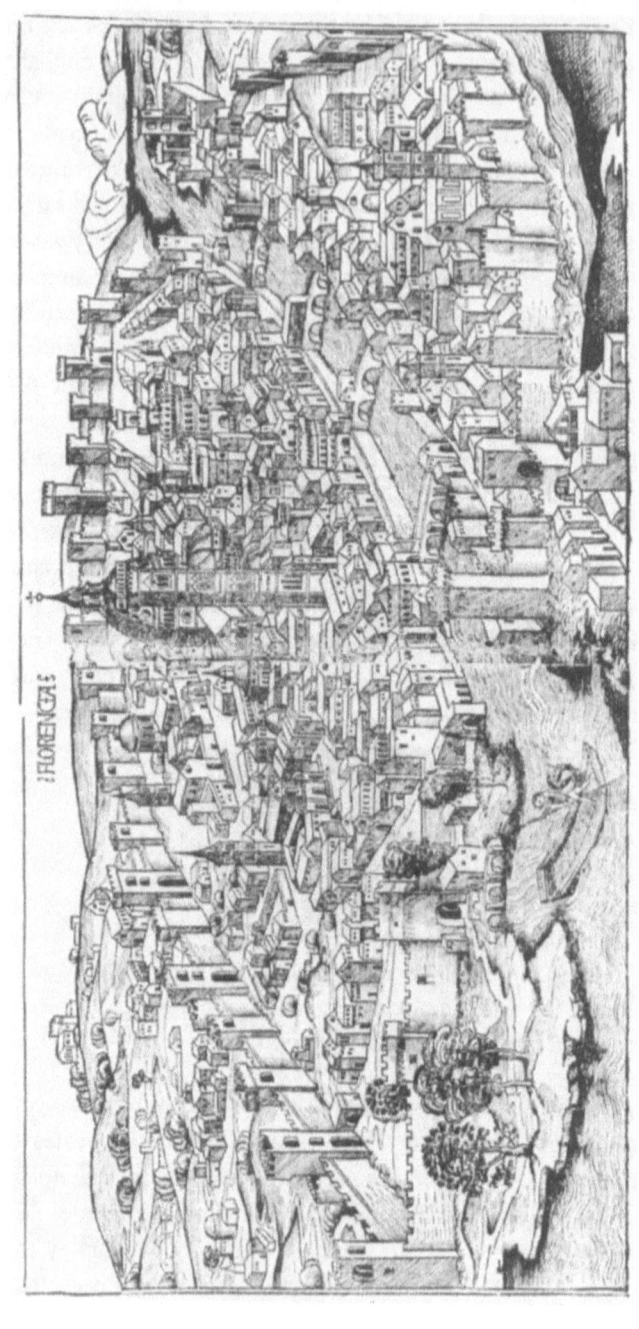

3. *Florence*, folio 33 from *Liber chronicarum* by Hartmut Schedel. Print Collection, Miriam and Ira D. Wallach Division of Art, Prints, and Photographs, the New York Public Library Astor, Lenox, and Tilden Foundations.

"to go to Saint Luke's to bid the priest be ready to come against you come with your appendix" (4.4.102–3), he appears to be stepping around the corner to something like the parish church where the blank-page Bianca is about to become her husband's index.

These scenes do not conjure up the classical contours of the temple within the *città ideale*. As an institution within Shakespeare's Italian city-state, the church readily serves the interests of the citizens, especially when they are in something of a hurry. We are given no reason to believe that anything more than wooing and grammar lessons took place in the garden outside Baptista's house, but the fair Bianca who cuts off Petruchio's attempt at some prenuptial banter with a bawdy exit line might have picked some parsley: "Am I your bird? I mean to shift my bush / And then pursue me as you draw your bow" (5.2.46–47).

The closest we come to a place of religious ceremony in Belmont is "the temple" where the suitors, like Morocco, must swear "never to speak to lady afterward / In way of marriage" if they choose the wrong casket (*The Merchant of Venice* 2.1.41–42). The lines that anticipate the wedding, which rewards the correct choice, represent the ceremony as a decidedly secular event. Bassanio compares himself to a victorious competitor, and Portia confirms his victory by describing the transfer of her ring and her possessions to "her lord, her governor, her king" (3.2.141, 165). Bassanio's feelings are compared to the reaction "among the buzzing pleased multitude" after the oration of a beloved prince (177–83). These lines keep the perspective within the secular world, where Portia has the authority to judge the competition, an authority that has passed to her through the father's will and is about to move to the new master with the wedding ring. Flustered precisely because Portia has made him the new lord and governor of Belmont, the young Venetian feels his way through this ceremony with protestations that will come back to haunt him (3.2.183–85). The only reference to a religious ceremony comes from Gratiano: "And when your honors mean to solemnize / The bargain of your faith, I do beseech you / Even at that time I may be married too" (3.2.192–94).

At the end of act 5, the couples move from the garden to the house, where they will read, at leisure, a letter from Bellario that explains Portia's disguise and another, which Portia chanced upon by "strange accident," that recounts the return of Antonio's argosies, as well as the "deed of gift" from Shylock to Lorenzo and Jessica. And when done reading, they will go to bed. But there is no mention of a wedding ceremony. This is not to say that the only religion in Belmont is to be heard in the music of the spheres. The messenger who announces Portia's imminent return reports that "she doth stray about / By holy crosses, where she kneels and prays / For happy wedlock hours" accompanied only by Nerissa and "a holy hermit" (5.1.30–34). The contrast between this activity and Portia's actual preparation for wedlock can be played for laughs. But in a play that includes the willing conversion of Jessica and the forced conversion of Shylock (4.1.287), there seems a conspicuous omission of reference to the religious ceremony that would, together with the consummation in bed, "solemnize" the marriage. Perhaps influenced by Venetian independence from papal Rome, Shakespeare creates Venetians who can cite Scripture (1.3.98) but who seal their bonds, including the marital variety, with a notary rather than a priest.

~

There is also a conspicuous absence of priest, consecrated roof, and wedding ceremony in *Othello*. We expect Iago and Roderigo to omit reference to anything that might make Desdemona's elopement less shocking to her father. As Roderigo proclaims in the street, Desdemona, "I say again, hath made a gross revolt, / Tying her duty, beauty, wit, and fortunes / In an extravagant and wheeling stranger / Of here and every where" (1.1.134–37). Only the word "Tying" suggests a legal bond, but even that phrase is peculiar, since it suggests that Desdemona is not tying herself to Othello by means of a ceremony, but rather entangling herself. Iago does ask Othello, "Are you fast married?" (1.2.11), but with Cassio he uses a nautical metaphor that distances the union from any holy place within the city: "Faith, he to-night hath boarded a land carract. / If it prove lawful prize, he's made for ever" (1.2.50–51).

Neither Othello nor Desdemona refers to a place where they might have been lawfully joined. Brabantio raises the question of Othello's enchantment, but no one asks who married them. Othello is almost as hard to understand as Iago when he says that were it not that he loved Desdemona, "I would not my unhoused free condition / Put into circumscription and confine / For the sea's worth" (26–28). His reference to the "sea's worth" echoes Iago's "land carract," while "circumscription" apparently refers to the marriage vow. Before her father and the Venetian senators, Desdemona identifies Othello as her husband, but only invokes a ceremony indirectly by recalling the precedent of her mother's marriage: "But here's my husband; / And so much duty as my mother show'd / To you, preferring you before her father, / So much I challenge that I may profess / Due to the Moor, my lord" (1.3.185–89). If we expect some equivalent of the Venetian church on Cyprus, all we find is a bed in act 5 that becomes alternately confessional, sacrificial altar, and tomb.

Everyone is so thoroughly grateful to Portia in act 5 of *The Merchant of Venice* that she hardly needs a priest to justify her Venetian expedition; a letter from cousin Bellario seems to be quite enough. We might compare her in this regard to Olivia, another young lady who governs her own household somewhere near the Adriatic coast. While Portia is constrained by the legal terms of her father's will, Olivia at first appears constrained by nothing other than the self-imposed mourning brought on by the deaths of her father and brother within the year (*Twelfth Night* 1.2.36–41). In direct response to Orsino's suit, she sends a message saying that she will not remove the veil of mourning for seven years: "But like a cloistress she will veiled walk, / And water once a day her chamber round / With eye-offending brine; all this to season / A brother's dead love, which she would keep fresh / And lasting in her sad remembrance" (1.1.27–31). However it is explained, the phrase a "brother's dead love" suggests that she is making a show of preserving something that is already dead by behaving like a "cloistress." Feste's catechism of Olivia makes the related point that there is some folly in the lady's ostentatious mourning for a brother whose soul she believes to be in heaven (1.5.70).

The church does not play a significant role in Olivia's life until she interrupts Sebastian's encounter with Sir Andrew and Sir Toby, takes the young man into her house, and then, with the priest in tow, proceeds to the altar. Sebastian accepts the haste as part of the peculiar atmosphere of a town that is, like the lady, error prone but not mad (4.3.10). The lady is wealthy, beautiful, clearly eager to engage with him at close quarters, but still not the type one might encounter at an inn like the Elephant. And her "stable bearing" is confirmed when she enters with the priest:

> Blame not this haste of mine. If you mean well,
> Now go with me, and with this holy man,
> Into the chantry by; there, before him,
> And underneath that consecrated roof,
> Plight me the full assurance of your faith,
> That my most jealous and too doubtful soul
> May live at peace. (4.3.22–28)

This private marriage will take place in Olivia's chapel, a place where daily masses might be said for the dead brother and father. Thinking of Cesario's ambiguous role as Orsino's servant and emissary in love, Olivia assures the youth that the marriage will be kept secret until he is "willing it shall come to note," whereupon they will have a more elaborate public celebration, "according to my birth" (29–31). The marriage ceremony is less a test of Cesario's intentions—whether he means "well"—than an acceptable way to catch a young man who has been as elusive as he is attractive. It marks the transition from the flirtatious pastimes of the garden to the more "stable bearing" required of married folk who take up residence within the house.

In act 5, the formality of the priest's speech on the "contract of eternal bond of love" (5.1.156) brings some of the controlling power of ritual to bear on the turbulent emotions that have been turned loose in the streets of Illyria. Shakespeare places the Malvolio and Sir Topas scene between Olivia's first encounter with Sebastian and their trip to the chantry. Malvolio requests light and paper to prove himself the victim of some error but no madman, and his lines are immediately echoed when Sebastian hopes Olivia's behavior "may be some error, but no madness" (4.3.10). While one man is rejected, the other is given rare gifts; one is in darkness and the other in the sun; one is tricked by a mock priest into questioning his identity and the other overcome by a "flood of fortune" that is ultimately ratified by a legitimate priest. While Feste mocks religion and those fools who think they can prove their sanity—"for as the old hermit of Prague, that never saw pen and ink, very wittily said to a niece of King

Gorboduc, 'That that is is'; so I, being Master Parson, am Master Parson; for what is 'that' but 'that,' and 'is' but 'is'?" (4.2.12–16)—Olivia uses the priest to prove that she is legally married and to allay Orsino's anger:

> A contract of eternal bond of love,
> Confirm'd by mutual joinder of your hands,
> Attested by the holy close of lips,
> Strength'ned by interchangement of your rings,
> And all the ceremony of this compact
> Seal'd in my function, by my testimony;
> Since when, my watch hath told me, toward my grave
> I have travell'd but two hours. (5.1.156–63)

The rhythm of the priest's speech prompts the audience to imagine an institution that helps soothe the discord caused by shipwrecks, love, and human foolishness. Though the church is not a dominating presence in Shakespeare's representation of the Italian urban scene, it is at hand, ready when the city's players are.

Twelfth Night ends with Orsino's anticipation of the marriage ceremony that will follow the sorting out of Malvolio's suit against the captain, who has Viola's "maiden weeds": "When that is known, and golden time convents, / A solemn combination shall be made / Of our dear souls" (5.1.382–84). The anticipation of a religious ceremony that will unite their dear souls might also be extended, by an appropriately inclusive gesture, to Olivia and Sebastian. In the public world of Illyria, both Olivia and the duke await the right, "golden" time for the kind of religious ceremony that befits their social standing. The private exchanges of vows, rings, and gestures, such as the giving of "hands," must be followed by the more official solemnity. From this perspective, the metatheatrical detail of getting Cesario to become Viola by a change of costume has a slightly different significance, for the public ceremony requires that all the social and legal details be in place. At the play's conclusion the stage is left to the clown, Feste, and to his song, which provides a less solemn picture of the transition to the married state: "But when I came, alas, to wive, . . . By swaggering could I never thrive" (5.1.397–99).

∽

Though Shakespeare first introduces Friar Lawrence as Romeo's spiritual adviser and confessor, it is Juliet who prompts the transition from the private contract in the garden to a place where a marriage can be solemnized: "If that thy bent of love be honorable, / Thy purpose marriage, send me word to-morrow, / By one that I'll procure to come to thee, / Where and what time thou wilt perform the rite, / And all my fortunes at thy foot I'll lay, / And follow thee my lord throughout the world" (2.2.143–48). Despite the somewhat ambiguous role of the nurse, whom Mercutio calls a bawd (2.4.130), and the connotation of Juliet's "procure," the lovers do not carry on a clandestine affair in or near the garden, nor do they risk their fortunes outside Verona "throughout the world." They attempt to move from the explosive energy of a contract that Juliet calls "too like the lightning, which doth cease to be / Ere one can say it lightens" (119–20), to a "rite" acknowledged by the whole community.

In this attempt they are assisted by the friar, who would use what he calls their "alliance," indicating his interest in the political implications of their relationship, to "turn your households' rancor to pure love" (2.3.93). The friar cannot be their assistant in "one respect" without assisting them in every respect once they have been married. The trip to Friar Lawrence's cell, where Juliet is to be "shriv'd and married" (2.4.182), is as clandestine as the rope-ladder that Romeo will use to climb into the house and consummate the marriage. Act 2, scene 6 is set in the cell, from which they exit to another place where the "holy act" will be performed: "For by your leaves, you shall not stay alone / Till Holy Church incorporate two in one" (2.6.36–37). We see little else of the church itself, though we have an extended scene back in the cell, where Friar Lawrence has an opportunity to demonstrate his ability as a counselor after the murder of Tybalt (3.3). The political implications of what the friar is attempting, or has been drawn into, are made clear in Romeo's lines: "Yet 'banished'? Hang up philosophy! / Unless philosophy can make a Juliet, / Displant a town, reverse a prince's doom, / It helps not, it prevails not. Talk no more" (3.3.57–60). For all his sage advice, the friar does not seem to have a plan that could, in fact, overcome the political authority by which the prince can banish Romeo. He temporizes and hopes to find a time "to blaze your marriage, reconcile your friends, / Beg pardon of the Prince, and call thee back" (151–52). The word "blaze" suggests a dramatic revelation of the secret marriage. How would that help? Who are the friends that need to be reconciled? What kind of influence does the friar have with the secular authority? The friar believes that the authority of the church can be used to overcome the social and political differences that plague Verona, but Shakespeare does not represent his methods as a variation on the Machiavellian policy that uses religion to promote the interests of the state. In Shakespeare's Verona, the friar remains identified with the humble confines of the garden and the cell; he is not identified with that powerful religious institution that might have been invoked in his reference to "Holy Church."

If we work back from Capulet's decision to proceed with the marriage of Juliet to Paris after Tybalt's death, it seems his family's ancient feast occurs on a Sunday, that the secret marriage takes place the next afternoon, and that Capulet's meeting with Paris, and Juliet's with Romeo, follow late that night. Informed that it is Monday, Capulet tells Paris that "We'n'sday next" is too soon for the marriage, and therefore "a' Thursday let it be" (3.4.17–20). In the following scene, Capulet is portrayed as a man who thinks of the church as a place where someone of his authority goes to have his daughter matched to "a gentleman of noble parentage, / Of fair demesnes" (3.5.179–80). He threatens to drag Juliet to "Saint Peter's Church" or to disown her and he does not seek the counsel of the friar, let alone ask ecclesiastical permission for the ceremony. It is Paris who conveys the decision to Friar Lawrence the following morning (Tuesday), describing the marriage as a form of therapy for Juliet's immoderate grief. Only after Juliet's apparent conversion to her father's will does Capulet mention the friar: "Now, afore God, this reverend holy friar, / All our whole city is much bound to him" (4.2.31–32). Capulet thinks nothing of moving the marriage up from next Thursday to the following morning (Wednesday), perfectly confident that not only Paris but the friar will respect his decision.

For his part, the friar turns the church into a theater where he performs a mock funeral in order to save Juliet and reconcile the clans. He relies on the fact that the Capulets will follow tradition when they bear Juliet in her "best robes, uncovered on the bier," her corpse adorned with rosemary for the journey to the "ancient vault" (4.1.110; compare 4.5.79). The exaggerated lamentations of Lady Capulet, the nurse, and

Paris, followed by the puns of Peter and the musicians, seem designed to arouse uneasy laughter in the audience over the friar's plan to make the church and the tomb the setting for a resurrection (4.5).

The action of the play moves from the bedroom to the churchyard, where the tomb of the Capulets stands. The audience would have been familiar with burial grounds within the precincts of the many churches in and around London. Shakespeare uses Paris's instructions to his page to describe the burial ground: "Under yond [yew] trees lay thee all along, / Holding thy ear close to the hollow ground, / So shall no foot upon the churchyard tread, / Being loose, unfirm, with digging up of graves, / But thou shalt hear it" (5.3.3–7). The ancient grudge has made Verona an unfirm city of the dead, a city that has collapsed into what Romeo calls "this hungry churchyard" (36). When Paris steps forward to challenge and apprehend Romeo, the churchyard mirrors the piazza, where Tybalt confronted Romeo, who attempted to avoid a fight, as he does once again with Paris. But its trees, even if they are yew trees, also recall the garden, for the signs of life that Romeo sees on Juliet's face as he enters the tomb can be traced back to the potion that the friar distilled from the earth, nature's "burying grave" and "her womb" (2.3.10–11). The tomb also becomes a residence, the "[palace] of dim night" where Romeo will dwell with his Juliet and the "worms that are thy chambermaids" (5.3.107–9). And finally the poison makes the tomb the final point of embarkation, recalling Juliet's willingness to "follow thee my lord throughout the world" (2.2.148), as well as Romeo's journey outside the walls of the garden and of Verona: "Come, bitter conduct, come, unsavory guide!" (116). And it is that journey, rather than the friar's call to leave "that nest / Of death, contagion, and unnatural sleep" and join "a sisterhood of holy nuns" (151–57), which Juliet undertakes.

The churchyard and "monument" then become an arena where the prince, the families, and the citizens of Verona gather to hear the friar "clear these ambiguities" and set the stage for the reconciliation. The statues in pure gold will be monuments to the lovers, "poor sacrifices of our enmity," as Capulet calls them (5.3.304). The statues are not identified with some commanding architectural presence within the city; they remain apart from the institutions of the state and the church. The friar does not proffer the religious platitudes he had recited as part of his performance after the supposed death of Juliet (4.5. 66–67). He simply offers his life to the rigor of the law.

The friar in *Much Ado About Nothing* enjoys greater success, but in the comic world of Messina threats come from the outside, from the contrived plot of Don John, rather than from within the basic social structure of the city. And luck plays a part. The watch from which Friar Lawrence flees becomes a group of bumbling saviors; the explosive patriarch Leonato is just as hard on his daughter Hero as is Capulet on Juliet, but the very public setting of her disgrace and of his rage provides the opportunity for a community to gather in her defense. Abandoned by her mother and her nurse, Juliet has no feisty cousin, like Beatrice, to stand by her. Authority within Messina seems more equally divided between Leonato's house, where the revels and the garden tricks are staged, and the church, which will be the setting for the wedding of Claudio and Hero.

But once again Shakespeare diminishes the authority of the church within the Italian city-state. The wedding ceremony toward which the action moves brings the leading residents of the city to the church, but Friar Francis is first instructed by Leonato to be brief and use "the plain form of marriage" and then interrupted by Claudio, who has his own script prepared—"Stand thee by, friar." Claudio seems to take it as a point of honor to use the church setting to denounce his erstwhile bride. The subsequent "catechizing" of Hero is an interrogation dominated by the court: "O God defend me, how am I beset! / What kind of catechizing call you this?" (4.1.77–78). When Claudio refers to Hero as "thou pure impiety and impious purity" (104), his oxymorons come from the Petrarchan religion of love rather than church doctrine.

Only when Hero faints does the friar step back to center stage to assuage the fury of Leonato, who regards the "pit of ink" into which his daughter has fallen as a blot on the family rather than on her eternal soul (4.1.129–43). Shakespeare gives Friar Francis the insight of a psychologist rather than the authority of a churchman: "Hear me a little, / For I have only been silent so long, / And given way unto this course of fortune, / By noting of the lady" (155–58). If Friar Lawrence is a student of mother nature's plants, Friar Francis is a student of human nature, who asks that his reading of Hero's looks and blushes be accepted as gospel. Shakespeare's friars seek to persuade by employing a combination of book learning and the "experimental seal" of worldly knowledge. They stand not above but amidst the citizens they serve. Friar Francis has the advantage of gaining the trust of the family and of working against those outsiders who have slandered Hero. He lends his authority to an elaborate performance whose "rites" answer, though he does not know it yet, the trick played by Don John: "Maintain a mourning ostentation, / And on your family's old monument / Hang mournful epitaphs, and do all rites / That appertain unto a burial" (4.1.205–8). When asked his purpose, the friar proposes that his scheme will "change slander to remorse" and that it will cause Claudio, in particular, to see Hero differently. Ever the psychologist, Friar Francis maintains that the idea of Hero's life "shall sweetly creep / Into his study of imagination" to stimulate remorse, "though he thought his accusation true" (224–25, 233). If all else fails, the family can conceal her wounded reputation "in some reclusive and religious life, / Out of all eyes, tongues, minds, and injuries" (242–43). Shakespeare will set the action within a church or cell, and make reference to a nearby sisterhood, but his friars address secular questions of reputation more than the spiritual questions of sin.

In or before the church, Beatrice asks Benedick to show his love and "kill Claudio" (289) for having "slander'd, scorn'd, dishonor'd my kinswoman" (302). Whether to characterize the Italians as more apt to think of the soul in terms of honor than salvation, or simply to avoid the representation of the church as a powerful institution within the city, Shakespeare makes it a place of trial or counsel rather than of religious ritual. When Claudio and Don Pedro do their penance at the "monument of Leonato" (5.3), Shakespeare distances the scene from any hint of Catholic ritual through the repeated use of classical allusions. When Hero is finally unveiled and recognized, the friar steps forward to redirect attention to the rites and institutions of the chapel.

Church doctrine does not play an important part in these maneuvers. Unlike Machiavelli's use of the church setting in *La mandragola*, Shakespeare never suggests that the priest's control over those who respect the institution of the church will be used for personal advantage, though that more cynical view does appear in the Vienna of *Measure for Measure*, at least as seen by Lucio. Even in his failure, Friar Lawrence of *Romeo and Juliet* is not represented as someone who reflects the corrupt ways of a religious institution that has lost its spiritual center. The presence of a friar who intervenes in the affairs of the city is no guarantee of a happy ending, but when seconded by the goodwill of others within the community, Shakespeare presents the consecrated roof of the church within his Italian city-states as contributing in a significant but not dominant way to the harmony that can take shape within the city's walls.

8

City Walls

OUR JOURNEY through the contours of Shakespeare's Italian cities leads beyond the walls to the open fields and forests. The port and the sea constitute one of the characteristic limits of Shakespeare's city-states, and a wilderness outside the control of the city might be seen as another region that defines the city by opposition. Another way to think of this urban geography would be as a series of concentric circles, tangible barriers and equally powerful social and political walls that can, depending on one's perspective, protect or imprison. The outsider who invades the protected space of the family and the state risks death or exile, while the control exercised by those who govern the household and the city inevitably creates a need to escape through windows, doors, and postern gates. Young women like Julia, Jessica, and Portia escape from the house or the city, often in disguise, to pursue their interests, while young men like Valentine and Romeo suffer banishment from the company of the women they love. The extra-urban excursion can be traumatic, but Shakespeare usually portrays the journey as an adventure undertaken with the implied or stated understanding that the city will not be closed to the adventurers who move for a time outside its walls.

The galleries of the public theater rising around the open area of the thrust stage reproduced for the audience the spatial sense of enclosure. Though London was spreading rapidly to the west beyond Ludgate and Newgate, it remained a city defined by its walls and gates. And beyond the walls we should imagine both the dangers and the attractions of open spaces and forests. John Stow laments the loss of open space within the city and extols the pleasure citizens derive from excursions into the surrounding fields (31, 148, 174). Both the river to the south and the fields north of the city's walls—West Smithfield, Moorfields, Spittlefields, and the Artillery grounds—provided release, while the great houses and courtly centers to the west contained their own bowling greens, tennis courts, and gardens. On the other hand, the sturdy beggar, the vagabond, or the player who lacked the protection of some lord's livery often found the passage from one town to the next precarious.

In contrast to the complex conditions of England, Shakespeare represents the territory between the famous Italian city-states as generally open to travel undertaken for the purposes of education, marriage, or business. When Baptista identifies Tranio as a stranger by his walk, the newcomer to Padua makes bold to introduce himself as a suitor who will be accepted because of his parentage: "This liberty is all that I request, / That upon knowledge of my parentage, / I may have welcome 'mongst the rest that woo, / And free access and favor as the rest" (*The Taming of the Shrew* 2.1.94–97). A loosely defined merchant/noble class not only enjoys the "liberty" to move between cities but expects "free access" within them. The impression of free passage between cities can also be observed in the transition from Padua to Petruchio's residence located somewhere outside "old Verona" (1.2.49). The "ways" may be foul (4.1.2), but they are dangerous only because of Petruchio's temper.

Shakespeare creates a somewhat different perspective in his treatment of the pedant, first identified as a "master, a mercantant, or a pedant" who reflects the sophisticated banking practices of Italy with his "bills for money by exchange" (4.2.63, 89) and something of the political problems that might threaten the Italian "mercantant" as he traveled from one city to another.

And Shakespeare's Italy is not entirely free of surprises on the road. The scene that shows Petruchio and Katherina traveling back to Padua introduces Lucentio's father, Vincentio, as a traveler who happens upon the last taming exercise designed to counter the "bias" in Kate's upbringing (4.5.25). Vincentio takes his "strange encounter" with the spirited couple in good spirits, identifies himself, and is embraced by Petruchio as his kinsman. Petruchio's sudden announcement that Vincentio's son has married the "sister to my wife, this gentlewoman" (62), seems as much a joke devised by "pleasant travellers" as his being addressed as "gentle mistress" (71–73). Vincentio subsequently faces the more serious threat of being arrested when he enters Padua, where the pedant has assumed his identity and Tranio his son's (5.1.108). But in Shakespeare's version of Italy, a world where identity and parentage circulate like bills of exchange, seeming threats become variations of the traveler's jest.

Occasionally the road leads not from one city to another but from the city's walls to the forest. The duke of Milan banishes Valentine from the court and consigns his daughter Silvia "to close prison" (*The Two Gentlemen of Verona* 3.1.237). Valentine and Speed encounter outlaws, who are identified by Speed as "the villains / That all the travellers do fear so much" (4.1.5–6). But they are called "friends" by Valentine, who represents himself as one, like them, who has been banished for killing a man in a fair fight. When one of the group swears by "the bare scalp of Robin Hood's fat friar" (36), the Italians banished for the "petty crimes" of "ungovern'd youth" (43) merge with the English tradition of a "wild faction" that is outside the city's law and yet governed by its own sense of justice. Valentine enters the forest as easily as he had the court, but has greater success among the outlaws, who make him their commander because of his self-control, his knowledge of foreign languages, and his attractive appearance, or "goodly shape." The banished gentlemen agree to "do no outrages / On silly women or poor passengers" because they "detest such vile base practices" (69–71). The band gets its treasure by attacking those who are neither innocent nor poor. Shakespeare is likely to have known something of the role of the political exile in Italian politics, from Dante to Machiavelli, but he represents the landscape outside the city as an area of passage, or transition, rather than of prolonged suffering, even for a Romeo.

When Silvia makes her escape from the prison of the court, she exits for the forest, "not three leagues off," by way of Friar Patrick's cell and the abbey wall (5.1). Shakespeare reinforces the impression that the forest is a short distance from the city when the duke reports that the escapees encountered the friar "as he in penance wander'd through the forest" (5.2.38). The duke instructs the pursuers to meet "upon the rising of the mountain foot / That leads toward Mantua, whither they are fled" (46–47). The region beyond the city's walls combines mountain, forest, and desert wilderness. It stands in opposition to the civilizing forces and to the injustices of the city. The abode of outlaws, it is also the appropriate setting for the friar's contemplation, or the "complaining notes" of the lover Valentine, who restrains his mates and his erstwhile friend. Once removed from "flourishing peopled towns," characters drop their masks, as they do in the garden; the would-be courtier Proteus shows himself to be an outlaw to civility, and the reformed outlaws regain their former "employment" (5.4.156–57). Valentine, who failed at courtly subterfuge, shows what he is made of when he confronts Thurio and takes Silvia for his very own. In the eyes of the duke, courage ennobles the young man and transforms him from a "base intruder" to the worthy companion of an empress: "Now, by the honor of my ancestry, / I do applaud thy spirit, Valentine, / And think thee worthy of an empress' love" (5.4.139–41). By recreating a reformed version of the court within the forest, Shakespeare asks the audience to laugh at and reflect on the relationship between these seemingly opposite worlds.

~

The open road that connects the cities of Shakespeare's "pleasant garden of great Italy" does not typically lose itself in the forest. More frequently a version of the wilderness opens up within the city. Most of Shakespeare's audience would have been aware of the Liberties, particularly the notorious Whitefriars district to the west of the Fleet River, or Blackfriars, where Shakespeare's company would attempt to open an indoor theater. These areas within or near the city's walls were exempt from the direct control of the city authorities because they had retained the independent legal status granted to religious institutions before the Protestant Reformation.

Though Juliet never travels outside Verona's walls, in the course of a very few days she journeys from a bedroom where her mother and the nurse prepare her for a conventional marriage to a bed where she prepares herself for a desperate escape from her family: "My dismal scene I needs must act alone" (4.3.19). When she imagines waking in the tomb before Romeo has arrived to redeem her, she fears being trapped again, "stifled in the vault" with "bloody Tybalt, yet but green in earth" (4.3.33–43). The friar has offered her an escape from what he calls the "present shame" of her marriage to Paris, "if no inconstant toy, nor womanish fear, / Abate thy valor in the acting it" (4.1.118–20). Anything but fearful, Juliet has shown herself more than eager to act her part, to commit suicide, or to search out parts of the city most distant from that room within the Capulet home where we first met her: "O, bid me leap, rather than marry Paris, / From off the battlements of any tower, / Or walk in thievish ways, or bid me lurk / Where serpents are; chain me with roaring bears, / Or hide me nightly in a charnel-house" (4.1.77–81). Shakespeare evokes the battlements of those Italian cities that were plagued by civil strife and blends the Italian setting with places more familiar to his audience. The "dismal scene" Juliet must act alone merges with marginal precincts of the city, including the arenas used for bearbaiting and theater.

The tomb embodies the ancient traditions of the family, but these traditions feed on the violence aptly represented by the "charnel-house" and the loathsome smells and "shrikes like mandrakes' torn out of the earth" (4.3.47). The forked mandrake root was thought to grow where the semen of a hanged man fell to the ground. In the Verona of this play Shakespeare creates a city that has impressive battlements, walls, houses, and gardens. But it is also a city that can become a wilderness of "roaring bears" and dead men's screams. It is a city, like London, whose citizens have a taste for blood that includes the sport of bearbaiting as well as the duels that kill Mercutio and Tybalt: "O, look! methinks I see my cousin's ghost / Seeking out Romeo, that did spit his body / Upon a rapier's point. Stay, Tybalt, stay!" (4.3.55–57).

The darkest corners of Shakespeare's Verona bring a dimension of psychological and social realism to Shakespeare's portrait of Italy. In Mantua Romeo speaks of sleep, dreams, and a strangely happy death: "I dreamt my lady came and found me dead—/ Strange dream, that gives a dead man leave to think!" (5.1.6–7). This dream reverses the friar's plan and foreshadows Juliet's attempt to join Romeo in death by kissing the poison from his lips. When Balthazar arrives with news of Juliet's apparent death, Romeo moves directly to the urban equivalent of a wilderness, the abode of exiles and outlaws. We know that the apothecary guild had shops in some of the best, but also many of the very poorest, wards of London. In Romeo's description Shakespeare mingles carefully observed detail with a sense of nightmarish fantasy that carries over from the talk of dreams. Like one of London's Liberties, the apothecary's shop is within the city but outside the laws of the secular world: "The world is not thy friend, nor the world's law, / The world affords no law to make thee rich; / Then be not poor, but break it, and take this" (5.1.72–74).

We imagine Verona's churchyard to be as close to the walls as the friar's garden, or that pastoral "grove of sycamore" where Romeo wandered in the role of a lovesick youth. It is a space that one naturally identifies with a church or the friar's cell. But it becomes a battleground for the county Paris, that "slaught'red youth" as Romeo calls him, who lies amidst "masterless and gory swords" in what should be a "place of peace" (5.3.84, 142–43). Verona remains a city on the verge of civil war, as we learn from Lady Capulet, who reports that "the people in the street cry 'Romeo,' / Some 'Juliet,' and some 'Paris,' and all run / With open outcry toward our monument" (191–93). Old Capulet still thinks in terms of blood feuds and the knife in the back when he sees Juliet with the dagger sheathed in her breast: "This dagger hath mista'en, for lo his house / Is empty on the back of Montague, / And is mis-sheathed in my daughter's bosom" (203–5).

~

Verona contains violent private quarrels, but Shakespeare's Italian city-states do not experience open civil war, nor are they under siege from armies camped outside their walls. This is in a way surprising since sixteenth-century Italy was a battleground for armies large and small, the home of famous *condottieri*, as well as equally infamous tyrant princes. But we also need to recall that Shakespeare's audience, unlike the Italians, did not experience the self-perpetuating warfare of professional, or mercenary, armies.

From the invasion of Charles VIII in 1494, an event to which Machiavelli returns in many contexts, Italy was to become the theater for military contests between the powerful nation states of France and Spain. Whether we consider the military *virtù* Machiavelli extols, or the polished skill of Castiglione's courtier, Italy was a country identified with the art and trials of war. Bassanio, who is said to be "a Venetian, a scholar and a soldier" (*The Merchant of Venice* 1.2.113), refers to cowardly men who, like the commedia dell'arte captains, "wear yet upon their chins / The beards of Hercules and frowning Mars" (3.2.84–5). But he and his aristocratic associates are more concerned with masques and marriage than with soldiering. Among Shakespeare's Italians, there are few Othellos, the professional soldier who moves between the military camp, which has shaped his character, and the city.

The Messina of *Much Ado About Nothing* seems easily to absorb the military gentlemen, Claudio the Florentine and Benedick of Padua. After an opening reference to the honor Claudio has earned by performing "the feats of a lion," Beatrice signals a transition from the wars to the city, where words and the tongue take precedence over swords and teeth: "I pray you, how many hath he kill'd and eaten in these wars? But how many hath he kill'd? for indeed I promis'd to eat all of his killing" (1.1.42–45). Benedick becomes food for Beatrice's disdain. However, an initial complication in the journey from camp to garden occurs when Claudio cannot use his own tongue to woo Hero (2.1.177). Though we are informed that Claudio has an uncle in Messina, he confides in his superior Don Pedro, who devises a military stratagem: "And in her bosom I'll unclasp my heart, / And take her hearing prisoner with the force / And strong encounter of my amorous tale; / Then after to her father will I break, / And the conclusion is, she shall be thine" (1.1.323–27). Claudio defers to his superior and quickly reverts to a soldier's stereotypical view of women to explain the prince's apparent duplicity, "for beauty is a witch / Against whose charms faith melteth into blood" (2.1.179–80). The attitudes of the camp invade the church and transform Hero from Diana to a camp follower, "a common stale" (4.1.65), as Don Pedro calls her. Though Leonato and his brother Antonio challenge the younger soldiers, the "boys, apes, braggarts, Jacks, milksops!" of the camp who have disrupted the city (5.1.91), Messina is never in danger of degenerating into the "grudge" that divides the Verona of *Romeo and Juliet*. Despite the disgrace Hero suffers, Benedick and Claudio both complete the transition from the camp's drum and fife to the city's tabor and pipe (compare 2.3.13 and 5.4.128).

Though we do not know what caused the original division within Verona, the bawdy puns used by Gregory and Sampson hint that sexual assault, or rape, certainly accompanied, if it did not initiate, the competition between the masters and servants of the feuding households. Speaking of Rosaline, Romeo rings the changes on the Petrarchan cliché of love as combat (1.1.212–13). Armed against Cupid's arrow and against "saint-seducing gold," Rosaline withstands assault within the citadel of her virginity. Romeo does not intend rape, nor is he ready for marriage. He uses the terms current among lovers, but as he delivers these lines in a street littered with weapons, Shakespeare anticipates the shift from assault as a figure of speech to the assault on the house and garden of the Capulets, which takes place within a city close to civil war. Verona experiences only moments of nervous respite, such as the break for the Capulets' "ancient feast." But it is a city that can revert to the atmosphere of a camp at any moment.

At the center of Mercutio's Queen Mab speech is the soldier's dream:

Sometime she driveth o'er a soldier's neck,
And then dreams he of cutting foreign throats,
Of breaches, ambuscadoes, Spanish blades,
Of healths five fadom deep; and then anon
Drums in his ear, at which he starts and wakes,
And being thus frighted, swears a prayer or two,
And sleeps again. (1.4.82–88)

As in Bassanio's lines, this picture of the soldier as one half braggart and the other coward owes something to the commedia dell'arte captains. But once Tybalt has identified a Montague, he is very serious about cutting Romeo's "foreign" throat. Verona is not governed by a prince who can, as Machiavelli recommends, direct the turbulent humors outward against some foreign power ("On Ambition" 97). In an urban center where, as Benvolio says, one cannot escape a fight, "for now, these hot days, is the mad blood stirring" (3.1.4), any act can become the occasion for a brawl. In Benvolio's reconstruction of the deaths of Mercutio and Tybalt, the events that have just transpired in the square take on the formal character of an engagement between two armies. Another fight passes into the narrative history of Verona's civil strife. One is reminded of Dante's exclamation: "those enclosed by the same wall and moat, even they are at each other's throats" (*Purgatory* 6.83–84).

Though Shakespeare does not introduce the threat posed to the city by foreign powers, anyone familiar with the history of Italy in the sixteenth century could easily imagine cities weakened by internal strife and overrun by the foreign armies that, as Machiavelli says, conquered Italy with little more than the chalk used to mark the homes where their troops would be billeted (*The Prince* XII). But with the exception of *All's Well That Ends Well*, Shakespeare does not journey to the Italy invaded by foreign troops. Nor does he take his audience on an imaginative journey to a country whose famous city-states were often at war with one another. England, not Italy, takes shape in his plays as the country of the politic Machiavel and the heroic warrior.

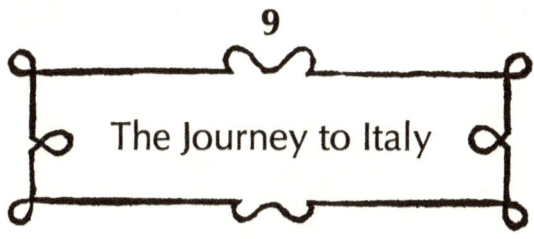

9
The Journey to Italy

ALL OF THE SETTINGS Shakespeare adopts for the concluding scenes of the Italian plays discussed in this book can be seen as variations on the piazza. Whether in the street before Olivia's house or the churchyard in Verona, citizens gather at the conclusion of each play. Even when the climactic events unfold within the protected confines of the court, as in *The Winter's Tale*, news spreads quickly to the outside world. The open exchange of ideas and experience is the essence of Shakespeare's Italy. Of course the scene I am describing typifies the comic genre, and any comedy set in Italy might include something like the dancing that revives the spirit of revelry at the end of *Much Ado About Nothing*. Nor are scenes of conflict and interrogation entirely forgotten. The concluding scene, with its recapitulation or acting out of tests and games, as in *The Taming of the Shrew* and *The Merchant of Venice*, can take on the character of a brief trial. And the churchyard as piazza, which provides the setting for the final scene of *Romeo and Juliet*, brings the citizens of Verona together as witnesses to a tragic catastrophe and to judgment: "Some shall be pardon'd, and some punished" (5.3.308).

The tragic ending might be considered more of a withdrawal from the dangerous openness of the Italian city-state, a return to the conventional restraints of London after the audience has made its imaginative journey. Italy drew Englishmen to its centers of learning, commerce, and courtliness, but as has been thoroughly documented, Italy was also considered a

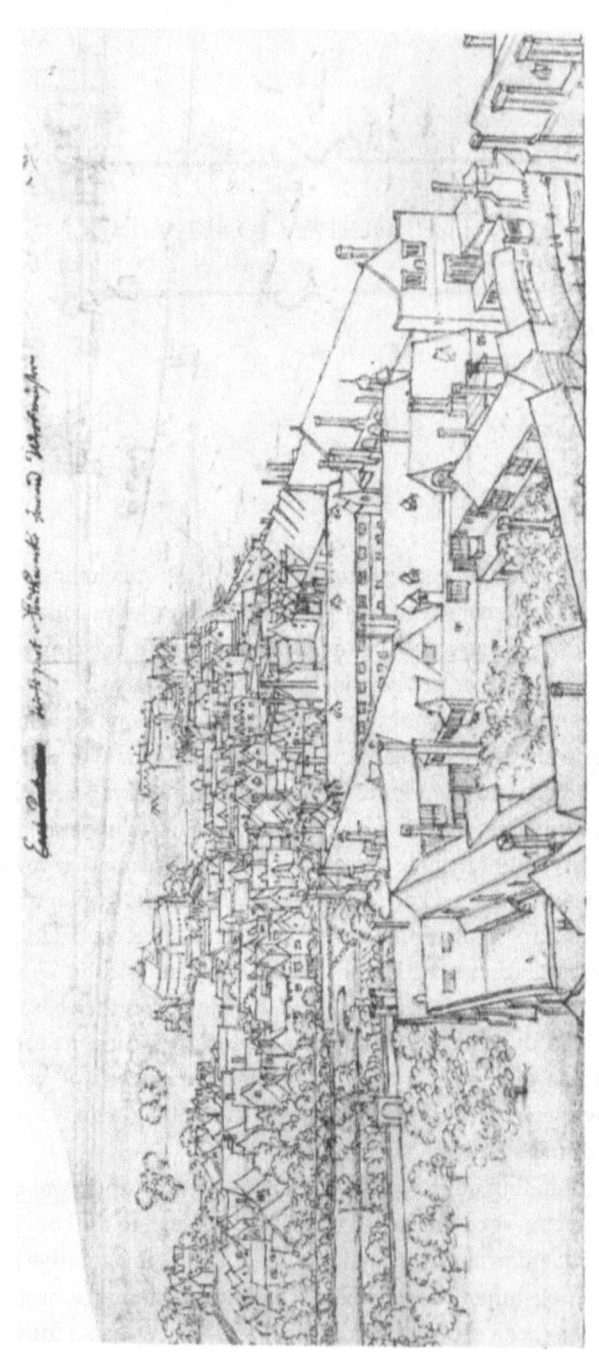

4. *A View from St. Mary's, Southwark, Looking Towards Westminster* by Wenceslaus Hollar. Yale Center for British Art, Paul Mellon Collection.

country of seductive dangers. The Italy where men can, apparently, move between notable cities with their bills of exchange and letters of introduction must have seemed inviting to some, while just as many spectators or readers of the plays may have perceived in this fluidity a symptom of the notorious dangers of Italy. With its revels and open roads, this Italy encourages, or at least facilitates, escapades—daughters elope, young women disguise themselves as boys, and the traditions identified with ancestors, whether represented by the ring Shylock received from his wife, Leah, or the ring that Bertram finally gives up to satisfy his desire for Diana, can be sacrificed for love or lust. This perspective is prominent when Italy is seen from the outside. In *All's Well That Ends Well* the young nobles who journey to Italy have to be warned by the king to watch "those girls of Italy" (2.1.19); in *Cymbeline* Imogen distinguishes the British court from a "Romish stew" (1.6.152) and later fears that her Posthumus is no match for the world of Machiavellian intrigue: "That drug-damned Italy hath outcraftied him" (3.4.15).

Cymbeline, which seems to straddle ancient and Renaissance Rome, moves from England to the Italian court. In Jachimo, Shakespeare combines the negative image of Italian courtesy, seen in his attempted seduction of Imogen (1.6), with the stereotype of the faithless Italian who, in the evil tradition of "Our Tarquin," violates the sanctity of Imogen's bedroom and of her person (2.2.31–33). Jachimo is, however, a diminished villain. Neither a Tarquin nor a Tereus, he becomes a mere thief, or cheap illusionist, who cannot touch Imogen's spirit. The contrast between England and that Rome where the true courtier has been replaced by the "false, Italian / (As poisonous tongu'd as handed)" (3.2.5–6) reappears in Jachimo's confession: "Being thus quench'd / Of hope, not longing, mine Italian brain / Gan in your duller Britain operate / Most vildly; for my vantage, excellent" (5.5.195–98).

Yet Shakespeare, ever ready to complicate matters, also undercuts this negative stereotype by giving the virtuous English courtier an Italian name (with perhaps a pun on the Italian *paesano*, or "fellow countryman"). Pisanio resembles Camillo of *The Winter's Tale*, for both men not only resist unjust orders but assist the intended victims their deluded masters would have them kill. They both fulfill the ideal of the courtier who must find a way to reconcile service with an innate sense of justice.

Pisanio assists Imogen in her escape, providing the clothes that she can use to disguise herself and enter the service of Lucius (3.4.169). Though the disguise only begins Imogen's adventures, it does counter Jachimo's diabolical use of properties, particularly the bracelet, to signify Imogen's betrayal.

The journey to Italy brings out the worst in Posthumus. Banished from the court for loving beyond his rank, he does not have the good fortune, like Valentine, to fall in with a band of outlaws. The Rome to which he travels is particularly deceptive because in it he encounters the genuine courtesy of Philario, whose name evokes a classical tradition, and the duplicitous scheming of Jachimo, denizen of the other Rome, the city of courtesans and of the courtliness Aretino satirized in his play *Il Cortegiano*. But Rome corrupts Posthumus by releasing sexual fantasies of a decidedly northern cast: "Perchance he spoke not, but / Like a full-acorn'd boar, a German [one], / Cried 'O!' and mounted" (2.5.15–17).

Italy is portrayed as a dangerous place for the inexperienced Briton to visit and the Italian, Jachimo, a dangerous man to entertain in your house. Shakespeare does not often represent the godless Machiavel on his home turf. The conniving villains who work behind doors, such as Proteus and Don John, are very general types defined by name or by professed melancholy. Shakespeare reserves the stereotype for the English history play, where his Richard III will "set the murtherous Machevil to school" (*3 Henry VI* 3.2.193). However, as Harold Goddard puts it, Jachimo is the last in a line of "Italianated" gentlemen condemned by Shakespeare (634). In the cross-cultural mix of the play, it is also possible that the name Jachimo, pronounced with the English-sounding "Jack" as its prominent syllable, would balance the British Pisanio. That is, this Jack is a familiar figure in and around London, as much a native product as the prostitutes who flourished in the English city quite as famously as in Rome. For English Puritans, London was in danger of becoming too much like Rome. But we also recognize that the gross assaults of the home-bred Cloten and the less than figurative poison of his mother threaten Imogen as much as the deceptive wiles of the Italianate villain Jachimo.

Imogen, like the audience, might have been quick to imagine the notorious courtesans of Rome, but Shakespeare leaves them in the imagination. The brothel, the inn, and the church were a part of the generic comic scene described and depicted by Sebastian Serlio (2:3 fol.25), but Shakespeare does not introduce a brothel in Rome, as he does in the Mytilene of *Pericles,* or a place of ill repute, like the house in the suburbs of Vienna visited by Elbow's wife in *Measure for Measure.*

~

In *All's Well That Ends Well* the king of France warns his courtiers about becoming captives rather than victors when they encounter the girls of Italy (2.1.19). Given the king's leering farewell to his young courtiers, one might expect the French camped outside Florence to look for "common houses" of the kind that dotted the suburbs of London, especially in the Bankside district. When the widow's house in Florence becomes the setting for a bed trick, the attendant "recompense" paid to the mother and daughter by Helena plays into the stereotype of Italy as a "mart," as Imogen calls it, for trade of all kinds. But we never get quite what the stereotype promises. The play offers the more familiar Shakespearean pattern of movement to a society that may have appeared dangerously seductive when viewed from the outside, but which allows someone like Helena deftly to transform vice to virtue. The intimate colloquy between the countess and Helena (1.3) reoccurs in the scenes in the widow's house in Florence. In both settings women govern a household and exhibit a degree of trust that allows them to take chances while maintaining order.

The freedom that Bertram enjoys in Florence derives from his rank and the opportunity that Italy offers young aristocrats to perform military service and to gain experience of the world. It reflects the same motivation for travel found in *The Two Gentlemen of Verona.* When encouraging Bertram to set out for Italy, Parolles puts the choice as between Venus and Mars: "He wears his honor in a box unseen, / That hugs his kicky-wicky here at home, / Spending his manly marrow in her arms, / Which should sustain the bound and high curvet / Of Mars's fiery steed. To other regions!" (2.3.279–83). While married love debilitates, the Italian wars inspire manliness. For Bertram, however, Italy merely provides the combination of camp and widow's house where he can find "breathing and exploit" on both fronts (1.2.17).

In the political history of Renaissance Italy commented on by Machiavelli, the incursion of the French under Charles VIII in 1494, which drew in Spain, led to what Machiavelli considered the ruin of Italy (*The Prince* XII). The fall of the Florentine republic in 1512 was for Machiavelli a personal disaster, while the sack of Rome in 1527 confirmed the Florentine's analysis of the weakness of political and military orders within the Italian city-states. Shakespeare's *All's Well That Ends Well* shows some awareness of the long-standing political alliance between France and Florence, as well as the long history of Florentine territorial expansion, which led to wars with Pisa and Sienna. Shakespeare touches on the interplay of Italian and European politics when letters from the duke of Austria to the king caution him that the Florentines will request aid; these letters, as the king says, "would seem / To have us make denial" (1.2.8–9). Following these diplomatic hints, the king denies the Florentines direct aid but does grant the gentlemen of his court leave to fight on either side in this "Tuscan service," which will serve as a "nursery" for their unpracticed *virtù* (1.2.14–17). The war thus functions as a proving ground for the "warlike principles" that will be profitable to the French (2.1.1–4). Though the duke of Florence alludes to "fundamental reasons" for the war and the French lord covers for his king with appropriately diplomatic circumlocutions, it would seem that the thirst for blood represented by this Italian conflict derives from a courtly need to "physic" the surfeit of ease among the nobles (3.1.19).

In *The Discourses* (book 3, chapter 16), Machiavelli comments on the problems republics face in times of peace, when spirited citizens need to distinguish themselves through war, and in *The Art of War*, a dialogue set in the Rucellai gardens of Florence, he attempts to revive the ancient principles of war that the Romans practiced. One of Machiavelli's abiding objectives was to create a sense of military professionalism that would reform the desultory battles led by mercenaries and ineffective nobles (*The Discourses* book 2, chapters 16–18).

Shakespeare is aware of the danger posed by aristocrats who rely on warfare to maintain their privilege and who, "sick" in times of peace, seek occasions for "breathing and exploit." Seen in its political perspective, the journey to Italy in *All's Well That Ends Well* takes the audience to a city that was the home of an important Renaissance thinker who was not the stage Machiavel, but rather a man who sought to expose the folly of fashionable soldiering, much as the play exposes the complementary emptiness of Parolles and Bertram. The king had warned his departing courtiers not to fall captive *before* they served in battle. When Helena follows Bertram to Florence, she joins a group of women who have gone outside the walls to observe the troops as they return to the city from the field. But the "girls" of Italy have not gone out to tempt the soldier; rather Bertram, who has done "worthy service" in battle, has begun to lay siege to Diana (3.5.48). Having informed Helena of Bertram's amorous intentions, the women identify the leading gentlemen-soldiers as they pass, Bertram being distinguished by his gallant plume and Parolles by his scarves. The scene recalls a courtly procession or tournament, with the audience of women taking an active role in the proceedings when they jeer at Parolles for being Bertram's go-between, or "ring-carrier," a reference which foreshadows the exchange of rings that will trap Bertram. Shakespeare's audience is in an imagined place like the actual space it occupies. When viewed from Machiavelli's critical perspective, the Renaissance field of battle itself had become a mere theater of war, a place very much like a theater where none of the combatants actually dies (*The Florentine Histories* book 5). How many courtly processions contained a performer like Parolles, downcast because he has lost Mars's drum, jeered at by the spectators? How often were the tournaments accompanied by asides like Diana's "I would he lov'd his wife," asides that uncover less than gallant truth about aristocrats who serve Venus more than Mars?

Shakespeare interlocks the camp scenes, where the lord directs the gulling of Parolles, with scenes in the widow's house, where Helena directs the bed trick. Parolles is more than eager to reveal the "secrets of our camp" to save his life, just as Bertram, during this same period between ten o'clock (4.1.24) and midnight, will give up the ring that, as Helena says, "downward hath succeeded in his house / From son to son, some four or five descents" (3.7.23–24) to a young woman whose name he does not know—"They told me that your name was Fontibell" (4.2.1).

The dramatic effectiveness of Shakespeare's imagination derives from the focus that theater, the instrument of his imagination, provides. A camp outside Florence comes to life through a trick that centers on a drum, an instrument important to combat and to theater. In what is called the fog of war, the signals provided by the trumpet and the drum can turn mayhem into an orderly theater of operations. When asked during his interrogation about Captain Dumaine's expertness in war, Parolles answers sarcastically, "Faith, sir, h'as led the drum before the English tragedians" (4.3.266). While Parolles, who is being exposed as one who merely plays the role of soldier, denigrates Dumaine, the reference to the drum and the English stage underscores the metatheatrical character of the events being played out in the Florentine camp. The drum, which becomes a prop in the play staged to set up Parolles, is the instrument used by actors to draw attention as they enter a city.

No sooner has Bertram agreed to the midnight meeting with Diana than news of his amorous siege reaches the Florentine camp. The second lord, to whom Bertram had desired to show "the lass," reports that "this night he fleshes his will in the spoil of her honor" (4.3.16–17) and that he has given Diana his "monumental ring." None of this will "dwell darkly." The camp-as-stage reveals truths and half-truths of all kinds, for men are "trumpeters" of their "unlawful intents" (27). News that a peace has been concluded mixes with the story of Helena's death, the "intelligence" that will allow Bertram to return to France: "I have to-night dispatch'd sixteen businesses, a month's length a-piece, by an abstract of success: I have congied with the Duke, done my adieu with his nearest; buried a wife, mourn'd for her, writ to my lady mother I am returning, entertain'd my convoy, and between these main parcels of dispatch [effected] many nicer needs. The last was the greatest, but that I have not ended yet" (4.3.85–92). By "not ended," Bertram means that he is afraid that he might "hear of it hereafter," while the audience knows that it is not ended because he has been trapped by a performance that will have consequences like those Parolles is about to suffer.

Shakespeare brings together many threads in this scene. The Florentine camp represented on his stage draws on the tradition of courtly and popular entertainments, the tournament, and the satirical dialogue, as well as the scaffolds where criminals were put on display to confess their crimes: "Bring him forth, h'as sate i' th' stocks all night, poor gallant knave.... He hath confess'd himself to Morgan, whom he supposes to be a friar" (101–9). When he discourses on the vices of Captain Dumaine and his brother, we do not know whether Parolles is revealing truths or is performing with a theatrical zest that almost redeems him—"He hath out-villain'd villainy so far, that the rarity redeems him" (273–74). The best he can say about Captain Dumaine's expertness in war is, as we have seen, that at a place in England called Mile-end he taught "the doubling of files" (270). The multilingual Florentine camp, where soldiers profess "the whole theoric of war" (142), is seen through Mile-end, where Londoners received elementary training to the sound of a drum, no doubt stumbling about like a group of actors (Fortescue 113–14). The sudden adjustments in perspective, between the widow's house and the camp, or between Florence and Mile-end, perfectly suit the interweaving of lies and truths: "The web of our life is of a mingled yarn, good and ill together" (4.3.71–72).

Could Shakespeare have created the same effects by moving the action to a camp outside some other city, to a country other than Italy, regardless of his sources? Though Helena has ventured from Rossillion to the court in Paris, it is not until she arrives outside Florence that she finds the conditions that will allow her to capture and, perhaps, redeem Bertram. But we do not feel that the Florentine transaction will be integrated within the institutions of a revitalized community. Though she has designed the encounter that consummates their marriage, and which, we are to suppose, will give her the child that Bertram's letter demands, Helena has also been used and must continue to use others. When Helena rouses herself to prepare for the return to France, she sees briars in her way, even if they will have sweet leaves in summer:

> But with the word the time will bring on summer,
> When briers shall have leaves as well as thorns,
> And be as sweet as sharp. We must away:
> Our waggon is prepar'd, and time revives us.
> All's well that ends well! still the fine's the crown;
> What e'er the course, the end is the renown. (4.4.31–36)

Helena is being optimistic, but she is not alone in thinking that Bertram will always be a thorn. Even the word "sweet" echoes the problematic "sweet use" of the midnight encounter and recalls the difficult role Helena has played in Florence, arranging an assignation that is all too like the more sordid prostitution that went on near military camps. Like players,

Helena, the widow, and Diana must pack up and leave on their "waggon," heading for the final performance to be staged at the French court.

For Bertram, the journey to Italy represents an escape; for the young French lords, an expedition in pursuit of honor; for Helena, something between a pilgrimage, a test, and a hunt. The city and camp, which the audience experiences from the inside, turn out to be neither the "higher Italy" of statecraft and honor, nor the seductive abode of those "girls" the French do not have the language to deny (2.1.12, 19). It is in fact a place where you can make up your own language, as the French do when tricking Parolles. The audience follows Bertram to a camp where he is free to abandon the higher ideals of the Italian Renaissance and follow his baser instincts; but if the audience expected to be titillated by the Italy of seductive looseness, it encounters, instead, the virtue of Diana and the integrity of the widow. To the extent that it provides a young man like Bertram the stage on which he can act out his foolishness and vice, Shakespeare's version of Italian society is dangerously open. But Italy also provides Helena the opportunity to develop her skill as a stage manager who can use the very theatricality of the Italian city to force Bertram into a more virtuous performance than he intends.

~

What may be Shakespeare's first and last plays, *The Comedy of Errors* and *The Tempest*, provide distant views of Italy. From across the Mediterranean Sea, Egeon and Prospero recollect the Syracusa and Milan of their past. These are nearly invisible, generic cities—the Syracusa of "marts and fairs" and of Egeon's happy marriage and "prosperous voyages" (*The Comedy of Errors* 1.1.17, 40) and Prospero's "poor Milan" and "fair Milan."

In *The Tempest* Prospero takes his daughter Miranda through the "dark backward and abysm of time" to a city that she left at the tender age of three (1.2.50). Prospero's memories focus on the two salient characteristics of the Italian city of the Renaissance: the court and the library, politics and the liberal arts. Whereas Egeon's life story revolves around business and the family, when Prospero turns his thoughts to Milan, it is to a city dominated by the political. Miranda has trouble connecting her father and the duke of Milan, and her father is something less than intimate in his recollections of family life: "Thy mother was a piece of virtue, and / She said thou wast my daughter" (1.2.54–57). In his reconstruction of the traumatic past, politics and the family are one, for Prospero's political trust in his brother Antonio, "like a good parent, did beget of him / A falsehood in its contrary" (94–95). The Italian city-state Prospero sees in his mind's eye has two centers of power: the seat of government he "cast" upon his brother and the library that became his private dukedom.

What I consider to be the defining characteristic of Shakespeare's Italy, its openness, becomes the undoing of Prospero's "fair Milan" when the treacherous brother opens the gates of the city to the king of Naples. Even Shakespeare's Milan has its generic "port," where Prospero and Miranda are set adrift in a leaky boat. Ambition makes openness and trust liabilities at court, but the liberal character of Italy also has its place in "fair Milan." The love the people bore Prospero kept his enemies from ordering his outright murder, and the charity of the Neapolitan counselor Gonzalo provided the exiles with "necessaries" and with books from Prospero's beloved library (141, 164). Openness begets the betrayal, but the books also liberate, as when Ariel is liberated from the pine (292). And just as Prospero's secret studies awoke an evil nature in his brother (93), the betrayal ultimately begets acts of love and charity, which redeem Prospero from his own need for revenge. Seen across time and space, the city is reduced to the competing spheres of the court and the library, a political world where one must be constantly on guard against the evil nature of humankind, and a library where trust and reflection ultimately beget love and charity.

The geography of the poet's imagination collapses north and south to create an Italy in which the Kingdom of Naples usurps the powerful Dukedom of Milan. We are in the political landscape Machiavelli described, where loyalty to a family or a city does not impede ambition. And the Naples to which Stephano and Trinculo hope to return with Caliban merges with the London of expeditions to the new world: "Were I in England now (as once I was) and had but this fish painted, not a holiday fool there but would give a piece of silver" (2.2.27–30). The "fair" tradition of Renaissance university towns can be traced in Gonzalo's learned discourse on "plantation of this isle" (2.1.144–65). The island mirrors the courtly intrigues of Renaissance Italy, as well as the more benign courtliness seen in Ferdinand's wooing of Miranda (3.1.39–48).

Though the content of the wedding masque Prospero creates for the young lovers is mythological and pastoral, the pageant recreates a form of theater that emerged within the Italian courts of the Renaissance. And when the recollection of Caliban's "foul conspiracy" causes the entertainment to dissolve, Prospero compares the melting of the "baseless fabric of this vision" to the fading away of cities: "The cloud-capp'd tow'rs, the gorgeous palaces, / The solemn temples, the great globe itself" (4.1.151–53). Italian cities gave rise to a form of theater capable of representing the city, with its towers and palaces, painted and designed in perspective. It is a sign of Prospero's anger or pride that he equates human creations, the pageant and the city, with God's creations, the earth and its inhabitants. All such creations are, it seems, the ephemeral stuff of dreams (155–56). The open character of the Italian city has returned to haunt Prospero, for his momentary failure to protect himself against Caliban has triggered a "thought" that dissolves the masque. Lost in his pageant, as he once lost himself in his library, the powerful magus is once again exposed. Even within the pageant, Prospero attempts to exclude from the vision what he cannot trust—the dangers represented by Venus and her son (87). The exuberant openness of creativity collides with the need to protect and to close the gates against "dusky Dis" (89), symbol of all potential invaders and rapists.

The island, like the vision of an ideal city, exists in the imagination. It is this quality of the isle that makes it, among other things, more like a theater in a city than a geographical place fixed solidly on God's globe. It provides the stage for Antonio to work his evil magic by exercising his "strong imagination" (2.1.207) and for Caliban to hear strange music, to dream, and to watch clouds dissolve into riches (3.2.135–43). But Prospero is the stage manager of this island theater.

The ideal city is at the center of a dream that challenges the heavens with its cloud-capped towers. But the island itself has no city, only a cell and a variable landscape. In his utopian dream of "plantation," Gonzalo imagines a society defined in opposition to the city, for he says, "I' th' commonwealth I would, by contraries, / Execute all things" (2.1.148–49). The contraries enumerated in this famous reworking of Montaigne dissolve the city in theory as surely as Prospero's "revels" speech dissolves its architecture, for without traffic, magistrate, letters, property, or handicrafts there can be no city (150–56). The landscape of the island is similarly composed of contraries, variations on "barren places and fertile" (1.2.338, compare 2.2.160–72). Evidence of the island's fruitfulness comes to us from Caliban and parallels Gonzalo's dream of an innocent people sustained by nature's unassisted abundance (2.1.164), as well as the ideal of fertility and natural bounty evoked in Prospero's marriage masque (4.1.106–17). Caliban knows the fertile places of the island well, but he has no experience of the city, nor of the commedia dell'arte clowns that cities like Naples let loose on the world.

Gonzalo and Prospero create intellectual and artistic visions of a world without cities, visions which are themselves the product of the city, of the library and of the court, of philosophy and theater. When Antonio and Sebastian mock Gonzalo and the downcast Alonso says "thou does talk nothing to me" (2.1.171), the old counselor effectively agrees that his discourse is a form of "merry fooling" (177) designed to distract Alonso from thoughts of his drowned son. It is also nothing because by canceling the city it cancels itself, for the speech is firmly rooted in the city's intellectual tradition of thinking by contraries, a kind of philosophical fooling. The philosopher, the master of courtly theater, and the magus can play with making themselves disappear and with making their stage, the city, nothing. But they never leave the magic circle of its walls. The books that gave Prospero the power to stage his marriage masque, with its vision of natural abundance, came from a city, and though he has survived on the island, the city remains central to his conception of human fulfillment. Everything Prospero does on the island, from staging the tempest to staging the wedding masque, works toward a return to the towers and palaces of a lost city. When his vision turns to nothing, Prospero's disturbed mind turns to an image of the city dissolving. It is the language, mythology, music, and artistic creativity of the city that give his vision its fabric. And, conversely, the dissolution of the vision threatens the very fabric of the city-as-theater.

The hermetic knowledge closed within the library opens a vision that equates human creativity with the godlike power to control nature (5.1.33–57). The magus gives up that power in order to return to the city, the Naples of the play, or the London of the play's performance, a fact underlined by the direct address employed in the epilogue, which completes a series of "unmaskings" by presenting the person of the actor to the audience (Demaray 130–31). All of the unmaskings point to the central paradox of the city, particularly the Italian city whose creative energy derives from the power to change shapes and to transform reality. Prospero feels pain when he thinks of structures dissolving, but his magic enters through open eyes and ears and works because of its capacity to alter perception.

There is a similar magic in Prospero's willingness to open his heart to Ariel's courtierlike prompting and follow virtue rather than vengeance (5.1.28). We are shown the redemptive power of that very fluidity which caused Prospero's momentary despair. Ariel reprises, with greater success, the role of the good counselors Camillo, Pisanio, and Gonzalo, when he opens Prospero to the power of forgiveness.

Moved to drop his guard and return to Naples, Prospero speaks an epilogue that closes the play with the word "free." The city to which the voyagers return is a city of the temple where the nuptials of Miranda and Ferdinand will be solemnized (5.1.309–10), of the towers and palaces where the chess game of politics and ambition will continue to play itself out (5.1.171), and of the theater where the magic circle can be found. That "rough magic" Prospero abjures is identified with nature's sun, winds, sea, and earth, but not with the city's structures. The gentler magic that grows out of the city and has the power to create visions leads back to the lost city and its theater.

∽

Kenneth Branagh's film version of *Much Ado About Nothing* draws the audience into a contemporary version of Shakespeare's Italy by means of a painting that dissolves to become a picturesque Tuscan landscape. Viewed from this cinematic perspective, Italy is that warm place where hypocrisy and inhibition seem to dissolve, where the northern traveler finds love, art, and perhaps a soul. Though I see Shakespeare's representation of Italy as focused on the city rather than the countryside, the movie catches that freedom to change which emerges within *Much Ado*

About Nothing in the dramatic transformation from soldier to lover, or constable to ass. I have argued that Shakespeare builds the representation of Italian city-states from the essential elements of his stage and his city. The dramatic characters who journey between the archipelago of those Italian cities do so with a freedom that is just dangerous enough to be exciting to the audience and familiar enough to be funny.

One can imagine the spectators emerging from the Globe in Southwark and moving into a world that had, like the moving picture image, dissolved during the "two hours' traffic" of the stage to become something else. Wenceslaus Hollar's pen-and-ink study for his print *The Long View of London from Bankside* shows the rebuilt Globe at the edge of a cluster of houses situated not far from the Thames. One recognizes the essentials of the urban landscape that Shakespeare recreated within the circle of his theater. In the clustered houses, the lanes, and alleys concealed by peaked rooftops, a walled garden, an enclosed square or courtyard, the river, and the open space beyond the theater, we find the vocabulary of his urban world. Here are the properties that will become the domestic and commercial cityscapes of Shakespeare's stage. Hollar records a particular section of the city as it appeared at a particular time; *A View from St. Mary's, Southwark, Looking Towards Westminster* is in its particularity quite unlike the Albertian harmonies of the *città ideale*. No landmark church, palace, or tower dominates the view, but one's eye is drawn to the theater building, where Shakespeare recast the familiar contours of his city to create a unique vision of Italian city life. And it is Shakespeare's conception of the life lived within the Italian cities that informs his sense of place.

Bibliography

Adelman, Janet. "Iago Alter Ego: Race as Projection in *Othello.*" *Shakespeare Quarterly* 48 (1997): 125–44.

Agnew, Jean-Christophe. *Worlds Apart: The Market and the Theater in Anglo-American Thought, 1550–1750.* New York: Cambridge University Press, 1986.

Alberti, Leon Battista. *The Family in Renaissance Florence.* Translated by Renée Neu Watkins. Columbia: University of South Carolina Press, 1969.

———. *On the Art of Building in Ten Books.* Translated by Joseph Rykwert, Neil Leach, and Robert Tavernor. Cambridge, Mass.: MIT Press, 1988.

Alvarez, Leo Paul de, translator. *The Prince.* Niccolò Machiavelli. Irving, Tex.: University of Dallas Press, 1980.

Anderson, Michael. "The Changing Scene: Plays and Playhouses in the Italian Renaissance." In Mulryne, *Theatre of the English and Italian Renaissance,* 3–20.

Anglo, Sydney. *Spectacle Pageantry and Early Tudor Policy.* Oxford: Clarendon Press, 1969.

Archer, Ian W. "The Nostalgia of John Stow." In Smith, Strier, and Bevington, *The Theatrical City,* 17–34.

———. *The Pursuit of Stability: Social Relations in Elizabethan London.* New York: Cambridge University Press, 1991.

Aretino, Pietro. *Ragionamento, Dialogo.* Introduction by Giorgio Bàrberi Squarotti and commentary by Carla Forno. Milan: Rizzoli, 1988.

Ariès, Philippe, and Georges Duby, general editors. *Passions of the Renaissance.* Translated by Arthur Goldhammer. Edited by Roger Chartier. Cambridge, Mass.: Harvard University Press, 1989. Vol. 3 of *A History of Private Life.* 5 vols. 1987–1991.

———. *Revelations of the Medieval World*. Translated by Arthur Goldhammer. Edited by Georges Duby. Cambridge, Mass.: Harvard University Press, 1988. Vol. 2 of *A History of Private Life*. 5 vols. 1987–1991.

Armstrong, Philip. "Spheres of Influence: Cartography and the Gaze in Shakespearean Tragedy and History." *Shakespeare Studies* 23 (1995): 39–69.

Ascham, Roger. *The Scholemaster*. Edited by John E. B. Mayor. London: Bell and Daldy, 1863; reprint, New York: AMS Press, 1967.

———. *The Schoolmaster (1570)*. Edited by Lawrence C. Ryan. Ithaca, N.Y.: Cornell University Press, 1967.

Barber, C. L. *Shakespeare's Festive Comedy: A Study of Dramatic Form and Its Relation to Social Custom*. Princeton, N.J.: Princeton University Press, 1959.

Barish, Jonas. *The Antitheatrical Prejudice*. Berkeley: University of California Press, 1981.

Barker, Felix, and Peter Jackson. *The History of London in Maps*. London: Barrie and Jenkins, 1990.

Bartlett, Kenneth R. "The Strangeness of Strangers: English Impressions of Italy in the Sixteenth Century." *Quaderni d'italianistica* 1 (1980): 46–63.

Barton, Anne. "Livy, Machiavelli, and Shakespeare's *Coriolanus*." *Shakespeare Survey* 38 (1985): 115–29.

Bates, Catherine. *The Rhetoric of Courtship in Elizabethan Language and Literature*. New York: Cambridge University Press, 1992.

Beier, A. L., and Roger Finlay, eds. *London 1500–1700: The Making of the Metropolis*. New York: Longman, 1986.

Berger, Harry, Jr. "Impertinent Trifling: Desdemona's Handkerchief." *Shakespeare Quarterly* 47 (1996): 235–50.

Bergeron, David M. *English Civic Pageantry, 1558–1642*. Columbia: University of South Carolina Press, 1971.

Bertelli, Sergio, Franco Cardini, and Elvira Garbero Zorzi. *The Courts of the Italian Renaissance*. Translated by Mary Fritton and Geoffrey Culverwell. New York: Facts on File, 1986.

Bloom, Harold. *Shakespeare: The Invention of the Human*. New York: Riverhead, 1998.

Bossy, John. *Giordano Bruno and the Embassy Affair*. New Haven, Conn.: Yale University Press, 1991.

Botero, Giovanni. 1596. *Delle cause della grandezza delle città*. Edited by Luigi Firpo. Turin: Tipografico Torinese, 1948.

———. *The Greatness of Cities*. 1606. Reprint, translated by Robert Peterson. London: Routledge, 1956.

———. *The Reason of State*. 1591. Translated by P. J. Waley and D. P Waley. London: Routledge, 1956.

Boulton, Jeremy. *Neighborhood and Society: A London Suburb in the Seventeenth Century.* New York: Cambridge University Press, 1987.

Bradbrook, M. C. *The Living Monument: Shakespeare and the Theatre of His Time.* New York: Cambridge University Press, 1976.

Braudel, Fernand. *The Structures of Everyday Life.* Translated by Siân Reynolds. Vol. 1. New York: Harper and Row, 1981.

Brockett, Oscar G. *The Theatre, an Introduction.* New York: Holt, Rinehart and Winston, 1964.

Brown, John Russell. *Shakespeare's Plays in Performance.* London: Edward Arnold, 1966.

Brown, Patricia Fortini. *Venice and Antiquity: The Venetian Sense of the Past.* New Haven, Conn.: Yale University Press, 1996.

Bruster, Douglas. *Drama and the Market in the Age of Shakespeare.* New York: Cambridge University Press, 1992.

Bullough, Geoffrey, ed. *Narrative and Dramatic Sources of Shakespeare.* 8 vols. New York: Columbia University Press, 1957–75.

Burford, E. J. *Bawds and Lodgings: A History of the London Bankside Brothels c. 100–1675.* London: Peter Owen, 1976.

Burke, Peter. *The Fortunes of the "Courtier": The European Reception of Castiglione's "Cortegiano."* University Park, Pa.: Pennsylvania State University Press, 1996.

———. *The Historical Anthropology of Early Modern Italy: Essays on Perception and Communication.* New York: Cambridge University Press, 1987.

———. *The Italian Renaissance: Culture and Society in Italy.* Rev. ed. Cambridge, Mass.: Polity Press, 1987.

Cairncross, Andrew S. "Shakespeare and Ariosto: *Much Ado About Nothing, King Lear,* and *Othello.*" *Renaissance Quarterly* 29 (1976): 178–82.

Calderwood, James L. "Appalling Property in *Othello.*" *University of Toronto Quarterly* 57 (1988): 353–75.

Campbell, O. J. "*Love's Labour's Lost* Re-studied." In *Studies in Shakespeare, Milton and Donne,* 1–45. New York: Macmillan, 1925.

———. "*The Two Gentlemen of Verona* and Italian Comedy." In *Studies in Shakespeare, Milton and Donne,* 49–63. New York: Macmillan, 1925.

Capocci, Valentina. *Genio e mestiere: Shakespeare e la commedia dell'arte.* Bari: Laterza, 1950.

Castiglione, Baldassare. *The Book of the Courtier.* 1561. Translated by Sir Thomas Hoby. New York: Dutton, 1928.

Chambers, David, and Brian Pullan, eds. *Venice: A Documentary History, 1450–1630.* Cambridge, Mass.: Blackwell, 1992.

Clark, Peter, and Paul Slack. *English Towns in Transition 1500–1700.* New York: Oxford University Press, 1976.

Clubb, Louise George. *Italian Drama in Shakespeare's Time*. New Haven, Conn.: Yale University Press, 1989.
Cody, Richard. *The Landscape of the Mind*. Oxford: Clarendon Press, 1969.
Coghill, Nevill. *Shakespeare's Professional Skills*. New York: Cambridge University Press, 1964.
Cohen, Walter. *Drama of a Nation: Public Theater in Renaissance England and Spain*. Ithaca, N.Y.: Cornell University Press, 1985.
Cole, Alison. *Virtue and Magnificence: Art of the Italian Renaissance Courts*. New York: Harry N. Abrams, 1995.
Cole, Howard C. *The "All's Well" Story from Boccaccio to Shakespeare*. Urbana: University of Illinois Press, 1981.
——— . "The 'Full Meaning' of *The Two Gentlemen of Verona*." *Comparative Drama* 23 (1989): 201–27.
Cook, Ann Jennalie. *The Privileged Playgoers of Shakespeare's London, 1576–1642*. Princeton, N.J.: Princeton University Press, 1981.
Cope, Jackson I. *Secret Sharers in Italian Comedy: From Machiavelli to Goldoni*. Durham, N.C.: Duke University Press, 1996.
Coryat, Thomas. *Coryat's Crudities*. 2 vols. 1611. Glasgow: James MacLehose, 1905.
Cosgrove, Denis E. *The Palladian Landscape: Geographical Change and Its Cultural Representations in Sixteenth Century Italy*. University Park: Pennsylvania State University Press, 1993.
——— . *Social Formation and Symbolic Landscape*. London: Croom Helm, 1984.
Coulanges, Fustel de. *The Ancient City: A Study on the Religion, Laws and Institutions of Greece and Rome*. 1894. Reprint, New York: Dillingham, 1956.
Coursen, H. R. *Watching Shakespeare on Television*. Rutherford, N.J.: Fairleigh Dickinson University Press, 1993.
Cox, Virginia. *The Renaissance Dialogue: Literary Dialogue in Its Social and Political Contexts, Castiglione to Galileo*. New York: Cambridge University Press, 1992.
Crane, Thomas Frederick. *The Italian Social Customs of the Sixteenth Century: And Their Influence on the Literatures of Europe*. New Haven, Conn.: Yale University Press, 1920.
D'Amico, Jack. "Machiavelli's Borgia: Founder and Failure." *Rivista di Studi Italiani* 5, no. 2 (1987–88): 18–30.
——— . "Poetic and Theatrical Perspectives in Ariosto's *Il Negromante* and Jonson's *The Alchemist*." *Italica* 66 (1989): 312–22.
——— . "Power and Perspective in *La Mandragola*." *Journal of Machiavelli Studies* 1 (1987): 5–16.
——— . "The Treatment of Space in Italian and English Renaissance Theater: The Example of *Gl'Ingannati* and *Twelfth Night*." *Comparative Drama* 23 (1989): 265–83.

Danson, Lawrence. "'The Catastrophe Is a Nuptial': The Space of Masculine Desire in *Othello, Cymbeline,* and *The Winter's Tale.*" *Shakespeare Survey* 46 (1994): 67–79.

Davis, Robert C. *The War of the Fists: Popular Culture and Public Violence in Late Renaissance Venice.* New York: Oxford University Press, 1994.

Demaray, John G. *Shakespeare and the Spectacles of Strangeness: "The Tempest" and the Transformation of Renaissance Theatrical Forms.* Pittsburgh: Duquesne University Press, 1998.

Dessen, Alan C. *Elizabethan Drama and the Viewer's Eye.* Chapel Hill: University of North Carolina Press, 1977.

———. "'Taint Not Thy Mind . . .': Problems and Pitfalls in Studying Plays at the New Globe." In Hildy, *New Issues in the Reconstruction of Shakespeare's Theatre,* 135–58.

Dimsey, Sheila E. "Giacopo Castelvetro." *Modern Language Review* 23 (1928): 424–31.

Draper, John W. "Shakespeare and Florence and the Florentines." *Italica* 23 (1946): 287–93.

Dundas, Judith. "The Refusal to Paint: Shakespeare's Poetry of Place." *Comparative Drama* 23 (1989–90): 331–43.

Ehrenberg, Victor. *The Greek State.* Oxford: Blackwell, 1960.

Einstein, Lewis. *The Italian Renaissance in England.* New York: Burt Franklin, 1902.

Elam, Keir. "The Fertile Eunuch: *Twelfth Night,* Early Modern Intercourse, and the Fruits of Castration." *Shakespeare Quarterly* 47 (1996): 1–36.

Enterline, Lynn. "'You speak a language that I understand not': The Rhetoric of Animation in *The Winter's Tale.*" *Shakespeare Quarterly* 48 (1997): 17–44.

Faherty, Teresa J. "*Othello dell'Arte:* The Presence of *Commedia* in Shakespeare's Tragedy." *Theatre Journal* 43 (1991): 179–94.

Farnham, Willard. "England's Discovery of the *Decameron.*" *PMLA* 39 (1924): 123–39.

Ferrone, Siro. *Attori, mercanti, corsari: la commedia dell'arte in Europa tra Cinque e Seicento.* Turin: Einaudi, 1993.

Flaumenhaft, Mera J. *The Civic Spectacle: Essays on Drama and Community.* Lanham, Md.: Rowman and Littlefield, 1994.

Fletcher, Anthony, and John Stevenson, eds. *Order and Disorder in Early Modern England.* New York: Cambridge University Press, 1985.

Florio, John. *His First Fruites.* 1578. Reprint, New York: Da Capo Press, 1969.

———. *Queen Anna's New World of Words.* 1611. Reprint, edited by R. C. Alston. Menston: Scolar Press, 1968.

———. *Second Frutes.* 1591. Facsimile with introduction by R. C. Simonini, Jr. Gainesville, Fla.: Scholars' Facsimiles and Reprints, 1953.

Fortescue, J. W. "The Army: Military Service and Equipment." In *Shakespeare's England: An Account of the Life and Manners in His Age,* 1:112–26. New York: Oxford University Press, 1916.

Fortier, Mark. "Married with Children: *The Winter's Tale* and Social History; or, Infanticide in Earlier Seventeenth-Century England." *Modern Language Quarterly* 57 (1996): 579–603.

Frantz, David O. *"Festum voluptatis": A Study of Renaissance Erotica.* Columbus: Ohio State University Press, 1989.

———. "Florio's Use of Contemporary Italian Literature in *A Worlde of Wordes.*" *Dictionaries* 1 (1979): 47–56.

Frugoni, Chiara. *A Distant City: Images of Urban Experience in the Medieval World.* Translated by William McCuaig. Princeton, N.J.: Princeton University Press, 1991.

Frye, Northrop. *Anatomy of Criticism: Four Essays.* Princeton, N.J.: Princeton University Press, 1957.

———. *A Natural Perspective: The Development of Shakespearean Comedy and Romance.* New York: Columbia University Press, 1965.

Fumerton, Patricia. *Cultural Aesthetics: Renaissance Literature and the Practice of Social Ornament.* Chicago: University of Chicago Press, 1991.

Gaeta, Franco. "Alcune considerazioni sul mito di Venezia." *Bibliothèque d'Humanisme et Renaissance* 23 (1961): 58–75.

Gatti, Hilary. *The Renaissance Drama of Knowledge: Giordano Bruno in England.* New York: Routledge, 1989.

Gibbons, Brian. *Jacobean City Comedy: A Study of Satiric Plays by Jonson, Marston and Middleton.* Cambridge, Mass.: Harvard University Press, 1968.

Gillies, John. *Shakespeare and the Geography of Difference.* New York: Cambridge University Press, 1994.

Gillies, John, and Virginia Mason Vaughn, eds. *Playing the Globe: Genre and Geography in English Renaissance Drama.* Madison, Wis.: Fairleigh Dickinson University Press, 1998.

Girouard, Mark. *Cities and People: A Social and Architectural History.* New Haven, Conn.: Yale University Press, 1985.

Goddard, Harold C. *The Meaning of Shakespeare.* Chicago: University of Chicago Press, 1951.

Grafton, Anthony, and Lisa Jardine. *From Humanism to the Humanities: Education and the Liberal Arts in Fifteenth- and Sixteenth-Century Europe.* Cambridge, Mass.: Harvard University Press, 1986.

Grazia, Margreta de. "Shakespeare, Gutenburg and Descartes." In Hawkes, *Alternative Shakespeares,* 63–94.

Grazia, Sebastian de. *Machiavelli in Hell.* Princeton, N.J.: Princeton University Press, 1989.

Greenblatt, Stephen. *Renaissance Self-Fashioning: From More to Shakespeare.* Chicago: University of Chicago Press, 1984.

Greene, Thomas M. "Ceremonial Play and Parody in the Renaissance." In *Urban Life in the Renaissance,* edited by Susan Zimmerman and Ronald F. E. Weissman, 281–93. Newark: University of Delaware Press, 1989.

Grubb, James S. "When Myths Lose Power: Four Decades of Venetian Historiography." *Journal of Modern History* 58 (1986): 43–94.

Guazzo, Stefano. *The Civile Conversation of M. Steeven Guazzo.* 1581. Reprint, translated by George Pettie and Bartholomew Young, edited by Edward Sullivan. 2 vols. 1925. New York: AMS, 1967.

Gurr, Andrew. "The Bare Island." *Shakespeare Survey* 47 (1994): 29–43.

———. "The Date and the Expected Venue of *Romeo and Juliet.*" *Shakespeare Survey* 49 (1996): 15–25.

———. *Playgoing in Shakespeare's London.* 2nd ed. New York: Cambridge University Press, 1996.

———. *The Shakespearean Stage 1574–1642.* 3rd ed. New York: Cambridge University Press, 1992.

Hager, Alan. *Shakespeare's Political Animal: Schema and Schemata in the Canon.* Newark: University of Delaware Press, 1990.

Hale, J. R. *England and the Italian Renaissance: The Growth of Interest in Its History and Art.* London: Faber and Faber, 1954.

Hattaway, Michael. *Elizabethan Popular Theatre: Plays in Performance.* Boston: Routledge, 1982.

Hawkes, Terence. *Alternative Shakespeares.* Vol. 2. New York: Routledge, 1996.

———. *Shakespeare's Talking Animals: Language and Drama in Society.* London: Edward Arnold, 1973.

Hazlitt, William. *Characters of Shakespeare's Plays.* Vol. 4 of *The Complete Works of William Hazlitt.* Edited by P. P. Howe. 21 vols. 1930. Reprint, New York: AMS, 1967.

Helgerson, Richard. *Forms of Nationhood: The Elizabethan Writing of England.* Chicago: University of Chicago Press, 1992.

Hendricks, Margo. "'The Moor of Venice'; or, The Italian on the Renaissance English Stage." In *Shakespearean Tragedy and Gender,* edited by Shirley Nelson Garner and Madelon Sprengnether, 193–209. Bloomington: Indiana University Press, 1996.

Henke, Robert. *Pastoral Transformations: Italian Tragicomedy and Shakespeare's Late Plays.* Newark: University of Delaware Press, 1997.

———. "*The Winter's Tale* and Guarinian Dramaturgy." *Comparative Drama* 27 (1993): 197–217.

Hildy, Franklin J., ed. *New Issues in the Reconstruction of Shakespeare's Theatre.* New York: Peter Lang, 1990.

Hodgdon, Barbara. "The Making of Virgins and Mothers: Sexual Signs, Substitute Scenes and Doubled Presences in *All's Well That Ends Well.*" *Philological Quarterly* 66 (1987): 47–71.

Hodge, Nancy Elizabeth. "Making Places at Belmont: 'You Are Welcome Notwithstanding.'" *Shakespeare Studies* 21 (1993): 155–74.

Hoenselaars, A. J. "Italy Staged in English Renaissance Drama." In Marrapodi et al., *Shakespeare's Italy*, 30–48.

———, ed. *Reclamations of Shakespeare*. Amsterdam and Atlanta: Rodopi, 1994.

Hoppe, Harry R. "John Wolfe, Printer and Publisher, 1579–1601." *The Library* 4th series, 14, no. 3 (1933): 241–88.

Hotson, Leslie. *Shakespeare's Wooden O*. New York: Macmillan, 1960.

Howard, Jean E. "Renaissance Antitheatricality and the Politics of Gender and Rank in *Much Ado About Nothing*." In *Shakespeare Reproduced: The Text in History and Ideology*, edited by Jean E. Howard and Marion F. O'Connor, 163–87. New York: Methuen, 1987.

Hunt, John Dixon, and Peter Willis. *The Genius of the Place: The English Landscape Garden 1620–1820*. Cambridge, Mass.: MIT Press, 1975.

Hunter, G. K. *Dramatic Identities and Cultural Tradition*. New York: Barnes and Noble, 1978.

———. "Italian Tragicomedy on the English Stage." *Renaissance Drama* n.s. 6 (1973): 123–48.

Ingram, William. *The Business of Playing: The Beginnings of the Adult Professional Theater in Elizabethan London*. Ithaca, N.Y.: Cornell University Press, 1992.

James, Max H. *"Our House Is Hell": Shakespeare's Troubled Families*. New York: Greenwood Press, 1989.

Jardine, Lisa. *Reading Shakespeare Historically*. New York: Routledge, 1996.

———. *Still Harping on Daughters: Women and Drama in the Age of Shakespeare*. New York: Columbia University Press, 1989.

———. *Worldly Goods: A New History of the Renaissance*. New York: Doubleday, 1996.

Jones, Robert C. "Italian Settings and the 'World' of Elizabethan Tragedy." *Studies in English Literature* 10 (1970): 251–68.

Kastan, David Scott. "Is There a Class in This (Shakespearean) Text?" *Renaissance Quarterly* 24 (1993): 101–21.

Kernan, Alvin. *Shakespeare, the King's Playwright: Theater in the Stuart Court 1603–1613*. New Haven, Conn.: Yale University Press, 1995.

King, T. J. "Shakespearean Staging, 1599–1642." In *The Elizabethan Theatre III*, edited by David Galloway, 1–13. Waterloo, Ont.: Archon Books, 1971.

Kirkpatrick, Robin. *English and Italian Literature from Dante to Shakespeare: A Study of Source, Analogue and Divergence*. New York: Longman, 1995.

Knowles, Ronald. "Carnival and Death in *Romeo and Juliet:* A Bakhtinian Reading." *Shakespeare Survey* 49 (1996): 69–85.
Korda, Natasha. "Household Kates: Domesticating Commodities in *The Taming of the Shrew.*" *Shakespeare Quarterly* 47 (1996): 109–31.
Kostof, Spiro. *The City Shaped: Urban Patterns and Meanings Through History.* Boston: Bulfinch Press, 1991.
Lane, Frederick C. *Venice: A Maritime Republic.* Baltimore: Johns Hopkins University Press, 1973.
Laroque, Francois. *Shakespeare's Festive World: Elizabethan Seasonal Entertainment and the Professional Stage.* Translated by Janet Lloyd. New York: Cambridge University Press, 1991.
Lavin, J. A. "Shakespeare and the Second Blackfriars." In *The Elizabethan Theatre III,* edited by David Galloway, 66–81. Waterloo, Ont.: Archon Books, 1971.
Leggatt, Alexander. *Citizen Comedy in the Age of Shakespeare.* Toronto: University of Toronto Press, 1973.
Levin, Harry. "Shakespeare's Italians." In Marrapodi et al., *Shakespeare's Italy,* 17–29.
Levine, Laura. "Men in Women's Clothing: Anti-theatricality and Effeminization from 1579 to 1642." *Criticism* 28 (1986): 121–43.
Levith, Murray J. *Shakespeare's Italian Settings and Plays.* New York: St. Martin's, 1989.
Lewalski, B. K. "Love, Appearance and Reality: Much Ado About Something." *Studies in English Literature* 8 (1968): 235–51.
Lievsay, John L. *The Elizabethan Image of Italy.* Ithaca, N.Y.: Cornell University Press, 1964.
Locatelli, Angela. "The Fictional World of *Romeo and Juliet:* Cultural Connotation of an Italian Setting." In Marrapodi et al., *Shakespeare's Italy,* 69–84.
Lombardo, Agostino. "The Veneto, Metatheatre, and Shakespeare." In Marrapodi et al., *Shakespeare's Italy,* 143–57.
Machiavelli, Niccolò. *The Chief Works and Others.* 3 vols. Translated by Allan Gilbert. Durham, N.C.: Duke University Press, 1965.
———. *Opere.* 8 vols. Edited by Sergio Bertelli and Franco Gaeta. Milan: Feltrinelli, 1960–65.
Mahler, Andreas. "Italian Vices: Cross-cultural Constructions of Temptation and Desire in English Renaissance Drama." In Marrapodi et al., *Shakespeare's Italy,* 49–68.
Mallin, Eric S. *Inscribing the Time: Shakespeare and the End of Elizabethan England.* Berkeley: University of California Press, 1995.
Manley, Lawrence. "Of Sites and Rites." In Smith, Strier, and Bevington, *The Theatrical City,* 35–54.

———, ed. *London in the Age of Shakespeare: An Anthology*. London: Croom Helm, 1986.

Marcus, Leah S. *Puzzling Shakespeare: Local Reading and Its Discontents*. Berkeley: University of California Press, 1988.

Marrapodi, Michelle. "'Of that fatal country': Sicily and the Rhetoric of Topography in *The Winter's Tale*." In Marrapodi et al., *Shakespeare's Italy*, 213–28.

———, ed. *The Italian World of English Renaissance Drama: Cultural Exchange and Intertextuality*. Newark: University of Delaware Press, 1998.

Marrapodi, Michelle, et al., eds. *Shakespeare's Italy: Functions of Italian Locations in Renaissance Drama*. New York: Manchester University Press, 1993.

Martines, Lauro. *Power and Imagination: City-States in Renaissance Italy*. New York: Knopf, 1979.

McCoy, Richard M. "'Thou idol ceremony': Elizabeth I, *The Henriad*, and the Rites of the English Monarchy." In *Urban Life in the Renaissance*, edited by Susan Zimmerman and Ronald F. E. Weissman, 240–66. Newark: University of Delaware Press, 1989.

McKerrow, Ronald B. *The Works of Thomas Nashe*. 5 vols. 1904–5. Reprint, Oxford and London: Basil Blackwell, 1966.

McPherson, David C. *Shakespeare, Jonson, and the Myth of Venice*. Newark: University of Delaware Press, 1990.

McWilliam, G. H. *Shakespeare's Italy Revisited*. Leicester: Leicester University Press, 1974.

Melchiori, Giorgio. "'In fair Verona': *Commedia erudita* into Romantic Comedy." In Marrapodi et al., *Shakespeare's Italy*, 100–111.

Mitchell, Bonner. "The Triumphal Entry as a Theatrical Genre in the Cinquecento." *Forum Italicum* 14 (1980): 409–25.

Moisan, Thomas. "Interlinear Trysting and 'Household Stuff': The Latin Lesson and the Domestication of Learning in *The Taming of the Shrew*." *Shakespeare Studies* 23 (1995): 100–119.

———. "'Knock me here soundly': Comic Misprison and Class Consciousness in Shakespeare." *Shakespeare Quarterly* 42 (1991): 276–90.

Molmenti, Pompeo. *La Storia di Venezia nella vita privata dalle origini alla caduta della repubblica*. 4th ed. Bergamo: Istituto Italiano D'Arti Grafiche, 1906.

Montrose, Louis A. "A Kingdom of Shadows." In Smith, Strier, and Bevington, *The Theatrical City*, 68–86.

Moore, Olin H. "Shakespeare's Deviations from *Romeus and Juliet*." *PMLA* 52 (1937): 68–74.

Morris, Brian, ed. *The Taming of the Shrew*. New York: Methuen, 1981.

Moryson, Fynes. *Itinerary*. 1617. Reprint edited by Charles Hughes. 2nd ed. New York: B. Blom, 1967.

Muir, Kenneth. *Shakespeare's Sources.* Vol. 1, *Comedies and Tragedies.* London: Methuen, 1957.
Mukherji, Subha. "'Lawful Deed': Consummation, Custom, and Law in *All's Well That Ends Well.*" *Shakespeare Survey* 49 (1996):181–200.
Mullaney, Steven. *The Place of the Stage: License, Play and Power in Renaissance England.* Chicago: University of Chicago Press, 1988.
Mullini, Roberta. "Streets, Squares and Courts: Venice as a Stage in Shakespeare and Ben Jonson." In Marrapodi et al., *Shakespeare's Italy,* 158–70.
Mulryne, J. R. "History and Myth in *The Merchant of Venice.*" In Marrapodi et al., *Shakespeare's Italy,* 87–99.
Mulryne, J. R., and Margaret Shewring, eds. *Theatre of the English and Italian Renaissance.* New York: St. Martin's Press, 1991.
Mumford, Lewis. *The City in History: Its Origins, Its Transformations, and Its Prospects.* New York: Harcourt, Brace and World, 1961.
Muraro, Maria Teresa. "La festa a Venezia: le compagnie della calza e le *momarie.*" In *Storia della cultura Veneta dal primo quattrocento al Concilio di Trento,* edited by G. Arnaldi and M. Pastore Stocchi, 3:315–41. Vicenza: Neri Pozza, 1976.
Olivieri, Achillo. "Eroticism and Social Groups in Sixteenth-Century Venice: The Courtesan." In *Western Sexuality,* edited by Philippe Ariès and André Béjin, translated by Anthony Forster, 95–101. London: Blackwell, 1985.
Orgel, Stephen. *The Illusion of Power: Political Theater in the English Renaissance.* Berkeley: University of California Press, 1991.
———. "Nobody's Perfect: Or Why Did the English Stage Take Boys for Women?" *South Atlantic Quarterly* 88 (1989): 7–29.
Orlin, Lena Cowen. "The Performance of Things in *The Taming of the Shrew.*" *Yearbook of English Studies* 23 (1993): 167–88.
———. *Private Matters and Public Culture in Post-Reformation England.* Ithaca, N.Y.: Cornell University Press, 1994.
Orr, David. *Italian Renaissance Drama in England before 1625: The Influence of 'Erudita' Tragedy, Comedy and Pastoral on Elizabethan and Jacobean Drama.* Chapel Hill: University of North Carolina Press, 1970.
Orrell, John. "The Architecture of The Fortune Playhouse." *Shakespeare Survey* 47 (1994): 15–27.
———. *The Human Stage: English Theatre Design, 1567–1640.* New York: Cambridge University Press, 1988.
Orsini, Napoleone. *Studii sul rinascimento Italiano in Inghilterra con alcuni testi inglesi ineditii.* Florence: Sansoni, 1937.
Osborne, Laurie E. "Dramatic Play in *Much Ado About Nothing*: Wedding the Italian *Novella* and English Comedy." *Philological Quarterly* 69 (1990): 167–88.

Oz, Avraham. "Dobbin on the Rialto: Venice and the Division of Identity." In Marrapodi et al., *Shakespeare's Italy*, 185–209.

Palladio, Andrea. *The Four Books of Architecture*. 1726. Translated by Giacomo Leoni. Reprint, New York: Dover, 1965.

Panizza Lorch, Maristella de. "Honest Iago and the Lusty Moor: The Humanistic Drama of *Honestas/Voluptas* in a Shakespearean Context." In Mulryne and Shewring, *Theatre of the English and Italian Renaissance*, 204–20.

Parker, Brian. "An English View of Venice: Ben Jonson's *Volpone* (1606)." In *Italy and the English Renaissance*, edited by Sergio Rossi and Dianella Savoia, 187–201. Milan: Unicopli, 1989.

Parker, Patricia. "Fantasies of 'Race' and 'Gender': Africa, *Othello* and Bringing to Light." In *Women, "Race," and Writing in the Early Modern Period*, edited by Margo Hendricks and Patricia Parker, 84–100. New York: Routledge, 1994.

Parks, George B. "The Decline and Fall of the English Renaissance Admiration of Italy." *Huntington Library Quarterly* 31 (1968): 341–57.

———. *The English Traveler to Italy*. Vol. 1. Stanford, Calif.: Stanford University Press, 1954.

Paster, Gail Kern. *The Idea of the City in the Age of Shakespeare*. Athens: University of Georgia Press, 1985.

Peat, Derek. "Looking Back to Front: The View from the Lord's Room." In *Shakespeare and the Sense of Performance*, edited by Marvin Thompson and Ruth Thompson, 180–94. Newark: University of Delaware Press, 1989.

Pelling, Margaret. "Appearance and Reality: Barber-Surgeons, the Body and Disease." In Beier and Finlay, *London 1500–1700*, 82–112.

Pfister, Manfred. "Shakespeare and Italy; or, the law of diminishing returns." In Marrapodi et al., *Shakespeare's Italy*, 295–303.

Porter, Roy. *London: A Social History*. Cambridge, Mass.: Harvard University Press, 1995.

Power, M. J. "The East and West in Early-Modern London." In *Wealth and Power in Tudor England*, edited by E. W. Ives, R. J. Knecht, and J. J. Scarisbrick, 167–85. London: Athlone Press, 1978.

———. "East London Housing in the Seventeenth Century." In *Crisis and Order in English Towns, 1500–1700: Essays in Urban History*, edited by Peter Clark and Paul Slack, 237–62. Toronto: University of Toronto Press, 1972.

———. "The Social Topography of Restoration London." In Beier and Finlay, *London 1500–1700*, 199–223.

Praz, Mario. *The Flaming Heart: Essays on Crashaw, Machiavelli, and Other Studies in the Relations Between Italian and English Literature from Chaucer to T. S. Eliot*. Gloucester, Mass.: Peter Smith, 1958.

Pressler, Charlotte. "Passing from Play to Play: The Novella as Mediator Between Italian and English Renaissance Drama." *Theory @ Buffalo* 4 (1998): 91–121.

Raab, Felix. *The English Face of Machiavelli: A Changing Interpretation 1500–1700*. London: Routledge, 1964.
Rappaport, Steve. *Worlds Within Worlds: Structures of Life in Sixteenth Century London*. New York: Cambridge University Press, 1989.
Redmond, Michael J. "'I have read them all': Jonson's *Volpone* and the Discourse of the Italianate Englishman." In Marrapodi, *The Italian World of English Renaissance Drama*, 122–40.
Rhu, Lawrence. "Agonies of Interpretation: Ariostan Source and Elizabethan Meaning in Spenser, Harington, and Shakespeare." *Renaissance Drama* 24 (1993): 171–88.
Rich, E. E., and C. H. Wilson, eds. *The Cambridge Economic History of Europe*. Vol. 4. New York: Cambridge University Press, 1967.
Richmond, Hugh. "Shakespeare's *Verismo* and the Italian Popular Tradition." In Mulryne and Shewring, *Theatre of the English and Italian Renaissance*, 179–203.
———. "Technique for Reconstituting Elizabethan Staging." In Hildy, *New Issues in the Reconstruction of Shakespeare's Theatre*, 159–84.
Roberts, Jeanne Addison. *The Shakespearean Wild: Geography, Genus, and Gender*. Lincoln: University of Nebraska Press, 1991.
Rose, Mary Beth. "Where Are the Mothers in Shakespeare?: Options for Gender Representation in the English Renaissance." *Shakespeare Quarterly* 42 (1991): 291–314.
Rosenthal, Margaret F. *The Honest Courtesan: Veronica Franco, Citizen and Writer in Sixteenth Century Venice*. Chicago: University of Chicago Press, 1992.
Rossi, Sergio. "Duelling in the Italian Manner: The Case of *Romeo and Juliet*." In Marrapodi et al., *Shakespeare's Italy*, 112–24.
Roston, Murray. *Renaissance Perspectives in Literature and the Visual Arts*. Princeton, N.J.: Princeton University Press, 1987.
Ruffini, Franco. "L' 'Invenzione' Umanistica del Teatro: Il 'Teatro' del Filarete." *Forum Italicum* 14 (1980): 311–55.
Rutter, Carol Chillington, ed. *Documents of the Rose Playhouse*. Manchester: University Press, 1984.
Salingar, Leo. "The Idea of Venice in Shakespeare and Ben Jonson." In Marrapodi et al., *Shakespeare's Italy*, 171–84.
———. *Shakespeare and the Traditions of Comedy*. New York: Cambridge University Press, 1974.
Schelling, Felix E. *Foreign Influences in Elizabethan Plays*. 1923. New York: AMS, 1971.
Sedinger, Tracy. "'If sight and shape be true': The Epistemology of Crossdressing on the London Stage." *Shakespeare Quarterly* 48 (1997): 63–79.
Sellars, Harry. "Italian Books Printed in England Before 1640." *The Library* 4th series, 5, no. 2 (1924): 105–28.

Sells, Lytton A. *The Italian Influence in English Poetry: From Chaucer to Southwell.* Bloomington: Indiana University Press, 1955.

Serlio, Sebastian. *The Five Books of Architecture.* 1611. Reprint, New York: Dover, 1982.

Seta, Cesare de. *La città europea dal xv al xx secolo.* Milan: Rizzoli, 1996.

Shaheen, Naseeb. "Shakespeare's Knowledge of Italian." *Shakespeare Survey* 47 (1994): 161–69.

Shakespeare, William. *The Riverside Shakespeare.* 2nd ed. Edited by G. Blakemore Evans and J. J. M. Tobin. New York: Houghton Mifflin, 1997.

Shapiro, James. *Shakespeare and the Jews.* New York: Columbia University Press, 1996.

Shapiro, Michael. *Gender in Play on the Shakespearean Stage: Boy Heroines and Female Pages.* Ann Arbor: University of Michigan Press, 1994.

Singleton, Esther. *The Shakespeare Garden.* London: C. Palmer, 1933.

Smith, Bruce R. "L[o]cating the Sexual Subject." In Hawkes, *Alternative Shakespeares,* 95–121.

Smith, David L., Richard Strier, and David Bevington, eds. *The Theatrical City: Culture, Theatre and Politics in London, 1576–1649.* New York: Cambridge University Press, 1995.

Snyder, Susan. "Ideology and the Feud in *Romeo and Juliet.*" *Shakespeare Survey* 49 (1996): 87–96.

Somerset, Alan. "'How chance it they travel'? Provincial Touring, Playing Places, and the King's Men." *Shakespeare Survey* 47 (1994): 45–60.

Stephens, John. *The Italian Renaissance: The Origins of Intellectual and Artistic Change Before the Reformation.* New York: Longman, 1990.

Stone, Lawrence. *The Crisis of the Aristocracy 1558–1641.* Oxford: Clarendon Press, 1965.

Stow, John. *The Survey of London.* 1598. Reprint, New York: Dutton, 1956.

Styan, J. L. "In Search of the Real Shakespeare; or, Shakespeare's Shows and Shadows." In Smith, Strier, and Bevington, *The Theatrical City,* 185–205.

———. *Shakespeare's Stagecraft.* New York: Cambridge University Press, 1967.

Summerson, John. *Architecture in Britain 1530–1830.* 9th ed. New Haven, Conn.: Yale University Press, 1993.

Susinno, Stefano. *La veduta nella pittura italiana.* Florence: Sansoni, 1974.

Teague, Frances. *Shakespeare's Speaking Properties.* Lewisburg, Penn.: Bucknell University Press, 1991.

Thomas, William. *The History of Italy.* 1549. Reprint, edited by George B. Parks. Ithaca, N.Y.: Cornell University Press, 1963.

Thurley, Simon. *The Royal Palaces of Tudor England: Architecture and Court Life 1460–1547.* New Haven, Conn.: Yale University Press, 1993.

Trease, Geoffrey. *London: A Concise History*. London: Book Club Associates, 1975.
Underdown, David. *Revel, Riot, and Rebellion: Popular Politics and Culture in England 1603–1660*. Oxford: Clarendon Press, 1985.
———. "The Taming of the Scold: The Enforcement of Patriarchal Authority in Early Modern England." In Fletcher and Stevenson, *Order and Disorder*, 110–36.
Vaughan, Virginia Mason. *Othello: A Contextual History*. New York: Cambridge University Press, 1994.
Vitkus, Daniel J. "Turning Turk in *Othello:* The Conversion and Damnation of the Moor." *Shakespeare Quarterly* 48 (1997): 145–76.
Warren, Roger. *Staging Shakespeare's Plays*. Oxford: Clarendon Press, 1990.
Weimann, Robert. *Shakespeare and the Popular Tradition in the Theater: Studies in the Social Dimension of Dramatic Form and Function*. Edited by Robert Schwartz. Baltimore: Johns Hopkins University Press, 1978.
Weissman, Ronald F. E. "The Importance of Being Ambiguous: Social Relations, Individualism, and Identity in Renaissance Florence." In *Urban Life in the Renaissance*, edited by Susan Zimmerman and Ronald F. E. Weissman, 269–80. Newark: University of Delaware Press, 1989.
Welsford, Enid. *The Court Masque: A Study in the Relationship Between Poetry and the Revels*. 1927. Reprint, New York: Russell and Russell, 1962.
Williams, Norman Lloyd. *Tudor London Visited*. London: Cassell, 1991.
Worthen, N. B. "Staging 'Shakespeare': Acting, Authority, and the Rhetoric of Performance." In *Shakespeare, Theory and Performance*, edited by James C. Bulman, 12–28. New York: Routledge, 1996.
Wright, H. G. "How Did Shakespeare Come to Know the *Decameron?*" *Modern Language Review* 49 (1955): 45–48.
Wright, Louis B. "Will Kemp and the *Commedia dell'Arte*." *MLN* 41 (1926): 516–20.
Yates, Frances A. *Giordano Bruno and the Hermetic Tradition*. New York: Random House, 1964.
———. *John Florio: The Life of an Italian in Shakespeare's England*. 1934. Reprint, New York: Octagon, 1968.
Zorzi, Ludovico. *Carpaccio e la rappresentazione di Sant Orsola*. Turin: Einaudi, 1988.

Index

Agnew, Jean-Christophe, 7, 23
Alamanni, Luigi, 14
Alberti, Leon Battista, 21, 26, 37, 73, 74, 77, 80, 82, 95, 119, 175
Anglo, Sydney, 24
Archer, Ian, 45, 62
Aretino, Pietro, 17, 78, 90, 164
Ariosto, Ludovico, 30, 90
Armstrong, Philip, 9
Arnaldi, G., 74
Arragon, 110, 112, 125
Ascham, Roger, 13, 15–16, 18–19
Audience, 3–5, 9, 11, 24, 59, 67–68, 86, 93, 124, 126, 134, 152, 167, 174, 175

Bandello, Matteo, 18
Bankside, 21, 26, 57, 78, 128, 165, 175
Barish, Jonas, 19–20
Bartlett, Kenneth R., 15–16, 25
Barton, Anne, 18
Bedingfield, Thomas, 17
Beier, A. L., 38
Bembo, Pietro, 133
Bergeron, David M., 24, 36
Bertelli, Sergio, 98
Bibbiena, Bernardo Dovizi, 91
Bloom, Harold, 38

Boccaccio, Giovanni, 18
Borgia, Cesare, 46
Botero, Giovanni, 7, 8, 23
Branagh, Kenneth, 174
Braudel, Fernand, 7, 24, 57, 71
Brooke, Arthur, 27
Brown, John Russell, 11
Brown, Sir Thomas, 132
Bruno, Giordano, 18
Bruster, Douglas, 6
Buchell, Arend van, 28
Bullough, Geoffrey, 18, 89, 90
Buondelmonti, Zanobi, 14
Burke, Peter, 10, 13, 74, 115
Burton, Richard, 85
Byron, George (Lord), 12, 21, 41

Carnival, 39, 41, 65, 74, 89, 92
Caro, Annibal, 93
Carpaccio, Vittore, 82
Castiglione, Baldassare, 12, 13, 16, 73, 103, 109, 114–16, 133; *sprezzatura*, 34, 49, 110, 114
Catholicism, 9, 12, 16, 71, 124–25, 130, 138, 150
Cecchi, Giovan Maria, 90
Cecil, Sir William, 13

Chambers, David, 39, 40, 75, 79, 133
Characters: Alonso, 173; Angelo, 91; Antonio (The Merchant of Venice, 38–44, 88, 104–8, 135, 142; Much Ado About Nothing, 158; The Tempest, 171–73; Twelfth Night, 53, 60–61, 70–71, 126, 128; The Two Gentlemen of Verona, 27, 98); Ariel, 171, 174; Arragon, 104; Balthazar (Romeo and Juliet, 156; The Merchant of Venice, 88, 105); Baptista, 30–31, 33–34, 36, 62–63, 73, 84, 93, 106, 121, 123, 141, 153; Bassanio, 38–40, 42–43, 49, 65, 88, 106–8, 131, 133–35, 141, 158–59; Beatrice, 110–13, 117, 125–26, 149–50, 158; Benedick, 110–11, 113, 117, 125–26, 130, 150, 158; Benvolio, 48, 50, 65, 81, 159; Bertram, 91–92, 111, 163, 165, 167–69, 170; Bianca, 33–35, 63, 77, 84, 91, 93, 121–23, 139, 141; Biondello, 139; Borachio, 67, 91, 112–13; Brabantio, 61, 68–69, 73–77, 93, 103, 106, 142; Caliban, 171–73; Cambio/Lucentio, 33–34, 121–22; Camillo, 114–16, 163, 174; Captain, the, 54, 129, 145; Capulet, 46–51, 65, 73, 80, 82–83, 86, 93, 147–49, 157; Cassio, 68, 77–79, 104, 136, 142; Cesario/Viola, 53–54, 60–61, 87, 90, 108–9, 126–29, 144, 145; Claudio, 66–67, 111–13, 125–26, 149–50, 158; Cleomines, 113; Cleopatra, 20; Cloten, 118, 164; Conrade, 67, 112–13; Countess, the, 92, 165; Crab, the dog, 59–60, 89; Curtis, 63; Desdemona, 74–9, 103, 136, 142–43; Diana, 91, 92, 158, 163, 167, 168, 170; Dion, 113; Dogberry, 67, 112–13; Don John, 66–67, 91, 112, 125–26, 149, 150, 164; Don Pedro, 52–53, 97, 110–12, 125, 150, 158; Duke of Milan, 29, 64, 86–87, 98–101, 103, 154, 155; Duke of Venice, 35, 43, 51, 69, 76, 103, 105, 107; Dumaine, 168–69; Edgar, 20; Egeon, 170; Elbow, 165; Escalus, Prince, 46–47, 51, 97, 110; Fabian, 126; Falstaff, 20; Ferdinand, 172, 174; Feste, 53–54, 60–61, 70, 89, 109, 127, 131, 143–45; French Lord, 166; Friar Francis, 68, 112–13, 138, 149–50; Friar Lawrence, 51, 82–84, 124–25, 137–38, 146–49,156, 157; Friar Patrick, 86, 154–55; Gonzalo, 171–74; Gratiano, 38–39, 41, 43, 49, 64–65, 105, 135, 141; Gregory, 47, 63, 159; Gremio, 33, 77, 139; Grumio, 34, 62; Hamlet, 20; Helena, 92–93, 165–70; Hermione, 4, 111, 116, 137; Hero, 66–68, 91, 111–13, 125–26, 149–50, 158; Hortensio, 33–34, 62–63, 68, 122; Iago, 68–69, 74, 76–77, 104, 136–37, 142–43; Imogen, 117, 163–65; Isabella, 91; Jachimo, 117–18, 163–64; Jessica, 39, 43, 60, 64–66, 74, 83–84, 86, 106–7, 131, 132, 142, 152; Julia, 29, 59–60, 64, 87–89, 99–100, 102, 106, 123, 152; Juliet, 46, 48, 51, 64, 66, 80–84, 86, 91, 106, 124–25, 136, 146–49, 155–57; Katherina, 31, 33–35, 51–52, 62–63, 83–85, 88, 121, 123; King of France, 165; Lady Capulet, 51, 82–83, 147, 157; Launce, 59, 89, 102; Launcelot, 130–31; Leonato, 67–68, 73, 97, 110, 112, 125, 149, 158; Leontes, 55, 95, 97, 105, 111, 114–18, 137; Lord (The Taming of the Shrew, 29, 30–31, 33, 63, 85); Lorenzo, 39, 41, 64–66, 84, 130–32, 134–35, 142; Lucentio, 31–35, 62–64, 68, 84, 85, 91, 119, 121, 122, 139, 153; Lucetta, 88, 123; Lucio, 150; Malvolio, 54, 89–90, 109–11, 126–27, 129, 131, 144, 145; Margaret, 66, 91, 126; Maria, 110, 126; Mercutio, 46–47, 49–51, 56, 65–66, 146, 156, 159; Miranda, 170–72, 174; Montague, Lord, 47–48; Morocco, 104, 141; Nathaniel, 63; Nerissa, 60, 88, 130, 135, 142; Nurse, 46, 49, 81–82, 86, 106, 146–47, 155; Olivia, 53–54, 60–61, 71, 87, 89, 90–91, 106, 109–10, 126–31, 143–45, 161; Orsino, 53–54, 60–61, 87, 108–9, 117–18, 127–28, 143–45; Othello, 56, 73–79, 93, 103, 136–37, 142–43, 158; Page, the, 31; Panthino, 59, 98–99; Paris, 48, 82, 147–48, 156–57; Parolles, 165, 167–68, 170; Paulina, 55, 95, 116–18, 137; Pedant, the, 34–35, 62–64, 122–23, 153–54; Perdita, 95, 118, 137;

Petruchio, 30, 34–36, 62–63, 68, 84–85, 121–23, 139, 141, 153–54; Philario, 117, 164; Philip, 63; Pisanio, 163–64, 174; Polixenes, 55, 114, 116–17; Portia, 40, 43, 60, 88, 104–8, 130–31, 133–35, 141–43, 152; Posthumus, 117–18, 163–64; Priest, the, 53, 143–45; Prince Escalus, 46–47, 51, 97, 110; Prospero, 170–74; Proteus, 27, 29, 59, 64, 86–87, 89, 98–102, 123, 139, 155, 164; Roderigo, 61, 68–69, 76, 142; Romeo, 27, 48–51, 64–66, 70, 81–84, 91, 124, 146–48, 152, 154, 156–57, 159; Rosaline, 48, 159; Salerio, 40, 64; Sampson, 47, 159; Sebastian (*The Tempest*, 173; *Twelfth Night*, 53, 60–61, 70–71, 90–91, 126–29, 143–45); Sebastian, Julia (*The Two Gentlemen of Verona*, 87, 102); Shylock, 37, 39–44, 47–48, 54, 61–62, 64–65, 74, 79–80, 93, 104–8, 111, 131, 142, 163; Silvia, 29, 60, 64, 86–87, 89, 98–102, 154–55; Sir Andrew, 61, 89, 126, 128, 143; Sir Toby, 61, 89, 90, 110, 126, 143; Sir Topas, 110, 129, 144; Sly, Christophero, 29, 30, 31, 85; Speed, 29, 59, 154; Stephano, 171; Tranio, 18, 32–35, 62, 122–23, 153–154; Trinculo, 171; Tubal, 44; Tybalt, 46, 48–51, 74, 80, 146–48, 156, 159; Valentine, 27–29, 32, 34, 51, 59, 60, 64, 86, 98–100, 103, 118, 139, 152, 154–55, 164; Verges, 112; Vincentio, 34–36, 62–64, 123, 153–54; Viola, 54, 60, 87, 89, 106, 108, 110, 118, 127–29, 145; Widow (*All's Well That Ends Well*, 92, 165, 167, 169–70; *The Taming of the Shrew*, 122)

Charles VIII of France, 157, 166
Cinthio, Giraldi, 18
Cities and strangers, 10, 35, 42, 60, 71–72, 74–75, 110, 117, 142, 153; citadel, 48, 63, 79–80, 82, 92, 104; civic discord, 46; theatricality, 3, 24, 40, 170, 173
Città ideale, 14, 23, 37, 43, 46, 51, 53, 70, 85, 172
City comedy, 4–5, 56
Cole, Howard C., 18, 59

Commedia dell'arte, 5, 18, 33, 41, 59, 69, 86, 131, 158, 159, 173
Commedia erudita, 23
Condottieri, 157
Cope, Jackson I., 91
Coryat, Thomas, 8, 10, 18–19, 27, 32, 47, 64, 72, 76, 78–79, 119
Cosgrove, Denis, 73, 130, 133
Court of law, 72, 98, 103, 105, 110–11
Cox, Virginia, 115

D'Amico, Jack, 23, 36, 46, 59, 70
Dante Alighieri, 71, 154, 159
Davis, Robert C., 41
de Alvarez, Leo Paul S., 46
de Coulanges, Fustel, 138
de Grazia, Sebastian, 14
de Grazia, Margreta, 139
Dekker, Thomas, 23
Demaray, John G., 174
de Seta, Cesare, 36
de Witt, Johannes, 28
Dundas, Judith, 86

Ehrenberg, Victor, 138
Einstein, Lewis, 115
Elizabeth I, Queen of England, 17, 24, 89, 90
Evelyn, John, 121, 132
Exile, 4, 36, 51, 66, 83, 103, 118, 152, 154, 156, 171

Ferrone, Siro, 93
Ficino, Marsilio, 132
Fiorentino, Ser Giovanni, 17, 18
Flaumenhaft, Mera J., 37
Florence, 11, 27, 32, 34, 37, 45, 70, 71, 91–2, 94, 165–67, 169
Florio, John, 17, 47
Forest, the, 56, 60, 98, 100, 103, 126, 139, 152–55
Fortescue, J. W., 169
Fortier, Mark, 115
Frantz, David O., 16, 17
Frugoni, Chiara, 119

Frye, Northrop, 56, 63
Fumerton, Patricia, 42

Gascoigne, George, 30, 90
Gaspar, Lord, 103
Gibbons, Brian, 5
Gillies, John, 8
Giorgione, 31
Girouard, Mark, 35, 38, 42
Globe theater, 21, 26, 128–29, 175; reconstructed, 3
Goddard, Harold, 164
Greenblatt, Stephen, 9, 75
Greene, Robert, 56, 113
Gurr, Andrew, 5, 28

Hager, Alan, 112
Hazlitt, William, 63
Helgerson, Richard, 9
Henke, Robert, 17–18, 114
Hoby, Sir Thomas. *See* Castiglione, Baldassare
Hodge, Nancy Elizabeth, 130
Hoenselaars, A. J., 9
Holbein, Hans, 77
Hollar, Wenceslaus, 175
Hoppe, Harry R., 17
Hotson, Leslie, 3
Hunt, John Dixon, 121, 124, 133
Hunt, the, 29, 31, 63, 122, 126, 128
Hunter, G. K., 7, 17

Illyria and Italy, 53, 55
Italian city-states, 3, 6, 7; arts in, 25; and the church, 128, 145, 149; and discord, 35, 56, 70, 81, 157, 160; and exchange, 9–10, 15, 56, 58, 77, 81, 87, 104, 153, 170; and exiles, 66, 154; gardens in, 121, 136 governors of, 35, 47, 52, 85, 97; and humanism, 12–13, 32, 132; as lobyinth, 70; ports, 152; and theater, 1, 11, 20, 33, 49, 62
Italian society: Shakespeare's conception of, 1, 6, 7, 10, 13, 27, 32, 33, 36, 59–60, 82, 90–91, 108, 166; Shakespeare's representation of, 3, 9, 11, 14, 30, 39, 46, 49, 55, 58, 62, 93, 100, 116, 118, 125, 162
Italian theater: *beffa*, 30; *camera scura*, 91–92; *lazzo*, 34, 59, 62; pantaloon, 33, 39, 41, 56, 69, 75; scenic design 21, 36. *See* Commedia dell'arte, Commedia erudita
Italy: artists, 25, 31, 95; commerce, 11, 12, 38, 42; dueling, 47, 50; novelle, 18, 19; preconceptions of, 19; universities, 10, 12, 19; vendetta, 47

Jardine, Lisa, 78, 109
Jones, Robert C., 20
Jones, Inigo, 21, 26
Jonson, Ben: *Volpone*, 26, 28, 40, 58, 72

Kernan, Alvin, 9
Kirchner, Herman, 8

Lane, Frederick C., 132
Laroque, Francois, 67
Leggatt, Alexander, 5
L'Estrange, Nicholas, 89
Levin, Harry, 10
Levith, Murray J., 6
Locatelli, Angela, 6
Locus amoenus, 83, 121–22, 125, 136
Lombardo, Agostino, 104
London: anti-alien legislation, 7, 44; burial grounds, 148; civic disorder, 45, 48; commerce, 38, 44; common houses, 78, 165, 169; dominant structures, 22, 138; gates, 22; growth, 8, 11, 36, 58, 152; houses, 64, 84, 121; liberties, 155, 157; and Shakespeare's Italy, 1, 3, 5, 6, 30, 59, 63, 174; squares, 21; streets, 57, 62, 131; and theater, 8, 25, 28, 58; as theater, 23, 24, 58; and Venice, 137; walls, 25
Lyly, John, 74

Machiavelli, Niccolò, 18, 154, 159, 171; *The Art of War*, 14, 17, 166; and Cesare Borgia, 46; *The Discourses*, 14, 166; *The Florentine Histories*, 17, 167; *The Mandrake Root*, 17, 23, 37, 70, 90, 93, 138,

150; *The Prince*, 17, 46, 160, 166; stage Machiavel, 12, 164, 167; *virtù*, 157
Mahler, Andreas, 76
Manley, Lawrence, 20, 24, 25
Mantua, 34–35, 66, 96, 99, 119, 155
Marriage: *All's Well That Ends Well*, 169; *The Merchant of Venice*, 104, 107–8, 135, 141–42; *Much Ado About Nothing*, 110–12, 125, 149; *Othello*, 77, 143; *Romeo and Juliet*, 48, 81, 83, 146–47, 155–56; *The Taming of the Shrew*, 33–4, 63, 84, 121, 139; *The Tempest*, 173; *Twelfth Night*, 129, 144–46
Martines, Lauro, 10, 47, 70, 96, 108
Masque, the, 26; *Much Ado About Nothing*, 158; *Othello*, 75; *Romeo and Juliet*, 65, 80; *The Merchant of Venice*, 39, 41, 64–65; *The Tempest*, 172–73
Master-servant, 34, 59, 62, 67, 102, 109, 126, 131
Mayor, John E. B., 19
McCoy, Richard M., 24
McKerrow, Ronald B. 16
McPherson, David C., 42, 104
Melchiori, Giorgio, 5, 112
Merchants, Venetian and English, 38, 40, 42
Messina, 5, 67, 97, 110, 112, 158
Metatheater, 3, 6, 24, 84, 95–96, 125, 168
Milan, 11, 25, 27, 29, 32, 55, 58–59, 98–100, 102, 123, 154, 170–71
Mildmay, Sir Walter, 13
Moison, Thomas, 62, 131
Molmenti, Pompeo, 78
Montaigne, Michel de, 172
Muir, Kenneth, 18
Mullaney, Steven, 8
Mumford, Lewis, 7, 10, 71, 119
Muraro, Maria Teresa, 39

Nashe, Thomas, 16

Octavian, Lord, 116
Olivieri, Achillo, 78
Orgel, Stephen, 26
Orlin, Lena, 7, 52, 69, 74

Orsini, Napoleone, 18
Outlaws, 60, 103, 154–55, 164
Ovid, 34
Oz, Avraham, 103–4, 131

Padua, 5–6, 9, 11, 19, 29, 30–35, 58, 62–63, 68, 105–6, 121, 153, 158
Palace/palazzo: *banche*, 64; bedroom, 54–55, 66, 77, 81–82, 85–86, 90–92, 94, 155, 163; as city, 73; court, 95; *cubiculum*, 98; and ruler, 44, 47; as theater, 75; towers, 81, 172
Palla, Batista della, 14
Palladio, Andrea, 73, 119, 133
Parker, Brian, 115
Parks, George B., 16
Paster, Gail Kern, 45, 80
Pfister, Manfred, 5
Piccolomini, Allesandro, 91, 93
Plautus, 56
Porter, Roy, 57
Power, M. J., 21
Praz, Mario, 18, 28
Pressler, Charlotte, 18
Priscianese, 133

Raab, Felix, 12, 14, 18
Rappaport, Steve, 36, 45, 58
Redmond, Michael J., 72
Roberts, Jeanne Addison, 115, 124
Romano, Julio, 95
Rome, 10, 15, 93, 97, 117–18, 121, 123, 163–66
Rosenthal, Margaret F., 78
Roston, Murray, 70
Ruffini, Franco, 23
Ryan, Lawrence, 19

Sackville, Sir Richard, 13
Salingar, Leo, 5, 18, 90, 94, 106
Saturnalia, 55
Sellars, Harry, 17
Serlio, Sebastian, 117, 165
de Seta, Cesare, 36
Shaheen, Naseeb, 17

Shakespeare's plays: *All's Well That Ends Well*, 91, 92, 163, 165–67, 169; *The Comedy of Errors* (1.1), 170; *Cymbeline*, 117, 163–64; *Henry V* (Chorus), 4; *Measure for Measure*, 91; *The Merchant of Venice*, 17, 37–44, 49, 60–61, 64, 74, 80, 86, 88, 105–8, 130–35, 141–43, 158, 161; *Much Ado About Nothing*, 52, 66–68, 91–92, 97, 110–13, 125–26, 130, 138, 149–50, 158, 161, 174; *Othello*, 25, 52, 56, 61, 68–70, 74–79, 103, 136–37, 142–44; *Pericles*, 165; *Romeo and Juliet*, 1, 5, 44, 46–52, 55, 65–6, 68, 74, 80–83, 97, 110, 113, 124–25, 138, 150, 161; *The Taming of the Shrew*, 18, 27, 29–35, 52, 62–44, 68, 77, 83–85, 88, 90, 119, 121–23, 139, 153–54, 161; *The Tempest*, 58, 170, 171–74; *Twelfth Night*, 20, 53–54, 60–61, 71, 87, 89–90, 108–10, 126–29, 131, 143–46; *The Two Gentlemen of Verona*, 27, 32, 55, 59, 60, 64, 86–87, 98–102, 123, 139, 154–55, 165; *The Winter's Tale*, 3, 4, 55, 58, 95, 97, 105, 111, 113–16, 137, 161, 163
Shapiro, James, 40, 44
Sicilia, 4, 55, 97, 112–14, 137
Stage, 6, 55, 68; fluidity of, 14, 28, 65, 108, 113; and garden, 125, 128, 136; and interiors, 77, 81, 91; and Italy, 11, 62; *locus*, 3, 5–6, 59; and perspective, 3, 23, 30–31, 36–37, 53, 70, 80, 93, 100, 138, 172; *platea*, 5, 24, 59; Shakespeare's amphitheater, 4, 5
Stephens, John, 12, 14
Stone, Lawrence, 36, 38, 45, 50, 121
Stow, John, 20, 22, 38, 45, 121, 153
Strozzi, Lorenzo di Filippo, 14
Styan, J. L., 28
Summerson, John, 21, 95
Syracusa, 25, 170

Tasso, Torquato, 17
Taylor, Elizabeth, 85
Terence, 56, 93
Theater, 7–9, 11, 26–28, 31, 93, 129, 155; and church, 147; and the city, 24, 37, 172, 175; and courtroom, 105; and garden, 121, 128; and London, 25, 36, 78, 124; and piazza, 23–24; and puritans, 55, 164; and travel, 19, 58; and warfare, 167–68
Thomas, William, 10, 15–16, 18, 119
Thurley, Simon, 22, 23, 95, 96, 99
Titian, 31, 133
Travel, 8, 27–28, 30–33, 60, 62, 82, 154–55, 164–65, 174; and the city, 71–72; and Italy, 10, 12–13, 15–16, 19, 153; and London, 57; and theater, 7
Trease, Geoffrey, 21

Underdown, David, 109
Urbino, 12, 73, 96, 99

Venice, 5, 6, 9, 10, 17, 25, 35, 43–44, 55, 60, 68, 71; and Belmont, 39, 41–42, 44, 58, 64, 103–6, 108, 130–31, 133–34, 136, 141–42; *compagnie della calza*, 39; courtesans, 78; courtliners, 133; homosexuality, 40; the law in, 104–5, 107; and London, 38, 137; mountebanks, 74; republic, 27, 40, 51; and trade, 11, 37–38, 42, 77, 107
Verona, 1, 6, 9, 11, 25, 32, 47, 49, 51, 58, 66, 68–69, 98, 110, 124–25, 146–48, 161; antiquities in, 27–28, 46; and civil strife, 157–59; gardens in, 121; and London, 27, 59, 64, 156
Veronese, 31, 76
Vitkus, Daniel J., 75

Warfare, 157–60, 166–69
Warren, Roger, 113
Weimann, Robert, 5
Welsford, Enid, 39, 75, 81
Whitehorne, Peter, 14, 17
Wolfe, John, 17
Wolley, John, 44

Yates, Francis A., 16, 17, 18, 50

Zeffirelli, Franco, 85
Zorzi, Ludovico, 39, 83

Jack D'Amico is professor of English at Canisius College in Buffalo, New York. He is the author of *The Moor in English Renaissance Drama* (UPF, 1991) and coeditor of *The Legacy of Benedetto Croce: Contemporary Critical Views* (1999).

www.ingramcontent.com/pod-product-compliance
Lightning Source LLC
Chambersburg PA
CBHW020910230426
43666CB00008B/1396